SUPERNATURAL ENTERTAINMENTS

SUPERNATURAL ENTERTAINMENTS

VICTORIAN SPIRITUALISM AND THE
RISE OF MODERN MEDIA CULTURE

SIMONE NATALE

THE PENNSYLVANIA STATE UNIVERSITY PRESS
UNIVERSITY PARK, PENNSYLVANIA

Library of Congress
Cataloging-in-Publication Data
Natale, Simone, 1981– , author.
Supernatural entertainments : Victorian spiritualism and the rise of modern media culture / Simone Natale.
  pages   cm
Summary: "Explores the proliferation of spiritualist séances in mid-nineteenth-century Europe and the United States, and the connection to the contemporary evolution of the media entertainment industry"—Provided by publisher.
Includes bibliographical references and index.
ISBN 978-0-271-07104-6 (cloth : alk. paper)
ISBN 978-0-271-07105-3 (pbk. : alk. paper)
1. Spiritualism—United States—History—19th century. 2. Spiritualism—Great Britain—History—20th century. 3. Seances—United States—History—19th century. 4. Seances—Great Britain—History—19th century.
5. Popular culture—United States—History—19th century. 6. Popular culture—Great Britain—History—19th century.
I. Title.

BF1242.U6N36 2015
133.909'034—dc23
2015029606

Copyright © 2016
The Pennsylvania State University
All rights reserved
Printed in the United States of America
Published by
The Pennsylvania State University Press,
University Park, PA 16802-1003

The Pennsylvania State University Press is a member of the Association of American University Presses.

It is the policy of The Pennsylvania State University Press to use acid-free paper. Publications on uncoated stock satisfy the minimum requirements of American National Standard for Information Sciences—Permanence of Paper for Printed Library Material, ANSI Z39.48-1992.

Frontispiece: Illustration of a séance from *Frank Leslie's Illustrated Newspaper*, May 12, 1888. Photo courtesy Brandon Hodge (MysteriousPlanchette.com).

CONTENTS

LIST OF ILLUSTRATIONS VIII
ACKNOWLEDGMENTS IX

INTRODUCTION 1

PART 1: CONFIGURATIONS OF SÉANCES

1 The Medium on the Stage: Theatricality and Performance in the Spirit Séance 21

2 Parlor Games: Play and Social Life in the Haunted House 42

PART 2: HOW TO SELL A SPIRIT

3 Breaking the News: Controversy, Sensation, and the Popular Press 65

4 Mediums and Stars: Religion, Consumerism, and Celebrity Culture 82

PART 3: SPIRIT AND MATTER

5 Stranger than Fiction: Print Media, Automatic Writing, and Popular Culture 109

6 The Marvels of Superimposition: Spirit Photography and Spiritualism's Visual Culture 135

AFTERWORD 170

NOTES 175
BIBLIOGRAPHY 200
INDEX 231

At the outset of my career I saw that everything depended upon getting people to think, and talk, and become curious and excited about the "rare spectacle."

—P. T. BARNUM,
Struggles and Triumphs, 1869

ILLUSTRATIONS

1 The advertisement for a "grand social reunion" organized by London spiritualists 27
2 The new "Hall for Spiritualists" on "New Water Street, Station Road, Blackburn" 28
3 Physical demonstrations of spirit phenomena 34
4 Mediums dancing under the influence of different spirits 35
5 Conversation in the séance circle 46
6 Levitation of the séance table 52
7 Levitation of a musical instrument 54
8 The spiritoscope, designed by Robert Hare 57
9 Exposé of a spiritualist medium 77
10 Portrait of Katie King, the spirit guide of medium Florence Cook 87
11 Photographic portrait of medium Georgiana Houghton 88
12 Stereoscopic photograph of a séance with Eusapia Palladino 95
13 Eusapia Palladino's "My Own Story" 100
14 Exposure of the trickery of Eusapia Palladino 103
15 Cover of the *Medium and Daybreak* dedicated to a medium 118
16 A spirit-drawn illustration from *Hafed Prince of Persia* 125
17 Writing under the influence of spirits 129
18 Two persons joining hands to perform automatic writing 129
19 The "direct process" of automatic writing 130
20 The "electrical process" of automatic writing 131
21 William Mumler's spirit photograph of Mary Todd Lincoln with the spirit of her deceased husband 139
22 William Mumler's spirit photograph of Mrs. Tinkman with the spirit of her deceased daughter 140
23 Reproduction of a spirit photograph by Jay J. Hartman 143
24 Spirit photograph published as the frontispiece to Samuel Watson's *The Religion of Spiritualism* 148
25 Photograph commissioned from Eadweard Muybridge by Kate and Robert Johnson 151
26 William Mumler's *Three Spirits with a Photograph on a Table Propped Against a Vase with Flowers* 152
27 A fake spirit photograph illustrating W. K. L. and Antonia Dickson's *History of the Kinetograph, Kinetoscope, and Kineto-phonograph* 155
28 A photographic trick reproduced in Albert A. Hopkins's *Magic* 160
29 *A Spirit Photograph: The Wraith of Mr. Maskelyne Appearing to Dr. Weatherly* 162
30 *Jacoby in the Realm of His Ghosts: So-Called Spirit Photography* 163
31 *The Liberation of the Prestidigitator Jacoby* 164

ACKNOWLEDGMENTS

This book is populated by the sweetest spirits: those of the many persons who provided useful insights, supported me, and contributed in many ways to its creation. It is the result of studies, research, and writing across many different places in Italy, Canada, Germany, and the United States, and therefore bears the trace of various influences, environments, and friends. It could not have come into being in this form without those hectic international movements that many young scholars experience today. I began my research at the University of Turin in Italy, where I was fortunate enough to have a supervisor, Peppino Ortoleva, who did not fear to embark on an unusual topic and provided me with endless insights, comments, and ideas. Historian of photography Nicoletta Leonardi and film scholar Silvio Alovisio were of great help in developing my research from an interdisciplinary perspective, especially during its initial stages. I also found it useful to discuss my work with the group of students and researchers who attended the Media History Seminars, directed by Professor Ortoleva. I am thankful to Giulia Ceriani Ruggero Eugeni and Massimo Leone, who offered some key advice on how to improve my work. Massimo was the first to encourage me to find an international publisher for this book.

My experience as a visiting scholar in the Department of Communication Studies at Concordia University in Montreal, Canada, was essential. Thanks so much to Kim Sawchuk, who invited me to Concordia and introduced me to the faculty, students, and staff of the department, as well as the vibrant and stimulating environment of the Mobile Media Lab. I am also deeply indebted to Jeremy Stolow, who generously offered suggestions and hints about secondary literature; he made some crucial contributions to my reflections, giving advice with intelligence and friendliness.

The Alexander von Humboldt Foundation generously supported much of the research leading to the publication of this book through a postdoctoral research fellowship in 2012–13 at the University of Cologne in Germany. I would like to thank my postdoctoral supervisor, Irmela Schneider, for her great support and insights, as well as my colleagues at the Institute for Media Culture and Theatre, who helped provide an ideal environment in which to pursue my work. Subsequent revisions and research were supported by a research fellowship at the Italian Academy of Columbia University in New York City. In the Italian Academy's weekly seminar I found a context for discussion with scholars from different disciplines; the debate that followed my recounting of the story of medium Eusapia Palladino was inspiring. I would like to thank director David Freedberg, Barbara Faedda, the members of the staff, and the other fellows of the academy. I am also grateful to Courtney Bender, who invited me to give a talk at Columbia's Institute for Religion, Culture, and Public Life and helped give a broader contour to my approach to spiritualism from the perspective of religious studies.

In the final stages of the preparation of this book, I was involved in the meetings and discussions of the research network Social Innovation Through the Non-Hegemonic Production of Knowledge, funded by the DFG (German Scientific Community). I would like to thank all members of the network, and particularly Bernard Geoghegan, Christian Kassung, Anna Lux, Sylvia Paletschek, Uwe Schellinger, Erhard Schüttpelz, Maren Sziede, Ehler Voss, and Helmut Zander, for welcoming me so generously into this group.

I am thankful to the numerous people with whom I discussed my project and who read parts of this work. I have benefited from the help of so many individuals that I will surely forget some of them, and I offer my apologies for this. I exchanged information and references with Murray Leeder, who was writing on spiritualism and cinema at the same time that I was writing my book. Feedback from Alexandra Bacoupoulos Viau, Gabriele Balbi, Andrea Ballatore, Luca Barra, Barbara Carnevali, Donna de Ville, Matthew Solomon, and Ehler Voss was important. Additionally, discussions with Charles Acland, Stefan Andriopoulos, Eberhard Bauer, Karen Beckman, Zoe Beloff, Mireille Berton, Alessandra Campana, Giulia Anastasia Carluccio, Noam Elcott, Andreas Fischer, André Gaudreault, Robert Hardwick Weston, Louis Kaplan, Rosanna Maule, Margarida Medeiros, Franco Prono, Jeffrey Sconce, Alessandra Violi, Diana Walsh Pasulka, Tanja Weber, and Martin Willis helped me move on with my research at different stages of the project. Finally, I would like to thank Bill Becker, Madeleine Castro, Arseli Dokumaci, Riccardo Fassone, Roberto Franzosi, Sandra Gabriele, Giuliana Galvagno, Hannah Gilbert, Jack Hunter, Joseph Imorde, Elena Lamberti, Peter Lester, Birgit Lettmann, Fabio Levi, Christine Maillard, Peter Marx, Gerhard Mayer, Gloria Origgi, Paola Pallavicini, Sarah Pesenti, Sven Pötting, Robert Prenovault, Franco Prono, Leo Ruickbie, Julio César Sal Paz, Peter Scheinpflug, Ina Schmied-Knittel, Tamara Shepherd, George Smith, Jeff Twine, Maartje van Gelder, Darren Werschler, Grant Wythoff, and Andrea Zeffiro.

My acquisitions editor at the Pennsylvania State University Press, Ellie Goodman, was foolish enough to believe from the very beginning in a book project on spirits, séances, and other weird things submitted by a student at an Italian university; many thanks to her, as well as to editorial assistant Charlee Redman, who helped create this book. The commentaries and insights offered by the reviewers of my manuscript—Tatiana Kontou, Jeffrey Kripal, and the third anonymous reviewer—prompted me to think critically about my work, in ways that helped me improve it significantly. I am also thankful to Julie Schoelles for her accurate and extremely helpful editing, as well as to the other staff members at the press who contributed so professionally to the completion of this project.

Portions of this manuscript have appeared elsewhere in different forms. An earlier version of chapter 1 was printed as "The Medium on the Stage: Trance and Performance in Nineteenth-Century Spiritualism," *Early Popular Visual Culture* 9, no. 3 (2011): 239–55 (reprinted by permission of Taylor & Francis Ltd.). The section "From Mumler to Méliès: A Short History of Superimposition" in chapter 6 was published as "A Short History of Superimposition: From Spirit Photography to Early Cinema," *Early Popular Visual Culture* 10, no. 2 (2012): 125–45 (reprinted by permission of Taylor & Francis Ltd.). Finally, some of the ideas I develop in chapter 4 were first sketched in "Spiritual Stars: Religion and Celebrity in the Career of Spiritualist Mediums," *Celebrity Studies* 4, no. 1 (2013): 94–96 (reprinted by permission of Taylor & Francis Ltd.). Thank you to the journal editors and to the anonymous reviewers for their comments on earlier versions of these texts.

I would like to thank my beautifully enlarged family as warmly as this page can convey. I am lucky to have the support and closeness of my beloved parents, their soul mates, my sensitive and poetic brother, my funny and lovable sister, my cousins and relatives dispersed across different places and yet always so close to me. I also thank my wonderful friends Andrea, Cischi, Debora, Flavio, Giovanna, Giulia, Hermes, Matteo, Nael, Nicola, Rita, Tommaso, the Montreal gang, Roberto and Robert, and the many others; I feel lucky to know you.

This book is dedicated to two different beings. One is a spirit, the other a person. The spirit is that of my grandfather, whose stories about how he survived the war were told in such vibrant words that he ultimately taught me to hear the voices of history and to see myself as shaped by a family (with all its ghosts). The person is Francesca, who accompanied me through so many experiences and travels, inspiring me to think in different ways about spirits, people, animals, things, and the world around us.

INTRODUCTION

Most histories of spiritualism start inside a small cottage in Hydesville, a little town in upstate New York, where, in 1848, two adolescent sisters initiated communication with the rappings allegedly produced by the spirit of a dead man. The sisters, Kate and Margaret Fox, were to be remembered as the first mediums in history and the founders of the spiritualist movement.[1] Yet the most important location for spiritualism's early history is arguably another one: a lecture theater called the Corinthian Hall—the largest theater in the nearby city of Rochester. It was there, on 14 November 1849, that the Fox sisters demonstrated spirit communication for the first time before a paying public. According to reports, nearly four hundred people paid twenty-five cents each to witness the astounding "Hydesville rappings."[2] This spiritualist demonstration was destined to be just the first of countless public séances in which religious beliefs mingled with live entertainment, converting spiritualism into a popular attraction for several generations of American and British Victorians.[3]

Supernatural Entertainments argues that the rise of the spiritualist movement as a religious and cultural phenomenon was closely connected to the contemporary evolution of the media entertainment industry. Following the history of spiritualism in Great Britain and the United States from its onset in 1848 to the beginning of the twentieth century, the book documents how spiritualist mediums and leaders employed some of the same advertising strategies, performance practices, and spectacular techniques that were being developed within the field of spectacular entertainments. Their séances offered not just a confirmation of religious beliefs about the afterlife but also a brilliant form of amusement, with sensational effects embellishing a distinctly spectacular environment. More broadly, by stressing the distinctive ways in which spiritualists participated in nineteenth-century media culture, this book aims to demonstrate that beliefs in ghosts contributed to the rise of the entertainment industry as we know it. Rather than diverging from the ghosts that populated literary, theatrical, and visual culture in the Victorian age, beliefs in spirits should be regarded as part of a broader cultural turn that placed ghosts and other supernatural phenomena at the center of the fictional, the spectacular, and the religious imagination.

During the Victorian age, spiritualism was a very significant religious phenomenon in America and Britain, revolving around the belief that it was possible to exchange messages with the spirits of the dead.[4] My claim is that in order to comprehend spiritualism's prominence, it is essential to understand its inclusion in a growing market for leisure activities and spectacular attractions. As I discuss at length in the following chapters, in fact, performances of spiritualist mediums often had a theatrical character. Séances were held in theaters and public halls, establishing a theatrical situation in which the medium played the role of the performer, and the sitters the role of the spectators. Many spiritualist mediums were virtually indistinguishable from professional performers: they had managers and agents, advertised their performances in the press, and developed spirit phenomena characterized by a high degree of spectacularism and theatricality.

One might object that, despite the frequency of public demonstrations of spiritualism, spiritualist séances were most often conducted in private environments by closed circles of spiritualists. The sources examined in this book, however, point to the fact that spiritualist sittings staged in Victorian households also stimulated playfulness and amusement. Creating an opportunity for leisure, private séances integrated numerous elements that were connected to forms of domestic entertainment in nineteenth-century households, such as amateur prestidigitation tricks, parlor theaters, table games, and rational amusements. It was not by chance that spirit communication was performed through the use of tables, a domestic object frequently used to receive visitors, engage in conversation, and play cards. In order to establish a spiritualist circle, in fact, spiritualists opened their homes to strangers, organizing social events that played simultaneously with religious belief and with public performance and entertainment. As the well-known spiritualist medium Catherine Berry pointed out in 1876, "The sitters at my séances have been neither few nor unimportant, so that my [private] experiments have been conducted in public."[5]

Spiritualist mediums and leaders organized and conducted séances that were meant to be entertaining as well as uplifting; in doing so, they adopted strategies that were being developed and employed in the show trade. As James W. Cook points out, one of the most innovative marketing schemes in nineteenth-century show business resulted from the discovery that a degree of uncertainty about the authenticity of an attraction would contribute to the arousal of interest in the public and the popular press.[6] Showmen such as P. T. Barnum understood that doubts about the authenticity of their spectacular feats only added to their appeal, and they would thus openly stimulate public controversies as an advertising scheme. As I demonstrate, spiritualists largely profited from this same strategy: mediums and leaders of the movement found in these controversies a way to grab the attention of the press and pique the public's curiosity about spiritualism. Moreover, spiritualism benefited from the powerful publicizing mechanism connected to celebrity culture. Frequently, it was the appeal of famous mediums featured in the popular press that attracted the attention of the public. Celebrity mediums contributed to the cohesion of spiritualist communities by spreading the fame of the movement and by providing a shared ground of recognized personalities.

Indeed, one of the most significant characteristics of spiritualism is the extent to which it participated in the formation of modern media culture, defined, as Erkki Huhtamo proposes, as "a cultural condition, where large numbers of people live under the constant influence of media."[7] From the very beginning, spiritualists employed the newly established popular press as a vehicle for publicity, mirroring the seminal entertainment industry of the Victorian age, which found in the mass circulation of the press new opportunities for broadening its public and reach. Spiritualists published and circulated an astounding number of publications, establishing a circuit of spiritualist print media that played a key role in strengthening their sense of belonging to a dispersed but distinct community. They participated in the visual culture of their time, using photography and other visual media to produce images that functioned as religious items as well as attractions and visual curiosities. In short, as the following chapters will show, the rise of spiritualism coincided more than just chronologically with the rise of entertainment media that placed ghostly apparitions and supernatural phantasmagorias at the very core of popular culture.

Taken as a whole, my explorations into spiritualism's spectacular character help frame the Victorian supernatural within the formation of a new commodity culture that changed the way public entertainments were planned, administered, marketed, and consumed. As scholars such as Fred Nadis, Sadiah Qureshi, and James Cook have shown, the nineteenth century signaled the growth of forms of live performance based on nontheatrical exhibitions of scientific, magic, anthropological, and human attractions.[8] Freak shows, stage magic, popular scientific lectures, panoramas, and dime museums were part of a long-standing tradition of public display of wonders, by which unfamiliar objects and counterintuitive phenomena were offered to the gaze of curious viewers and spectators.[9] While not all of these exhibition practices originated in the nineteenth century, what was unmistakably new about these attractions was their insertion in circuits of public visibility comprising commercial advertising, large-scale enterprises, and sensational reports heralded by the press. Tony Bennett uses the term "exhibitionary complex" to group the wide range of practices and performances that were offered to a growing public of entertainment seekers.[10] Spiritualist séances, such as the one performed at the Corinthian Hall, shared many characteristics with these kinds of performances. The séance was set on a theatrical stage before a paying public and introduced by a short lecture. Advertising and publicity strategies were employed to attract potential audiences. Additionally, as in freak shows and other spectacular exhibits, the subject of attention was a "living curiosity," a phenomenon that escaped normality to enter the dimension of curiosity and wonder.[11] Séances, in this sense, participated in the exhibitionary complex that promoted the consumption of entertainment and leisure activities in the Victorian age.

Public demonstrations of spiritualism were also similar in many ways to popular scientific lectures, which presented technological and scientific novelties as sensational attractions.[12] Magic and science in the nineteenth century were not contrasted but rather intimately allied: in an effort to appeal to the senses of their audiences through elaborate spectacular effects and performative strategies, lecturers mingled scientific lectures with stage magic. In London, for instance, the Royal Polytechnic—an institution devoted to the popularization of science and technology—mixed scientific divulgation with up-to-date illusions of stage magic, including in its repertoire the use of optical illusions to create an apparition of ghosts.[13] The inclusion of elements of both science and magic in the exhibitionary complex of the nineteenth century is particularly relevant if we consider that one of the main characteristics of spiritualism, as highlighted by some of the most authoritative scholars in the field, was the insertion of its religious and spiritual viewpoints within a positivistic and scientific framework.[14] Belief in spirit communication required the constant confirmation of empirical evidence: only the accumulation of facts and phenomena made it possible to profess and believe. This attention to empirical evidence came together with the sense, shared by many believers, that spiritualism was a "scientific" religion and that spirit communication could be experimentally verified.[15] Moreover, spirit phenomena were explained by pointing to the agency of natural phenomena such as electricity, and spirit communication was frequently compared to communication technologies such as the telegraph.[16] This emphasis on science and technology suggests that audiences who gathered for spiritualist demonstrations, not much differently from those who attended scientific lectures, could be attracted by the fascination of magic and, at the same time, by the appeal of scientific inquiry and knowledge. In fact, as scholars have noted, popular scientific lectures as well as stage-magic shows also benefited from the quasi-magical status of natural phenomena such as electricity and magnetism.[17]

After the Fox sisters' "discovery" of spirit communication, belief in spiritualism spread beyond North America, reaching countries as different and far away as Britain, France, Germany, Italy, and Brazil. This book is mostly concerned with the British and American spiritualist movements, which maintained a relationship of continued exchange during the nineteenth century.[18] The first medium to introduce spiritualism to Britain was the Bostonian Maria B. Hayden; moreover, many of the most famous mediums, including the Fox sisters, the Davenport brothers, and Daniel Dunglas Home, would travel from one side of the Atlantic to the other. While most historical works on spiritualism have focused on a unique national context, my choice to adopt a transatlantic perspective is meant to underline spiritualism's international dimension. This was a characteristic that the movement shared with the new industrial-based show business. As the British magazine *Theatre* remarked in 1882, the "'circuits' of Bristol, Norwich and York of the last century are now replaced by those of the United States, South Africa, India and Australia, and a modern actor thinks as little of a season in Melbourne or New York as his grandfather did of a week's 'starring' in Edinburgh."[19] Just as shows, performers, and attractions moved across exhibition circuits throughout the United States, Britain, Canada, continental Europe, and the rest of the world, so did spiritualist mediums and leaders travel from one continent to another, touring different countries in an effort to find new audiences of believers and curious spectators. In this context, the spiritualist movements of Victorian Britain and the United States exhibited a particularly high degree of mutual integration. This does not mean that British spiritualism and American spiritualism were not different from each other. For instance, the United States in particular was regarded by spiritualists all over the world as a place where particular emphasis was given to the spectacular and theatrical character of séances. As one British medium put it, "American mediums are never lost for want of advertising; their light is not hid under a bushel."[20] Yet my analysis of the

British and the American spiritualist movements reveals that intermingling with show business, entertainment practices, and consumer culture was characteristic of them both.

The time frame of this book spans almost the entire Victorian era, from the foundation of the spiritualist movement in 1848 to the beginning of the twentieth century. During this period, belief in spirit communication spread throughout America and Europe. The invention and commercial development of the moving picture as the nineteenth century drew to a close provides one possible apex for the rising entertainment industry and, consequently, an opportune—if arbitrary—end point for this book.[21] The introduction of the moving image brought forth, as scholars have noted, the changes in the organization, marketing, and fabrication of attractions and celebrities that characterized nineteenth-century show business.[22] Including a discussion of the relationship between cinematic representations of ghosts and spiritualism's visual culture, this book aims to underline the continuity, rather than the rupture, between the spectacular entertainments of the nineteenth and the twentieth centuries.

While Victorian spiritualism is sometimes depicted as a phenomenon that especially concerned the upper classes, the audiences of spiritualist demonstrations and the participants in spirit séances were, in fact, quite diverse in terms of class, gender, and, to a lesser extent, even race. Spiritualist communities in America and Britain varied in regard to religious faith, provenance, and social status; moreover, public events that displayed mediumistic phenomena were organized in theaters as well as more inclusive locations such as fairs and public halls. The multiplicity of environments in which séances and demonstrations were set defies a simplistic characterization of spiritualism as a pastime for the aristocracy and the bourgeoisie.[23]

The development of the media entertainment industry was part of a wide range of transformations in the culture, the economy, and the social milieu of both British and American society. While the birth of the entertainment industry is most often identified with the rise of classical cinema at the beginning of the twentieth century,[24] this development was anticipated and readied by the transformations of spectacular entertainments and the show trade in the previous decades. Increasingly during the nineteenth century, large masses of people in Europe and the United States began to participate in leisure activities and recreation.[25] As a result, large audiences became available for the consumption of popular entertainments. In the United States—first in the metropolitan areas along the Atlantic Coast and later in other contexts—managers and showmen seized the new entrepreneurial opportunities offered by the show trade, developing novel forms of entertainment and employing a range of advertising strategies. They strongly relied on the mass circulation of the newly established "penny press" as a vehicle for publicity.[26] The rise of American show business was epitomized by the career of showman P. T. Barnum, who managed a system of spectacular attractions, including fairs, popular museums of curiosities, music, stage performances, and freak shows, and became one of the most famous personalities of his time.[27]

The creation of new audiences and new exhibition practices also took place in the British context. As Aileen Fyfe and Bernard Lightman observe, while Britain may have already become a consumer society by the eighteenth century,[28] "it was not until the nineteenth century that most of the population had the opportunity to participate in this new world of goods, as products proliferated and the gap between prices and available income lessened."[29] In the middle of the century, the growth of the middle class and the institutionalization of the Saturday half-holiday facilitated the development of an emergent field of showmanship and popular attraction.[30] This was particularly true in metropolitan areas such as London, where the population increased from 900,000 in 1801 to 3,000,000 in 1851 and to 6,000,000 in 1901. Here, attractions such as panoramas and dioramas, stage-magic shows, lectures on scientific and cultural issues, freak shows, and cabinets of curiosities rivaled the popularity of theatrical plays.[31]

Despite the attention that the history of the spiritualist movement has recently attracted in fields such as Victorian studies, cultural history, and the history of science, little emphasis has been placed on the movement's overlap with the rise of the entertainment industry in the nineteenth and early twentieth centuries. Spiritualism is usually interpreted through a rigid framework, which leaves out the possibility that faith in spiritualism did not contrast but rather was embedded with the spectacular and entertaining character of séances. Historical works in this area have mainly focused on political, social, scientific, and religious issues, ignoring the ways in which spiritualism also interacted with entertainment practices and the show trade.[32] As cultural historian Daniel Herman put it, most scholars have addressed spiritualism with "an almost grim seriousness that obscures its playfulness and its willingness to explore the profane as well as the sacred."[33] Although some scholars have acknowledged the fact that spiritualism was also a matter of entertainment and spectacle, their works have focused on the relationship of spiritualism with specific forms of entertainment, such as literature,[34] theater,[35] cinema,[36] or stage magic,[37] or they have not gone much beyond recognizing a degree of playfulness in the spiritualist experience.[38] My analysis of spiritualism suggests that occult beliefs and practices should be interpreted in a more complex way. Spiritualist séances, in fact, were not only religious rituals and collective investigations into the phenomenon of spirit communication. They were also spectacular and entertaining events.

Scholars in media history, such as Jeffrey Sconce and John Durham Peters, have noted that spiritualism originated roughly at the same time that electric telegraphy was introduced in the United States; early spiritualists appropriated this technology as a metaphorical reference to explain communication with the world of spirits.[39] Spiritualism, however, also coincided with another significant process in the history of media: the rise of show business and industrial entertainment during the nineteenth century. Beliefs in ghosts, haunted houses, and spirit communications existed (albeit in different forms) long before the advent of spiritualism.[40] Yet, in the middle of the nineteenth century, the spiritualist movement succeeded in incorporating these beliefs into the growing market for entertainment and spectacular attractions. The extent to which spiritualism participated in this market is a distinctive characteristic of the movement that most sets it apart from previous forms of belief in supernatural and ghostly entities.

More than 150 years after the Fox sisters' rappings inaugurated the nineteenth-century craze for spirit séances, ghosts and other supernatural phenomena continue to haunt the imagination of entrepreneurs and performers in show business and the entertainment industry. In this sense, this book is not only a history of the relationship between spiritualism and spectacular entertainments in the nineteenth century. It is also a media archaeology of how the supernatural entered into the very core of twentieth- and twenty-first-century media culture—from cinema to television, from radio to new media, from comics to video games. By looking at spiritualism in the Victorian age, one might find a signal moment in which belief mingled with the spectacular and entertainment became a central element of spiritual and religious experiences. Understanding how this happened provides us with better tools to comprehend the key role played by beliefs in ghosts and other supernatural phenomena in contemporary popular culture.

THE SPECTACLE OF SPIRITS

In its broader sense, a spectacle is the presentation of something that invites the attention of a public. This presentation, however, can take place in different environments, attract different kinds of audiences, and establish a different relationship between the spectator and the performer or attraction.[41] Freak shows, popular scientific lectures, the circus, stage magic, theatrical plays, popular museums of curiosities—these are only some of the entertainments that were offered to nineteenth-century audiences and contributed to the formation of show business as we know it. If spiritualism is to be approached as a form of spectacular entertainment, some important questions arise: What kind of spectacle was conceived and performed in spiritualist séances, and what did they have in common with other forms of popular entertainment in the nineteenth century?

In my view, three aspects of nineteenth-century spiritualism are crucial to understanding its spectacular nature: first, the participatory character of the spiritualist experience; second, the coexistence of claims of authenticity with a spectacular frame; and third, the openness to different, potentially divergent interpretations of the event. As I will show, each of these aspects is specific to spiritualist demonstrations and séances and, at the same time, helps connect them with other forms of entertainment in the nineteenth century.

The first aspect characterizing spiritualist séances as spectacular events is their participatory character. Whether in a demonstration of spiritualism on the stage of a public hall, or in a private session held for a limited number of sitters, taking part in a spiritualist séance usually required active involvement in the performance. Sitters participated in spirit communication, asked for particular evidences of spirit agency, and tried to ascertain whether there was any fraud. They sang hymns and recited invocations to summon the spirits, and they dialogued with the spirits through the intercession of the medium. They wanted to touch spirit phenomena with their own hands, rather than merely observe them. Séances were often described by spiritualists as occasions to *experiment* with spiritualism, underlining the active involvement of participants in a collective act of spiritual inquiry.[42] Spiritualist spectatorship was, therefore, interactive and performative in nature.

Such participation was not unique to spiritualism; on the contrary, it linked séances to other practices that had an overtly spectacular character. In fact, contrary to the particular mode of spectatorship established by classical cinema, in which the spectator functioned (at least predominantly) as a passive viewer, inclusive and participatory forms of live performance were paramount in the nineteenth century.[43] Spectators were invited to participate in spectacular events, contributing to the tricks performed onstage by professional magicians, or asked to judge the authenticity of a given attraction.[44] The audiences of popular scientific lectures and demonstrations were encouraged to observe scientific processes and to examine the functioning of technological innovations.[45] That is, the spectators of several other forms of spectacle in the nineteenth century were actively shaping, not merely attending, performances.

The second aspect of séances as spectacles is that, despite often displaying a high degree of sensationalism and theatricality, they were presented to viewers and participants as authentic manifestations of spirit agency. In other words, in spiritualist demonstrations, the spectacular frame coexisted, rather than contrasted, with the claim that there were no tricks involved in the development of these phenomena. This has prompted some historians to posit a strong boundary between demonstrations of spiritualism and public performances such as stage magic, which had a more explicit spectacular nature.[46] This view, however, does not fully acknowledge how categories such as authenticity and deceit operated within the field of show business, where the curiosity of the public was constantly kindled and manipulated. Magicians, popular lecturers, and showmen played with the public's fascination with the supernatural. They also emphasized the exceptional character of their attractions, demonstrations, and exhibits by maintaining a substantial ambiguity between rational explanation and extraordinary experience.[47] That séances were presented as authentic manifestations of spirit agency, therefore, does not distinguish them from spectacular attractions; on the contrary, it shows that they were inserted within a broader array of shows and exhibits that played with the blurring distinctions between authenticity and forgery.

Taking into account the case of late nineteenth-century Paris, Vanessa Schwartz argues that spectators participated in a number of entertainment forms whose popularity was sustained through a "spectacular depiction of reality."[48] According to this perspective, panoramas and dioramas, wax museums, and public visits to the Paris Morgue can all be understood as cultural forms that, by using their underlying realism to entertain audiences, forecasted the visual entertainment of cinema. By proposing that séance phenomena were authentic manifestations of spirit agency, spiritualism took part in this nineteenth-century tradition of realistic entertainment. The ever-increasing spectacularism of spirit manifestations, which can be observed throughout the history of the movement in the nineteenth century, reveals a trajectory toward a kind of "total spiritualism," which transformed séances into ultra-realist and, concurrently, astonishing and spectacular events. Similar to other "spectacular realities," in spiritualist séances, spectacle and realism were not contrasted but rather intimately allied. Levitation, table movements, and materializations were among the most successful features of spirit shows that promised sitters a pervasive and multisensory involvement in the realm of spirits.

The third and last aspect of spiritualism as a spectacle is its openness toward different interpretations of the events observed at séances. Committed spiritualists were not the only ones invited to join séances. Mediums also welcomed people who were simply curious and willing to learn more about spiritualism, as well as those who were skeptical about spiritualist claims.[49] The openness to different kinds of spectatorship and involvement (the skeptic, the curious, the believer) was a characteristic that spiritualism shared with several other forms of spectacular entertainment from the nineteenth century. In an attempt to appeal to a broad public, in fact, the promoters of freak shows, magic shows, sensational attractions, and scientific lectures avoided positing one interpretation over others. The audiences of these shows could experience different kinds of involvement and consider different ways of engaging with the spectacle. For instance, when P. T. Barnum exhibited the alleged remains of a mermaid in his New York museum in the 1850s, or when sophisticated trompe l'oeil paintings displayed in public venues played with the distinctions between illusion and reality, viewers wavered between acceptance and skepticism, but were nonetheless drawn to the exhibits.[50] Likewise, the spectators at a magic show could regard the performance as the result of tricks, but they may sometimes have also wondered whether the magician had real supernatural powers.[51]

The fact that mediums were open to different interpretations of spectacular events suggests not only that there were different publics represented at séances, but also that the reaction of every single participant could involve different and concomitant responses. Participants in séances demonstrated flexible interpretations of their own involvement: they professed to believe, for instance, that they were witnessing real phenomena of spirit agency, but at the same time confessed that they were having fun.[52] Mediums welcomed manifestations of delight, amusement, and even laughter at spirit séances and did not consider them as opposing the goal of spiritual inquiry.[53] Spiritualist séances could be considered playful and entertaining also—and perhaps especially—by those who believed in spiritualism.

Acknowledging the spectacular nature of spiritualism, therefore, means taking a more nuanced approach to the way in which beliefs and convictions interact with the entertaining nature of an event. This book, in this sense, involves a discussion of two worlds that apparently diverge yet are closely allied: those of religious beliefs and mass entertainments. My argument is that the entertaining and spectacular nature of séances did not contrast but coexisted with their religious character. Rather than proposing to consider spiritualism as a spectacular entertainment *instead* of a religious movement, I am interested in the intermingling of these realms.

MATERIAL SPIRITUALISM

Although their doctrine mingled with other mystical and religious discourses, and despite their concomitant call to the authority of science, spiritualists frequently demarcated the boundaries of their faith, distinguishing spiritualism from superstitious beliefs and from other religious faiths. How can we reconcile, then, the spectacular nature of spiritualist séances with the religious character of the spiritualist experience? In what way did issues such as commerce, money, and spectacle interact with the religious context in which spiritualism was framed?

Scholars in religious studies and the anthropology of religion have recently deepened a perspective that points to the relevance of material culture in religious practice and belief and focuses on the presence of religion in popular culture and the media. In her groundbreaking study on the material culture of Christianity, Colleen McDannell argues that our understanding of religious beliefs is usually informed by a dichotomy between the sacred and the profane, spirit and matter, piety and commerce. Yet, she points out, in order to comprehend how religion works in the real world, we have to refuse these oppositions and consider religion as something interconnected with money, amusement, and spectacle.[54] Historians of spiritualism and the supernatural have taken up this framework, questioning the role of material objects—such as the table in spirit séances—and the material culture of spiritualism.[55] This book aims to continue pursuing this line of research, placing particular emphasis on the relevance of issues such as material culture, commerce, and entertainment in the development of the British and American spiritualist movements.

The intermingling of theatrical performances and religious ceremonies is a characteristic common to other religions, including Christianity. This is evident from the theatrics involved in many religious rituals.[56] Religious ceremonies such as those practiced by the Shakers in the United States, for instance, employed the phenomenon of trance in pseudotheatrical performances before the advent of the spiritualist movement.[57] As anthropologists such as Richard Schechner and Victor Turner have shown, rituals from numerous other religious faiths likewise contributed to performative situations bearing a strong theatrical character.[58] Religious communities and institutions, moreover, often organized and promoted forms of popular entertainment. One of the most evident examples of this tendency is seen in American revival meetings, whose spectacular and sometimes rather extravagant nature has inspired scholars of nineteenth-century American religion to regard them as a sort of religious theater.[59]

Yet there were arguably very few instances of religious communities where entertainment and spectacle played such a relevant role as they did in spiritualism. In certain cases, public events organized by spiritualist groups were directly comparable to early cinema shows, as both had a paying public, musical accompaniment, the condition of darkness, and magic-lantern projections.[60] Furthermore, even when sittings took place in domestic settings rather than in theatrical venues, several symbolic elements in the séances suggest that they played simultaneously with belief and entertainment. Spirit communication, as noted, was performed through the use of tables, a domestic object frequently used to engage in forms of domestic entertainment. Mediums also typically employed musical instruments, which were magically played by the spirits during séances. In this regard, spiritualist séances symbolically reenacted typical leisure activities and had much in common with amateur prestidigitation tricks, music, parlor theaters, philosophical toys, and other forms of domestic entertainment that were popular in nineteenth-century households.

In *The Stars Down to Earth*, a 1947 book based on a content analysis of newspaper horoscopes, the German sociologist Theodor W. Adorno remarks that "much like cultural industry, astrology tends to do away with the distinction between fact and fiction: its content is often overrealistic while suggesting attitudes which are based on an entirely irrational source."[61] Adorno refers here to the constant allusions to earthly activities and everyday life that appear in astrological forecasts; in his argument, these function as a way to cover up the underlying irrationality of the horoscope. A similar mechanism was at play in Victorian séances. The necessity of bringing spiritualism—to paraphrase Adorno—"down to earth" might explain why phenomena featured in spiritualist séances were most often described as trivial and worldly. Instead of offering religious and spiritual revelations, spirits were eager to produce mechanical manifestations, such as the movement of tables and other objects, and often entertained sitters with conversations of an everyday character.[62] Material objects and goods, moreover, circulated widely within the spiritualist movement. Spiritualists promoted cultural goods such as printed books, spiritualist journals, and photographic reproductions, and thereby contributed to and were part of the rise of consumerism in the nineteenth century. Although the invention of the printing press dates back to the fifteenth century, it was in the nineteenth century that print media became an industrial commodity in both Britain and the United States. The publication and successful marketing of texts within the spiritualist movement were part of this newly established mass commerce of books. Spiritualist journals, pamphlets, books, and biographies of mediums became hot items in the book market at the end of the nineteenth century. Another commodity successfully commercialized within the spiritualist movement was spirit photography, which was based on the belief that the photographic plate could record the presence of spirits invisible to the human eye. The fact that prints of spirit photographs were sold and advertised in spiritualist journals suggests that spiritualism's visual culture was framed by the new market for visual goods that emerged in the second half of the nineteenth century, when photographic prints and stereographic cards became industrial goods.[63]

Examining the history of spiritualism, therefore, recalls the complex relationship of religious discourses and praxis with commerce and money. Explicitly or implicitly, the market formed the background for virtually all explorations of the otherworld attempted by spiritualist circles in Victorian America and Britain. Mediumship was considered a profession, and those who performed trance phenomena did not make much of an effort to hide their pecuniary benefits, charging admission to their séances or relying on the institution of patronage. Contemporary accounts of the careers of famous mediums openly mentioned the amounts of money they were being paid for holding séances, suggesting that this might be a useful indicator of the prominence of their powers and the success of their sittings.[64] The most famous mediums received high sums. In 1854, for instance, the inventor and manufacturer Horace H. Day employed Kate Fox for a year, paying her a salary of 1,200 dollars to give "free" sittings.[65] Symbols for money were common in spiritualist séances: phenomena experienced by sitters included, for instance, the temporary disappearance of wallets or other objects from their pockets.[66]

Spiritualism's inclusion of strategies and practices typical of commercial sectors such as show business was often a source of concern among spiritualists. The fact that they sometimes lamented the commercialization of spiritualism, however, should not lead us to think that commerce and entertainment were marginal aspects of the experience of spiritualist believers. While debates on money's role in mediumistic activities were often lively and in some cases even harsh, spiritualist leaders and writers most frequently defended the professional nature of mediumship. Mediums, many pointed out, had the right to earn their own living and should be appropriately rewarded for the use of their time and gifts. Likewise, most spiritualists realized the necessity of appealing to the human senses and openly approved, to some degree, of spectacularism in spiritualist séances. Mediums were encouraged to employ any means that would facilitate the diffusion of their faith, and they did not refrain from stimulating the interest of the public by developing the most elaborate manifestations. As one put it, it was necessary "to break the ice of materialism and scepticism by first demonstrating to our senses of seeing, hearing, and feeling that spirits do exist."[67]

Take, for instance, the case of Eusapia Palladino, who became, at the turn of the nineteenth century, the most celebrated spiritualist medium of her time. Perhaps more than any other medium, she demonstrated the capacity to manipulate the attention of the public and the popular press. Judging from the extent to which Palladino and her agents invited journalists to participate in séances and encouraged public controversies about her phenomena, they were well aware that this would kindle the attention of the press and ultimately bolster her fame. Yet the use of marketing strategies and the elaborate staging of her séance demonstrations do not mean that she was not sincere and committed in her belief. Certainly, spiritualists could employ strategies from show business and at the same time believe in what they were doing.[68] In this regard, the perspective of material religion suggests that commerce and belief should be regarded as two sides of the same coin, rather than as conflicting elements.

SUPERNATURAL ENTERTAINMENTS

This book argues that the emergence of spiritualism in the nineteenth century was based on the entanglement of ancient beliefs in ghosts, haunted houses, and spirit rappings with the rise of commercial entertainment. Relying on a wide array of spiritualist and antispiritualist publications, it develops provocative and challenging questions regarding the intersection of religious experience with popular culture and mass media.

Part 1, "Configurations of Séances," examines the role of entertainment and spectacle in spiritualist sittings and demonstrations. In nineteenth-century spiritualism, "private" and "public" séances were often differentiated: the former referred to those held within the domestic sphere, with the participation of a small number of sitters, while the latter took place in theaters and halls before public audiences. The first two chapters take up this distinction to examine how séances were meant to be not only religious and spiritual but also entertaining and spectacular events. In chapter 1, public séances are analyzed as a form of spectacular entertainment. After sketching the history of the presence of spiritualist mediums on the stage and discussing the role of professionalism in mediumship, I focus on the trance as a specific performance strategy. I examine how the spiritualist trance combined principles of automatism, theatricality, and absorption, allowing for the coexistence of spectacular features and claims of authenticity in spirit séances. In chapter 2, private séances are regarded as events that created opportunities for social gatherings and parlor entertainment in nineteenth-century households. Spirit communication is compared and linked to other domestic pastimes that were common in the Victorian age, such as parlor theaters, table games, and philosophical toys.

Part 2, "How to Sell a Spirit," investigates the inclusion of spiritualism in the nineteenth-century show trade. The history of the rise of modern show business is also the history of the development of new strategies for advertisement and publicity. Spectacular attractions needed to be fabricated, marketed, and prepared for consumption, and the ways in which these operations were performed constituted one of the main innovations led by impresarios, managers, and showmen throughout the nineteenth century in Britain and the United States. The chapters in this section argue that spiritualists adopted many of these strategies. Chapter 3 examines how controversies over spiritualism were actively stimulated in order to create media hype and enhance the popularity of mediums and the movement as a whole. This was a well-established strategy in the show trade, as managers discovered that public disputes added to the appeal of attractions and performers. Chapter 4 employs the concept of celebrity to discuss how famous mediums contributed to the popularity of spiritualism. Relying on insights developed within the field of celebrity studies, I argue that celebrity functioned as a strategy that helped individual mediums and ultimately the entire movement to increase their presence and visibility within the public sphere.

Part 3, "Spirit and Matter," tackles the role of print and visual media. In spiritualism, where every sign could be interpreted as a message from spirits, objects took on special meaning as well. Spirit communications were not always as volatile as the voice of mediums; they were often inscribed in things that had their own materiality, durability, and value. The relationship of the spiritualist movement with consumer culture—already seen in spiritualism's dialogue with show business—was strengthened by the production, marketing, and consumption of material commodities. The final two chapters address issues regarding material culture, in relationship to religion and to beliefs in the supernatural. Chapter 5 frames the publication of spiritualist books, pamphlets, and journals within the industrialization of print media and the advent of popular literature in the nineteenth century. It shows how spiritualist print culture was informed as much by concerns about religion as by the effort to amuse and entertain the reader. Chapter 6 focuses on spirit photography, a spiritualist practice that emerged in the 1860s and was based on the belief that it was possible to capture the image of a ghost on the photographic plate. Examining the circulation of spirit photography as a curiosity and an attraction in the spiritualist movement, as well as the use of similar images in overtly fictional and spectacular contexts, I demonstrate that spiritualism's visual culture was strongly informed by tendencies toward consumerism, fictionality, and commerce.

Today, just as much as in the nineteenth century, psychic mediums and clairvoyants use marketing strategies and exhibit their alleged powers in a spectacular fashion. Moreover, representations of spirits and the supernatural continue to haunt contemporary popular culture, just as they haunted Victorian literature and early cinema. In the brief afterword, I consider the implications of this work for interrogating the role of the paranormal and ghosts in the contemporary age. Looking beyond the period examined in this book, I contend that popular culture is still characterized by its strong involvement with the theme of the supernatural. In this sense, the rise of the spiritualist movement was only the beginning of a longer trajectory that helps explain the popular appeal of spirits, mediums, and supernatural beliefs in contemporary media culture.

Supernatural Entertainments tells the story of the Victorians' fascination with the supernatural and how it came to intersect with a growing entertainment industry. I believe that this same fascination is at the core of both the diffusion of beliefs in the supernatural and the success of its fictional counterparts—whether ghosts, those with psychic powers, vampires, or other undead—in contemporary literature, film, and television. Perhaps this fascination is also the reason why supernatural beliefs have been pursued as a topic of research in scholarly literature in recent years. In a certain sense, then, this book is—not unlike ghost stories and horror movies—a product of popular culture.

PART ONE

CONFIGURATIONS

OF SÉANCES

1

THE MEDIUM ON THE STAGE

THEATRICALITY AND PERFORMANCE

IN THE SPIRIT SÉANCE

One afternoon in the 1880s, the spiritualist John Wetherbee and his two friends were uncertain about how to occupy their time, so they looked over a list of local mediums who were performing that day. "'Well,' said they, after the civilities were over, 'what is there going on this afternoon? Where can we go and see something?'—meaning spiritual manifestations. We looked over the list; there were five or six interesting choices, but we could choose but one."[1] Finally, they decided upon the Berry sisters. The abundance of choice in what to see was one thing that made Wetherbee proud of his city, Boston. Where, after all, could one find a greater concentration of spiritualist events? As he put it, "Look at the meetings for spiritualist teachings that this locality sustains. See the number of mediums that dispense the idea . . . ; and with regard to the more sensuous phenomena there seems to be in this city about all the time a dozen mediums for materialization, to say nothing about other physical phenomena."[2]

To today's reader, this anecdote by an amusement-seeking spiritualist in nineteenth-century Boston recalls the act of choosing among movies available in local theaters. Indeed, as documented by this and many other accounts, the sitters in Victorian séances often regarded these events not only as a mystical experience but also as a distraction, an entertaining activity. Similar to other popular live entertainments of the time, such as theatrical amusements, freak shows, and stage conjuring, spirit messages were often delivered within an openly spectacular frame, with the mediums performing trance phenomena on a theatrical stage before a paying audience. Some of them had come to spiritualism directly from the show trade, having had careers as theatrical performers before discovering the advantages of mediumship.³

While spirit séances have typically been analyzed as social constructs in which matters of politics, science, and religion were questioned, authors such as Alex Owen and Amy Lehman have recognized the presence of a theatrical frame that regulated communication with the spirits.⁴ In this chapter, I approach spiritualist séances from this perspective. Based on spiritualist accounts of public séances performed onstage, often before a paying public, I argue that séances were meant to function not only as moments of religious and scientific inquiry, but also as brilliant amusements in which theatrical effects embellished an exciting shared experience. The climax of these events culminated in the occurrence of spirit contact, which was often presented in dramatic ways, as a kind of coup de théâtre around which the entire event was shaped. As they waited for spirit messages, the sitters' expectations were shaped by a tension, or suspense, about the outcome of the phenomena—similar to what a viewer might experience when attending a dramatic sketch.

From the beginning of the spiritualist movement, mediums participated in the realm of show business, hiring managers, touring countries, and advertising in the press. Consequently, a nineteenth-century medium may be regarded as a sort of professional performer who, through the phenomenon of trance, shaped a complex dramatic space in which theatrical performance mingled with claims of passivity and authenticity. Although the repeated exposures of fraudulent mediums leave few doubts about the humbugs orchestrated by some of them, such a perspective does not necessarily imply that mediums and sitters did not believe in spiritualist claims. Séances were regarded as spectacular and entertaining events, particularly by persons who believed in spiritualism. The intermingling of performance and claims of authenticity, of spectacle and religious experience, did not represent a contradiction within spiritualist séances; on the contrary, it was at the very core of the spiritualist experience.

My claim, then, is that just because séances could be framed for their audiences as real does not mean that they were devoid of theatrical protocols. In this regard, it is useful to recall the argument employed by Peter Lamont, who relied on Erving Goffman's notion of frame to address the difference in reception to a magician's trick and to a psychic phenomenon reputed by viewers to be authentic.⁵ According to Goffman, a frame is the way in which an individual experiences a situation; she perceives an event in terms of a framework that gives meaning to her experience. What is particularly relevant in this analysis is how it allows for the possibility of incongruence between a situation and someone's frame: "From an individual's particular point of view, while one thing may momentarily appear to be what is really going on, in fact what is actually happening is plainly a joke, or a dream, or an accident, or a mistake, or a misunderstanding, or a deception, or a theatrical performance."[6] In the case of stage magic, a spectator would probably perceive the performance as a fictional spectacle that relies on trickery and sleight of hand; on the contrary, a spiritualist sitter at a séance might perceive it as a nonorchestrated event that opens a channel of communication with the beyond. This difference in interpretation, as Lamont suggested, contributes to marking a boundary between an entertaining magic trick and an allegedly genuine séance. Yet these demarcations were often less rigid than we might think. Both magic shows and spiritualist séances prompted attenders to form different and flexible interpretations of the events. In this sense, Goffman's contention that certain situations allow for the coexistence of different frames, or stimulate the change from one interpretative frame to another, applies very well to the case of spiritualism.

Throughout this chapter, I use the term "theatricality" in regard to spiritualist séances and demonstrations. Authors such as Joseph Litvak and Tracy C. Davis have underlined the multiple meanings that this word assumes, as it refers not only to a mode of representation but also to a broader range of ceremonies, rituals, festivities, and public spectacles that do not pertain to the world of theater per se, but create situations that are similar to theatrical performances.[7] Recently, the concept of theatricality has also been employed to study religious rituals, including spiritualist séances;[8] however, Davis and Postlewait contend that the apparent similarity between religious rituals and theatrical performances "is complicated by, on the one hand, the nature of belief and rite within religious practices and ritual action and, on the other hand, the nature of play and imagination in theatrical representations."[9] In contrast to this view, my analysis of spiritualism is based on the recognition that Victorian séances invited different but potentially concurrent modes of spectatorship and participation, including religious piety as well as playfulness, curiosity, imagination, and skepticism. In this chapter, I would like not only to document that mediums performed on the theatrical stage, but also to show how séances were characterized by the coexistence of theatricality with religious beliefs and claims of authenticity. As I will argue, such coexistence was made possible by a particular mode of spectatorship organized around the performance of trance. The development of trance phenomena contributed to establishing a situation that, despite being essentially theatrical, supported the claim of truthfulness in the mediums' performance.

SPIRITUALISM IN THE THEATER: FROM THE FOX SISTERS TO THE DAVENPORT BROTHERS

The founding myth of spiritualism—the story of the Fox sisters, who "discovered" spirit communication—mirrors spiritualism's movement from the private to the public sphere. Although the "Rochester rapping" that inaugurated the craze for spirit séances in 1848 was first heard in the haunted house occupied by the Fox family in Hydesville, the phenomenon soon moved to more inclusive spaces. In November 1849, the Fox sisters demonstrated their mediumship in Rochester's Corinthian Hall for three nights. On the first evening, four hundred people filled the hall to hear the mysterious noises.[10] Some months later, in June 1850, New Yorkers who were interested in attending a demonstration of the spirit rappings could see the Fox sisters at Barnum's Hotel, where the phenomenon was presented three times a day for an admission of one dollar.[11] The organization of these public séances, including a popular song written specifically to market them, testifies to the commercial approach of this first tour of the Fox sisters' table rapping.[12]

Such close ties to the world of show business continued to characterize spiritualism in its later history. Apparently, spiritualist mediums felt as much at ease in theaters and public halls as in the domestic space. Performing before large audiences was considered part of the medium's moral duty. Medium Catherine Berry wrote, "I have never regretted having devoted my services to the cause in so public a manner. On the contrary, I feel some degree of pride in having passed through such a trying ordeal *pro bono publico.*"[13] In many cases, the spectators attending such performances were subject—as with theater shows or public lectures—to the payment of an admission fee. Attending a séance was thus often a matter of theatergoing: mediums performed in halls and theaters as well as within the walls of the Victorian house. In doing so, they gave birth to a tradition of spectacular spirit manifestations and standardized mediumship as an activity to be conducted before the public.

A particularly successful type of spiritualist performance was trance lecturing. Replicating the figure of the lecturer—a well-established profession in the cultural field—mediums in the United States and later in Europe offered themselves as the channel through which spirits delivered discourses before large audiences. According to historian Ann Braude, trance lecturing provided one of the first opportunities for women to speak in public about sensitive issues in nineteenth-century America. Through them, their "spirit controls" delivered lectures that touched upon pressing social and political questions, including the institution of marriage and the condition of women in Victorian society.[14] Trance lecturers were often itinerant mediums and preachers who moved from one community to another presenting their spiritual and healing methods to different audiences.[15] Given the extent to which itinerant performers shaped the Victorian show trade, bringing attractions and new entertainments to local communities throughout Britain and the United States, it is tempting to consider itinerant mediums as part of a broader "exhibitionary complex" that contributed to the formation of a shared popular culture in the nineteenth century.[16]

Mediumship was also formally associated with public speaking. In August 1872, the popular British medium J. J. Morse joined the list of professional speakers in England. In his autobiography *Leaves from My Life*, Morse recounted the favorable reception of his first trance lecture on 21 April 1870, where his spirit control delivered a "regular address" through him: "The event was a complete success, and my advent as a trance-speaker was welcomed with pleasure by all." During his subsequent career as a public medium, he performed before "large and influential audiences in all the large towns in three out of the four divisions of the United Kingdom."[17] His spirit control, Tien-Sien-Tie, presented himself as the spirit of a Chinese mandarin of the second class and delivered discourses on religious, philosophical, and spiritual issues.

Public events organized by spiritualists included a wide range of performances and features. Instrumental music was played during exhibitions of spiritualist phenomena, including trance lecturing, as advertised in spiritualist magazines and publications.[18] Music also featured as a manifestation of spirit agency. In Athens County, Ohio, in 1852, the farmer Jonathan Koons built a log cabin that was exclusively used to conduct public séances with a strong musical component.[19] In Koons's spirit concerts, music performed with numerous musical instruments, including the trumpet, accordion, and percussion instruments, was attributed to spirit agency.[20] In other cases reported by spiritualist sources, mediums sang and played musical instruments in trance, allegedly under the guidance of spirits,[21] or accompanied spirit manifestations by playing the guitar.[22] The inclusion of music in spiritualist public events reflects its remarkably relevant role in spectacular entertainments and theatrical plays during the nineteenth century.²³ Spiritualism also inspired the production and commercialization of sheet music for popular songs—an important staple of the music industry in the nineteenth century, before the introduction of sound reproduction.²⁴

Spiritualist organizations often owned or rented rooms where it was possible to host a large number of people. The British magazine *Medium and Daybreak*, for instance, often advertised public evenings and exhibitions (fig. 1). In March 1885, the magazine formally announced the opening in Blackburn of a new "Hall for Spiritualists" (fig. 2), which was celebrated with an inaugural lecture, the projection of spirit drawings and spirit photographs, and selections of vocal and instrumental music.²⁵ In the United States, spiritualists went so far as to organize summer camp meetings.²⁶ J. J. Morse, in reporting his impressions after a journey to the United States, described these camps as merging spirit séances and entertainment. Among the events planned for the amusement of the campers, Morse listed the "phantom party," an evening festivity in which all the participants were costumed as ghosts, and the "Old Folks' Concert," an open-air event "in which all the performers were attired in the costumes of a century ago, and all the airs and words were dated back to the same period." At 10:30 P.M. each evening, "lights out" brought "the labours and pleasures of the day to a close."²⁷

Those who attended spiritualist demonstrations were able to observe all the stages of a séance even if they did not directly participate as sitters. The séance table was sometimes placed on a theatrical stage so that spectators could follow the interaction between spirits and the sitters.²⁸ In other cases, including a public séance performed in 1876 in New York, spectators watched at a distance from the table, where only the medium was allowed to sit.²⁹ Likewise, in a demonstration held at the Spiritual Institution in London, the participants in the séance sat in the back room, following precise instruction that had allegedly been provided by the spirits, while the public crowded into the front room. During this sitting, one of the spirits reportedly observed that the spectators were "packed like sardines in a box."³⁰ Although they were not included in the séance circle, viewers participated in the demonstrations in numerous ways, purporting to have seen or perceived spirits among them,³¹ analyzing the medium's performance for signs of fraud,³² or overstepping their role as spectators by setting up

FIG. 1   The advertisement for a "grand social reunion" organized by London spiritualists. This evening program featured lectures from well-known spiritualists, as well as "music, songs, and dramatic readings." From *Medium and Daybreak* 16, no. 778 (1885): 144.

The 37th Anniversary of the Advent of Modern Spiritualism.

On WEDNESDAY, MARCH 18, 1885,

A Grand Social Reunion of London Spiritualists,

AT CAVENDISH ROOMS, 51, MORTIMER STREET, W.

TEA in the Spacious and Elegant Refreshment Rooms, from 6.30 to 7.30.

MUSIC, PROMENADE and CONVERSATION in the HALL, from 6.30 to 8 o'clock.

Come Early! Meet the Friends of the Cause, and have a Happy Evening.

AT EIGHT O'CLOCK THE CHAIR WILL BE TAKEN.

A LONG PROGRAMME OF MUSIC, SONGS, AND DRAMATIC READINGS

WILL BE INTERSPERSED WITH

ADDRESSES FROM WELL-KNOWN SPIRITUALTISTS
SUITABLE TO THE OCCASION.

TICKETS NOW READY.
TEA AND ENTERTAINMENT, 1s. 6d., RESERVED SEATS, 2s. 6d.

Sold by Mrs. MALTBY, 46, Grove Road, St. John's Wood, and Mrs. BURNS, 15, Southampton Row, W.C.

SPIRITUAL WORKER'S EDITION.

THE SPIRITUAL LYRE.

Complete: in strong wrapper, 10s. per 100; in limp cloth, £1 per 100; in cloth boards, gilt lettered, £1 10s. per 100.

Everybody who attends Meetings buys a Hymn-book, now that the Spiritual Worker's Edition is on sale. It contains valuable Information on the Cause, and as it commands an immense circulation, its use greatly extends Spiritualism.

SEND STAMPS FOR SPECIMENS.

LONDON: J. BURNS, 15, SOUTHAMPTON ROW, HIGH HOLBORN, W.C.

"MENTAL MAGIC."

With Divining Frontispiece.

The A B C of Elementary Occultism, Experimental and Curative; also the New Phase of Mediumship. ALL *should read this Work, before procuring expensive Magic Mirrors, as it explains both how to cheaply make, and also use them.*

200 pp. post free, 5s. from J. BURNS, 15, Southampton Row, Holborn, London; or of the Editor, ROBT. H. FRYAR, Bath.

LONDON: 37, QUEEN SQUARE, BLOOMSBURY, W.C.

SHIRLEY'S OLD-ESTABLISHED TEMPERANCE HOTEL

BEDS, 1s. 6d. & 2s. BREAKFAST AND TEA, 1s. 3d.

THIS House has been established 30 years, is very central, quiet and convenient for the West End or City; about four minutes from Holborn, where there is a continuous line of Omnibuses to all Parts. It is the most central part of London for all the Railway Termini. The following Testimonials, taken from the Visitor's Book, in which there are many hundreds, will show the estimate in which the Hotel is held.

J. MACKENZIE ROBERTSON, Esq., Edinburgh.—"Have much pleasure in expressing my gratification at the comfort and courtesy I have experienced at this hotel during a stay of a week."

Rev. H. E. HOWAT, Reading.—"Much gratified with finding so comfortable a Temperance Hotel, and advantageously situated."

J. ROBERTS, Esq., Bourne.—"We are more than satisfied; we are truly delighted to find in London so quiet and comfortable a domicile. We shall certainly highly recommend SHIRLEY'S to all our friends."

J. POULTNEY, Esq., Birmingham.—"I should like to find such another house in every town I visit."

References also kindly permitted to Mr. BURNS, Publisher of the MEDIUM.

LONDON: Printed and Published by JAMES BURNS, 15, Southampton Row, High Holborn, W.C.

FIG. 2
Theaters and public halls often hosted public séances and spiritualist meetings. This illustration, published in a spiritualist journal, displays the new "Hall for Spiritualists" on "New Water Street, Station Road, Blackburn." From *Medium and Daybreak* 16, no. 778 (1885): 160.

a secondary, simultaneous séance on their own premises.[33] The dramatic character of these events was often stressed, and reports underlined the condition of expectation and suspense that was created among the audience at public séances.[34]

Spiritualist periodicals published and advertised the programs of spiritualist demonstrations, including such details as their time, location, and price of admission. The *Herald of Progress*, for instance, regularly printed a list of performances of mediums organized by numerous spiritualist societies, "for the convenience of Spiritualists visiting other towns." These lists reported dozens of events across England, Wales, and Scotland, including trance lectures, physical manifestations, and members-only private séances. The public performances of the most popular mediums, such as J. J. Morse, were listed in a dedicated space. Here, one could browse the details of all of Morse's public appearances in the upcoming months and find how to contact him; the paper noted that he could be engaged to perform additional lectures and demonstrations in all parts of the kingdom.[35]

Although most mediums relied primarily on patronage to finance their performances, many were supported at least in part by the paying public. Some of them specialized in a kind of spiritualist show that bore an evident resemblance to contemporary stage magic. The Russian physicist Dmitrij Ivanovič Mendeleev pointed out in the second of the three lectures he wrote on spiritualism that the difference between magicians and mediums was that the former usually stated that they were performing trickery.[36] Magicians such as Harry Houdini and John Nevil Maskelyne made it clear that the supernatural played no role in their shows; rather, everything was accomplished through sleight of hand, as well as optical and mechanical tricks. Yet the boundaries between mediumship and magic were often quite hard to distinguish, and some spiritualists went so far as to suggest that famous stage magicians might have psychic and spiritual gifts.[37] John Wetherbee, for instance, described magicians as mediums who had decided that it would be more profitable to use their mediumistic powers in the show trade: "It is a matter of dollars and cents with them. I could name a man who is a good medium for physical manifestations, but likes the popularity and the reputation that he gets from the skeptical world better than poverty with truth."[38] The difference between mediums and magicians was also a matter of performance style: as Peter Lamont notes, magicians tended to perform their tricks with apparent ease, while mediums appeared exhausted after séances, suggesting that their contact with the spirit world required an intense physical effort.[39]

Among mediums who performed spiritualist shows that were similar to stage magic, the Davenport brothers became particularly prominent. Touring the United States and Great Britain in the 1860s and 1870s, they performed séances on the stages of theaters and public halls, as well as in smaller rooms before a select audience. The fact that their feats were considered to be supernatural was central to the success of their shows. George Smith-Buck, writing under the pseudonym Herr Dobler, thoroughly described the Davenport brothers' shows in a book that was intended to unmask their tricks. The environment in which their séances were conducted was carefully designed. For instance, since séances were usually supposed to take place in darkness, a "spirit cabinet" placed on the stage allowed the Davenports to perform before a large audience without requiring the spectators to sit for a long time in the dark.[40]

Ira Erastus and William Henry Davenport were born in Buffalo, New York, in 1839 and 1841, respectively. Their mediumship was revealed during their early childhood: according to their biographer T. L. Nichols, the Davenport family was "disturbed" by spirit rappings as early as 1846, two years before the Hydesville rappings became public knowledge.[41] After news of their mediumship spread through Buffalo, Ira and William toured the United States, accompanied initially by their father and then by persons who acted as their agents and assistants. Among these were figures involved in the world of show business, such as Harry Kellar, who later became a leading American magician. At least one of the brothers' managers, a Mr. Palmer, also managed stage conjurors.[42]

At the beginning of their séances, the Davenport brothers were usually tied with ropes by someone from the public, in order to make sure that they did not manipulate the development of spirit phenomena. The participation of audience members, called onstage to confirm that the protocols were correctly followed, suggests that the success of the Davenports' spiritualist shows relied, like stage magic, on the public's engagement: spectators were encouraged to actively question the reality of spirit manifestations and the claims of spiritualism. As cultural historian James W. Cook convincingly showed, many spectacular demonstrations in the nineteenth century, including those promoted by show-business entrepreneur P. T. Barnum, stimulated the public to form personal opinions about the reliability of the attractions. Barnum increased the public's curiosity with his sophisticated use of the press, giving newspapers evidence either supporting or casting doubt on the authenticity of his attractions in order to spark rumors and debates.[43] Quite similarly, contemporary exposés of the Davenport brothers by magicians such as Maskelyne and Cook in London may have ultimately increased the Davenports' box-office success.[44] After all, testing the truth of spirit communication was the principal activity of sitters in spiritualist séances.[45]

Music played a very prominent role in the Davenports' shows. Their most famous and cited manifestation involved the playing of musical instruments by spirits. During a séance held in London, where they performed before a select audience of twenty-four people, the housekeeper sent someone to a neighboring music seller for six guitars and two tambourines to ensure that the instruments used would not be those that the mediums were familiar with. After the Davenports had been tied in the cabinet, the instruments magically started to play, and people in the audience claimed to have been grasped by spirit hands.[46] The Davenports' spirit concerts could include guitars and tambourines, as well as violins, horns, and bells.[47]

The attitude of spiritualists toward the mediumship of the Davenport brothers was one of ambivalence. As Arthur Conan Doyle put it in his history of the movement, in making a profession out of their gifts, the Davenports worked at a lower level than more traditional mediums, "and yet by their crude methods they got their results across to the multitude in a way which a more refined mediumship could not have done."[48] Many spiritualists defended the Davenports' work, responding to magicians who had tried to unmask their trickery. An oration delivered in London in 1873 attempted a counter-exposure of magicians' antispiritualist shows, pointing to the fact that "we have in London at this moment several conjurers who night after night attempt by mere trickery to show phenomena something like those that take place in the presence of spirit-mediums, and to burlesque and ridicule the whole subject of spirit communion."⁴⁹ Others, however, worried that an excessive spectacularization of spiritualism could have negative effects on the movement. J. J. Morse, for instance, openly criticized the more commercial approach of American mediums, who charged an admission fee and regularly advertised in the popular press; he noted that "it is somewhat disagreeable to see the function of mediumship reduced to the level of show business."⁵⁰ Likewise, recognizing the entertaining nature of many public séances, one spiritualist described a spiritualist concert—which included drums, tambourines, and violins—as "pretentious" and criticized its exceedingly spectacular approach.⁵¹

PROFESSIONAL MEDIUMS

As medium Emma Hardinge recognized, the roots of mediumship can be found in mesmeric performers who practiced the art known as animal magnetism, invented by the Austrian physician and occultist Franz Anton Mesmer at the end of the eighteenth century. Mesmerists relied on theories about vital fluids that governed the universe, whose manipulation by the healer could exercise a beneficial power on the patient.⁵² "In nearly every [American] city, town, or hamlet," Hardinge wrote in 1870, "the itinerant mesmerizer made his rounds, operating upon chance subjects as opportunity offered, and alternately exciting superstitious terror or wrathful antagonism by the exercise of his seemingly magical powers."⁵³ As Terry M. Parssinen documented, the entertaining nature of these performers' activities was often underlined by detractors as well as advocates of mesmerism. Such performers were entrepreneurs who made a living out of mesmerism, drawing on the traditions of popular entertainment, scientific lecturing, and lay healing.⁵⁴

Similar to mesmeric performances, the institution of mediumship was challenged by the apparent contradiction between the spiritualist belief and the commercial and professional approach of many practitioners. Spiritualists often acknowledged that performances by mediums could include some acting, at least to give some more "color" to the manifestations. John Wetherbee, who became a convinced spiritualist after the death of his firstborn son, admitted, "I have seen, of course, attempts to cheat by at least supplementing their powers by more or less imposition; not always meaning to do anything wrong, but, perhaps, to give more for the fee received than the spirits can do through them."⁵⁵ The analogy between stage performers and mediums was reinforced by the fact that some mediums had come to the spiritualist movement directly from the show trade. Hardinge's career, for instance, had started in theaters rather than in spiritual séances: before becoming a trance lecturer, she had tried unsuccessfully to make it as an actress and a singer.[56] Mediumship was understood not only as a natural gift but as a skill that could be improved by regular training. As biographical accounts testify, becoming a medium was a gradual process that required, like acting, abnegation and experience. George A. Redman wrote in his autobiography that after he had begun to develop mediumistic powers, he could perceive "wonderful progress" as each day rolled on.[57] Manifestations often improved in complexity and variety throughout a medium's career. As one spiritualist put it, "The gift of mediumship requires developing by constant sitting, in the same way that a musical or an artistic talent requires to be cultivated; and a person can therefore no more become at once a 'full-blown' medium than he could expect to be a proficient instrumentalist without previous practice."[58]

The link between mediumship and performance often prompted accusations of trickery and fraud and was therefore highly controversial within the spiritualist field. Given the number of documented exposures of fraudulent mediums, it was easy for opponents of spiritualism to argue that mediums were actors who did no more than perform an act. For this reason, polemics and debates surrounding the professionalism of mediums who charged the public a fee to attend their séances or relied on patronage were frequent. French physiologist Charles Richet lamented in his magnum opus on psychical research, *Traité de métapsychique* (Treatise on metempsychosis), that spiritualism was considered by some to be a promising source of monetary benefits. "Everywhere," Richet observed, "the credulity of the public tempts the cupidity of the fraudsters. So there has been public séance before paying audiences where, side by side with the circus and the magic theater, *spiritualist* performances were given."[59]

Most of the leading figures of spiritualism, however, kept defending the professional nature of mediumship. In 1878, for instance, a spiritualist claimed that paying a medium for performing his duty "is as praiseworthy as to employ the time and 'gifts' of a lawyer, doctor, baker, or any other tradesman who has goods for sale, mental or material," and that refusing to pay was "equivalent to pocket-picking." In fact, also in the spiritualist field, "the question of work and fees comes under the heading of 'supply' and 'demand,' and will be regulated accordingly."[60] Many mediums, after all, came from the working class and needed financial support to devote themselves full time to communing with spirits.⁶¹ In the spirit of self-entrepreneurship, successful mediums in the nineteenth century advertised in the press, toured their home countries and abroad, and promoted their businesses in every way they could.

Mediumship in the nineteenth century was a very competitive business. Every medium had a specialty, often claiming its superiority over other manifestations. For example, Redman, a direct-writing and materialization medium, lamented that in almost every spiritualist community one could find mediums and believers who expressed disgust for those "tangible manifestations of spirit presence" and who proclaimed the disciplines of the trance lecturer and the clairvoyant to be superior. His defense of rapping and direct writing accompanied an argument against the reliability of trance lecturing: "Every idea expressed through such channels, is tainted, more or less, with the characteristics of the brain through which it comes; and without doubt we may take seven-tenths of such matter at a discount. The only perfect mode of spirit communion free from mortal interference is, where the communication given is *wholly* mechanical, and disconnected entirely from the mind of the medium, which can be obtained in various ways,—by rapping, tipping, or writing in such a manner, that the medium cannot read it at the time."⁶²

In the early years following the advent of spiritualism, mediums discovered that they had to tailor their manifestations to the taste of the public. In order to widen the reach of the spiritualist faith, they were encouraged to do everything possible to attract public attention. Their performances could be trivial or spectacular, if the latter was the only way to make spiritualism acceptable and appealing to large masses of people.⁶³ This opened the way to an increasing spectacularization and sensationalism of spirit phenomena (fig. 3). As R. Laurence Moore noted, spirit concerts such as those delivered through the mediumship of the Davenport brothers had an important advantage: they could be performed before a crowd.⁶⁴ Various and increasingly original apparitions competed for attention within the spiritualist field, in part replacing the "old" phenomena of direct writing and trance lecturing. The French American medium Lucie Marie Curtis Blair, whose career began in 1872, toured the United States demonstrating her ability to paint flowers while blindfolded.⁶⁵ Others specialized in dance mediumship (fig. 4) or in the apparition of flowers.⁶⁶ As in stage magic and show business, innovation and novelty played a significant role in establishing the success of a professional medium. Innovations were as customary as imitations of successful phenomena. The American magician Harry Houdini, who thoroughly

FIG. 3   Physical demonstrations of spirit phenomena in Victorian séances were often quite spectacular, featuring the levitation of objects and persons. From Hiram Mattison, *Spirit Rapping Unveiled!* (New York: Mason Brothers, 1853), 13.

studied the history of spiritualism and published a book on this topic in 1924, noted that "even a casual examination of Spiritualistic history and development shows that just as soon as a medium forms a new alliance with the psychic power dispenser and produces phenomena unknown before, other mediums immediately begin to produce it also and the new manifestation becomes epidemic." This had been the case, for instance, with spirit photography: "No one had thought of such a possibility before Mumler [the first spirit photographer] invented the mystery, but talented mediums everywhere when they heard of his pictures began to produce them also."[67]

Spiritualism was not immune to the dynamics of precinematic stardom either. The most popular mediums, such as the Fox sisters, the Scotsman Daniel Dunglas Home, and later the Neapolitan Eusapia Palladino, were acclaimed by spiritualist circles in Europe and the United States and performed séances with prominent personalities and aristocrats sitting at their tables. The story of Daniel Dunglas Home is a perfect example of the rise of "star" mediums. According to Peter Lamont, the author of a biography of the medium, Home "performed so many extraordinary features, for so many witnesses and in such a wide range of circumstances, that he

FIG. 4 Spectacular spirit manifestations included dance mediumship, in which the medium, in trance, performed dance movements under the influence of spirits. Note the markedly racialized and gendered depiction of the different spirit characters. From Hiram Mattison, *Spirit Rapping Unveiled!* (New York: Mason Brothers, 1853), 81.

became one of the most famous men of his time."[68] Home began producing the mediumistic phenomenon that made him famous—levitation—in 1851.[69] This was a veritable turning point in his career: by 1853, at the age of just twenty, he was performing séances with personalities of the caliber of Washington Irving and William Makepeace Thackeray.[70] It was said that he had been able to float in the air in good light, before reputable witnesses including several lords in Great Britain and high French noblemen, more than a hundred times.[71]

In his history of the French spiritualist movement, John Warne Monroe gives an interesting account of the triumphant reception of Home's 1857 tour in France. Despite being doubtful about their authenticity, a journalist for *Le Siècle* so described Home's spectacular manifestations, which overcame any other spiritualist phenomena previously experienced in France: "Tables tilt without being touched, and the objects on them remain immobile, contradicting all the laws of physics. The walls tremble, the furniture stamps its feet, candelabra float, unknown voices cry from nowhere—all the phantasmagoria of the invisible populate the real world."[72] Home's charismatic character certainly played a role in stimulating public interest in this elegant and fashionable British man. His "astonishing career" convinced

Arthur Conan Doyle to depict him as "the greatest [medium] in a physical sense that the world has ever seen."[73]

THE SPECTACLE OF TRANCE

While the first two sections of this chapter have given an account of the theatrical nature of spiritualist demonstration and of the professionalism of mediums, the question of how mediums cued audiences to regard séances as distinct from overtly theatrical performances has yet to be answered. In what follows, I discuss how mediums succeeded in orchestrating a spectacle that, despite its underlying theatrical character, could be perceived as authentic by their sitters. I argue that this was primarily achieved through the apex of the mediums' performance: the state of trance, which strengthened spiritualism's claims of authenticity by recalling the principles of automatism, creative absorption, and reverie. Understanding mediumship as an activity that could have a theatrical character opens the way for an interpretation of trance's highly spectacular effects.[74]

When a medium fell into a trance, the actions she performed were considered to be disconnected from her own will. As one medium put it, the only perfect mode of spirit communion was "wholly mechanical, and disconnected entirely from the mind of the medium."[75] This argument, supporting spiritualism's scientific claims, was based on an understanding of machines as objective means to receive spirit communications. As authors such as Lorraine Daston and Peter Galison have demonstrated, automatism acquired an increasingly important status within the conceptualization of scientific evidence in the nineteenth century.[76] Spiritualism, which developed into a mass movement during the same period, was strongly influenced by this process. Mechanical devices were used to ensure the spontaneity of spirit phenomena and trance. Direct-writing mediums, for instance, often used the planchette to demonstrate that they were not consciously controlling the writing. Photography was also employed to furnish mechanical, "automatic" evidence of spirit phenomena. The use of these and other mechanical devices to record and document physical manifestations was customary in séances conducted under test conditions.[77] In this context, spiritualists also underlined the scientific value of messages and phenomena delivered *automatically* through the medium.

One of the arguments most often used by spiritualists seeking to demonstrate the authenticity of trance phenomena was the naïveté of spirit mediums. Since mediums served as mere channels through which spirit agency manifested itself, their ignorance and inexperience were often cited as further evidence that the hypothesis of trickery and fraud had to be rejected. It is perhaps for this reason that spiritualists frequently recognized mediumistic powers in children. The story of the Fox sisters relies on a similar understanding of childhood as a locus of spirit mediumship: the "discovery" of spirit communication was attributed to two teenagers. Childhood played such a role in this narrative that the younger Kate Fox was depicted as a more powerful medium than her sister: as Emma Hardinge pointed out, "The manifestation became more powerful in the presence of Kate, the youngest sister, than with any one else."[78]

This link between childish innocence and mediumship can be found frequently in the history of spiritualism during the nineteenth century and beyond. In 1878, the *Medium and Daybreak* announced that the Fox sisters' sensitivity to spiritual agency had been inherited by Kate's daughter. The child's powers had been manifest since she was a newborn: the magazine published "an account of writing done through the hands of the child when a babe five months old, a facsimile of the writing accompanying the record of the event."[79] Children of spiritualists were often encouraged to take part in spirit séances. An American spiritualist from Philadelphia, Joseph Hartman, reported how he had realized his daughter Kate possessed mediumistic powers. After this discovery, she started to deliver spirit messages through trance writing.[80]

Mediums' humble origins could also be given as evidence of their innocence and inability to perform tricks. John Wetherbee, for instance, discovered one day that the Irish nurse who was living in his house possessed "that constitutional quality that some people have, that in their presence and sometimes without contact, as was the case with this young woman, inanimate tables and other objects become animate, and intelligently move, it would seem, by the said objects' own volition." From then on, the nurse conducted spirit séances in his home, giving the family "two years of very valuable experience."[81] Emphasizing the ingenuousness of his domestic medium, Wetherbee pointed to the fact that at the moment he discovered her powers, "she did not, in her ignorance, know what Spiritualism meant."[82] She was Irish and Catholic, "a widow of about twenty,—ignorant, careless, and lively."[83] With Wetherbee's account in mind, it is perhaps easier to understand why, as Eve M. Lynch has noted, nineteenth-century ghost stories of the gothic genre often depict an alliance between the supernatural and the domestic servant.[84] In fact, mediums most often came from a lower cultural and social background than their benefactors—a circumstance that spiritualists stressed as reinforcing the credibility of their "automatism." For instance, the medium J. J. Morse—designated by journalist William Thomas Stead as the "Bishop of Spiritualism"[85]—had been a potboy in a public house before his mediumship was discovered. The difference between his waking and entranced states was also a matter of culture: he was as ignorant and uneducated while awake as he was erudite and well educated in trance.

While mediums often stressed their lack of education and knowledge, their previous involvement in theatrical performances or in show business sometimes went unmentioned, probably for fear of attracting accusations that they were merely acting during séances. Emma Hardinge, for instance, was a full-time actress in the 1840s, performing in plays brought to the stage of London theaters such as Sadler's Wells, as well as on New York's Broadway circuit.[86] Just one year before starting her second career as a trance lecturer, in January 1856, she was playing on Broadway.[87] After she became a reputed spiritualist medium, her previous experiences on the theatrical stage were overlooked in several autobiographical accounts.[88] Refusing to link her mediumship with her experiences as an actress, Hardinge pointed out that mediums were individuals whose senses could perceive the electrical and magnetic impulses sent by the souls of the dead; they should thus be compared to the operator in a telegraphic system or, more aptly, to the physical channel through which the message was sent. Their trance phenomena were the result of automatism, not of acting.[89]

The spiritualist fascination with automatism can be linked to the spectacles of clockwork automata, a common attraction since the late eighteenth century. The performance of trance mediums was certainly impacted by the display of a mechanical agency performing rational acts, such as the famous chess-playing automaton that astonished European and American audiences between the end of the eighteenth and the beginning of the nineteenth century—a trick that was performed by an operator hidden inside the machine.[90] The word "automatism" itself, as Lisa Gitelman noted in her discussion of typing, spiritualism, and psychology, derives from the older word "automaton."[91] Clockwork automata were scientific curiosities and attractions whose primary applications were scientific demonstrations, and they involved issues of showmanship as much as inventorship.[92] Demonstrations of automata were part of a broader Victorian culture of spectacularization of machines and technologies, epitomized in the nineteenth century by the display of mechanical modernity in the great industrial and scientific exhibitions.[93] While in the case of the chess-playing automaton the machine was assigned human characteristics, in trance mediumship the human person embodied mechanical automatism.

If most spiritualist accounts focused on the question of automatism and "mechanical" trustworthiness, trance mediumship was also frequently connected to the act of artistic creation and to intellectual life. Under the condition of trance, mediums delivered lectures, wrote messages, stimulated physical manifestations, even drew and painted. Descriptions of mediumistic phenomena mentioned their involuntary as well as aesthetic character, since these two aspects were intrinsically linked. Thus, Charles Hammond of Rochester, New York, reporting on the mediumistic phenomenon of trance dancing, wrote that "the movements are very eccentric, yet often exceedingly graceful."[94] Demonstrations such as the playing of the piano by persons who were not trained left audiences astonished by the wonder of trance automatism and the aesthetic value of the musical performance.

An early writing on spiritualism expressed this tension between spontaneous action and art. Considering the adequacy of automatic mental action, the author Charles Beecher explained, "Instrumental representative of mind, the brain is capable of spontaneous action, without mind. Such spontaneous action will be indistinguishable from mental operations proper. Musicians perform automatically. Printers set type mechanically. In revery, all manner of things are done unconsciously."[95] By bringing musical performance, typesetting, and reverie together, Beecher evoked the principles of mechanical automatism on one hand and creative absorption on the other. In a similar way, the author of an 1869 historical survey of spiritualism and clairvoyance, J. M. Peebles, compared mediumship with artistic inspiration, since mediums were influenced by the spiritual atmosphere—by spirits "pouring down upon us love-waves of heavenly inspiration, levelling up humanity at large, the same as the sun attracts and unfolds the floral beauties of all landscapes."[96]

Mediumistic trance was often linked with dreaming and visions. A medium described the process of falling into a trance as though a black curtain was placed before her eyes: "For a moment by looking down she can see the floor beneath her, then the curtain comes down with a rush, and all is blank."[97] In an article in the *Spiritual Magazine*, the boundaries between spirit communication and dreaming seem to blur: "Spiritual beings belong to inner life, and when they appear to us, and have power strongly to influence us,—to make us *en rapport* with them,—we are powerfully drawn towards that inner state of consciousness which we call sleep and dreaming,—and which is an abstraction from the waking consciousness."[98] Following this perspective, clairvoyance and trance were "forms of sleep less common than our nightly experience, and far more wonderful to us."[99]

Such accounts suggest that mediums' automatism had, at the same time, to do with the mechanical world and with one of the greatest manifestations of human agency—the act of creation. What seems to be a contradiction was, in reality, the product of a pre-Freudian psychology of unconscious life and dreaming, in which ideas about mechanical automatism and trance overlapped with artistic creation and reverie.[100] Writings that gave a theoretical frame to spiritualist phenomena, in fact, consistently relied on a number of earlier scientific and popular publications that situated dreams, illusions, and artistic inspiration in the automatic actions of the brain and perceptual organs.[101]

This overlapping of trance mediumship with artistic creation and dreaming helps explain how trance worked to frame the séance as a real, albeit spectacular, event. In his book *Absorption and Theatricality: Painting and Beholder in the Age of Diderot,* art historian Michael Fried identifies two dominant approaches to painting. The first one, absorption, refers to paintings in which the main figure is absorbed in her intent and does not directly regard the viewer. The second one, theatricality, refers to artworks where the subject is clearly represented in order to shape and direct the viewer's gaze. Fried gives several examples of absorption, pointing to paintings that depicted artists, philosophers, and writers caught up in the moment. The use of absorption responds to the aim of presenting images as though they were not explicitly intended to be regarded by an audience. The viewer is therefore drawn into the representation, made oblivious to the act of looking and thus to the fictional nature of the scene. On the contrary, theatricality tends to acknowledge the position of the spectator and the fictional interpretation of the situation.[102] One of the apparently most contradictory characteristics of nineteenth-century séances was that they simultaneously evoked conditions of theatricality and absorption. On the one hand, the complex dramaturgy and rituals shaped the viewers' situation in a way that could reinforce the understanding of their role as spectators. On the other hand, the state of trance, recalled in virtually every spiritual manifestation delivered through the mediums, was connected to an aesthetics of creative absorption that contributed to the spontaneous character of their performance.

Trance mediumship can thus be interpreted, even if or when it did not involve conscious acting, as a highly regulated modality of performance that spiritualist mediums employed before large crowds of sitters and spectators in the nineteenth century. By employing an aesthetics of absorption, mediums made the sitters oblivious to their position as spectators. This made possible the establishment of a situation that, despite being essentially theatrical, denied the fictional character of the mediums' performance. Although the denying of an overtly fictional situation is customary in drama, too, in the séance space, this entailed much more than a suspension of disbelief: the sitter's involvement in the ritual and, ultimately, the meaning of the séance spectacle itself relied on its claim of authenticity.

To employ Erving Goffman's notion of frame again, spiritualist séances were a spectacular device that played with the sitters' interpretation of the event. It was, in particular, through the state of trance that mediums erected a frame that discouraged the sitters to recognize themselves as spectators. Acknowledging the complex spectacularization of trance phenomena helps explain how séances and trance mediumship created theatrical environments, at the same time avoiding an explicit and overt acknowledgment of this shift from the world of religion to that of entertainment. Mediumistic trance contributed to defining the environment of spiritualist séances, where believers and skeptics gathered to attend a spectacle of "spontaneous" manifestations.

The entertaining nature of spiritualist séances not only characterized those that were performed before an audience of spectators. In private séances, too, mediums orchestrated a performative environment where sitters participated in an event resembling a social game. As the next chapter will show, séances held at home also created opportunities for leisure, social gatherings, and amusement. If public séances played a role in the history of show business, private séances participated in the introduction of new forms of domestic entertainment in the Victorian age.

2

PARLOR GAMES

PLAY AND SOCIAL LIFE IN

THE HAUNTED HOUSE

Leah Fox, the older sister of Kate and Margaret, left us some colorful descriptions of her family's communications with spirits. In many of them, the house serves as the privileged setting for the phenomena of mediumship, and spirit manifestations are portrayed as something similar to a parlor entertainment. One evening, for instance, Leah enjoyed the company of some friends, playing the piano and singing, and at the same time felt "the deep throbbing of the dull accompaniment of the invisibles, keeping time to the music as I played."[1] After they retired for the night, she was able to sleep for a couple of hours before being awakened by what she described as a spirit pantomime: "There seemed to be many actors engaged in the performance, and a large audience in attendance. The representation of a pantomime performance was perfect. After the first scene, there was great applause by the Spirit audience. Immediately following, one Spirit was heard to dance *as if with clogs*, which continued fully ten minutes. This amused the audience very much; and a loud clapping of hands followed. After this we heard nothing more except the representation of a large crowd walking away down-stairs, through the rooms, closing the doors heavily after them."[2] In Leah's account, the haunted house is described as a parlor theater. Spirits took part in the social gatherings that the medium enjoyed with her friends and family, as if they were guests invited to join a domestic party.

Although mediums often performed on the theatrical stage, Victorian spiritualist séances were most frequently held in domestic spaces. For many committed spiritualists, forming circles at home was, in fact, "the most satisfactory mode of testing the truth of the phenomena."³ This has been interpreted by some historians of spiritualism as symptomatic of the isolation of spiritualist circles within their own private space. Ann Braude, for instance, argued that séances held in the house "reflected the Victorian view that the home was the true locus of religiosity."⁴ Beliefs in the supernatural and spiritualist attempts to communicate with the otherworld should be understood, following this perspective, within a religious framework that tended to consolidate community relations and group membership. Scholars such as Robert S. Cox, Daniel Herman, Molly McGarry, and John Warne Monroe, however, have recently put forth a more subtle interpretation of spiritualist séances, including issues of entertainment and emotional commitment in their examinations of the experience of spiritualist sitters.⁵ Following from this line of thinking, this chapter aims at shedding light on how spiritualist séances shaped domestic environments as spaces open to social encounters and amusing pastimes. In the first section, I show that private séances were semipublic events in which sitters enjoyed the emotional rewards of friendship and social life. Then, in the second section, I propose to examine them as pertaining to the history of domestic media entertainments. Their playful and amusing nature suggests that we should look at their relationship with a range of domestic amusements conducted in Victorian households, from table games to parlor theaters, from musical entertainments to philosophical toys.

OPENING THE HAUNTED HOUSE

During the first half of the nineteenth century in the United States, a change in architectural design took place first in the households of the wealthy and then, by the 1850s, in those of the middle class. New townhouses were built with a barrier dividing the living room from the dining room, which could be removed in order to stage performances. This change transformed the parlor into a room used for display and into a comfortable setting for social ceremonies.⁶ It made the household a more inclusive place, and it influenced the choice of setting for many séances held in Victorian America. In fact, spiritualist sittings were usually carried out in those parts of the home, such as the living room, that were dedicated to social and familial gatherings.⁷ Such spaces, which were simultaneously private and public, allowed spiritualists to shape their events as religious experiences and, at the same time, as occasions for social encounters and playful activities. Consequently, séances held at home were often not too different from the theatrical versions of this ritual.

From the beginning, spiritualism established the parlor as a gathering space for those who wished to inquire about the mysteries of the spirit world. According to Arthur Conan Doyle, when the news of the discovery of spirit rapping spread through the town of Hydesville, neighbors of the Fox family came flocking to their door to see what it was about. "On the next Saturday," Mrs. Fox reported, "the house was filled to overflowing."[8] There were more than three hundred people present in the house, whose doors were open to anyone who wanted to see with her own eyes the phenomenon that had sparked so many rumors.

Many spiritualists acknowledged the blurred boundary between private and public mediumship. Catherine Berry, a well-known medium in Britain and the United States during the nineteenth century, divided her reports of spiritualist phenomena into two parts—the first dedicated to "séances at home," the second to "séances in public."[9] She reported how her apartment had become, during the years prior to the publication of her book in 1876, a gathering place for people interested in investigating the subject. Having convinced herself of the authenticity of spirit phenomena, Berry did all she could to convince others: "Whenever I had a séance with a good medium, and that was intervals of only a few days, I made a point of inviting my friends to participate in it, and also received enquirers who were introduced to me. The sitters at my séances have been neither few nor unimportant, so that my experiments have been conducted in public."[10]

Séance rooms were chosen for their capacity to host a large number of people. The author of *Confessions of a Medium*, debunking his own spiritualist mediumship as a fraud, recalled first entering a proper spiritualist circle in "a long room, capable of comfortably holding the thirty people present."[11] The following week, the medium returned to this house, noting that the company had been increased "by several others, who came from all parts of the town; some from the suburbs, and some from nearer home."[12] The dimensions of the room were also instrumental in the full development of spirit phenomena: the séance table, for instance, could be conveniently moved by the spirits "in all directions—from side to side—from end to end—and round and round—over a large room with great ease and smooth regularity."[13]

Private spiritualist circles were open to the participation of outsiders. Lists of mediums performing in domestic environments appeared in print, allowing spiritualists to choose the séances they were interested in visiting or to contact the organizer of a séance circle.[14] Since experimenting with spirit communication was the main path to participating in the spiritualist faith, spiritualists considered it a duty to provide neophytes with a warm and hospitable environment. Hence, one spiritualist could report that he was given the opportunity to visit a séance by a medium who, despite being "an entire stranger," welcomed him to her table.[15] The open nature of spiritualist sittings was noted not only by supporters but also by opponents of the movement, albeit with very different results. A skeptic, for instance, observed that all visitors were admitted to a medium's parlor provided that they had paid a fee, linking the monetary transaction to suspicions of trickery and fraud.[16] Others pointed out that spiritualist séances were open to everyone who wanted to be entertained.[17] From their viewpoint, spiritualism's emphasis on entertainment and spectacle contrasted with its alleged religious or scientific endeavors.

The setting and physical arrangement of the séances were designed in order to establish a welcoming and pleasant atmosphere. Although there existed variations among different spiritualist circles, the séance environment was progressively standardized over the course of the century. Spiritualist journals and publications gave advice to their readers on how to organize a successful spirit encounter. Felix Roubaud, the author of a book published in Paris in 1853, after reporting that news of the spiritualist phenomenon of "table dancing" had recently reached France, explained that the presence of affective feelings among the sitters was an important condition for a successful séance: "A woman whose maternal love is overexcited by some threat suspended over the cradle of her son, or a lover whose heart shakes while waiting for her beloved, will give movement to an inert body much faster and with much more energy."[18] Furthermore, Roubaud suggested that, if possible, the ratio of males to females should be equal in a séance, so that persons of a different sex might sit beside each other, "in order to shorten and distract from the boredom of the wait."[19] The organizer of a spirit circle had to purposefully compose a group of sitters, in the same way that a host might behave in sending out invitations for an evening gathering. If good guests make a good party, then good sitters seem to have been crucial for establishing a successful spiritualist circle. As Catherine Berry put it, "By carefully selecting my sitters I have ensured the best manifestations."[20]

Establishing contact with the beyond could be an enjoyable and amusing event through which small groups of people shared a collective experience.[21] Conversation and other pastimes were not excluded from the séance environment (fig. 5). An article in a British spiritualist magazine, listing

FIG. 5
Conversation was not excluded but often openly encouraged in séance circles, in order to unite the minds of those present in the common purpose of contacting the spirits. Frontispiece to *Confessions of a Medium* (London: Griffith and Farran, 1882).

séance conditions such as a good atmosphere, subdued light or darkness, and love of truth and mankind in the sitters' hearts, noted that "agreeable conversation, singing, reading, or invocation may be engaged in—anything that will tend to harmonize the minds of those present, and unite them in one purpose."[22] Although such rules perhaps also resulted from the need of fraudulent mediums to distract the sitters while they performed the "phenomena," the fact that chatting and singing were welcome in spiritualist séances contributed to shifting the atmosphere of these events from a serious religious experience toward entertainment and leisure—or, as John Warne Monroe put it, "from a pastime for amateur scientists into a titillating party game."[23]

Social encounters that derived from spiritualist séances sometimes had sexual connotations, too. As Marlene Tromp and Ann Braude have shown, spiritualist communities in the nineteenth century often combined spiritual activities with radical political views and social behaviors in such areas as marriage and gender issues.²⁴ Critics of spiritualism frequently condemned the movement's libertinage, and some fierce debates concerning the authenticity of spirit phenomena included allegations of promiscuity between the medium and her sitters. Thus, when the British press attacked the scientist William Crookes for his conversion to spiritualism, one of his opponents' main arguments revolved around the allegation that he had fallen in love with the medium Florence Cook; this challenged his credibility as a scientist and a witness.²⁵ The battle for social rights, such as the right to divorce and the right to free love, was paralleled, in the spiritualist realm of the séance, by an atmosphere that often tended to trespass the usual borders of prudence and puritanism. Promiscuity was the rule in private séances, and the condition of darkness (widely accepted as one of the essential requisites for contacting the spirit world) enhanced the sense that the relationship between sitters and mediums might have sexual implications.

The opening of the séance room to strangers interested in learning about spiritualist phenomena was emblematic of the permeability of the haunted house to an entity who came, in the strictest sense, from another world. In fact, opening a house to the participants in a séance also involved welcoming the spirits who would respond to the medium's call. During a séance conducted by the American medium Maria B. Hayden, the first to introduce spiritualism to England, the apartment of a British spiritualist hosted "eight or nine persons of all ages," in addition to a great number of spirits; their ages and sex could be recognized by the tone of their rapping, "the big needle sounds of the men, and the little ones of the women and children, being clearly distinguishable."²⁶ The variety in the character and behavior of spirits was such that an early witness of spiritualist manifestations reported to have sustained communication with ten or twelve "*invisible* actors" during a séance that exhibited "many of the characteristics of a regular drama."²⁷ If sittings were frequently compared to theatrical plays, another entertaining pastime that was frequently mentioned in reference to séances was social chatting. The unseen visitors could engage in enjoyable conversation through rapping, trance lecturing, and direct writing. In a letter to a spiritualist journal, a London lawyer described his encounter with the spirit of a James Lombard, with whom he had "some lively chat upon a variety of subjects, having reference especially to his own state and the conditions under which he was enabled to communicate with us." Judging from the tone and the vocabulary employed by this spirit, the writer thought that he was "an unlettered 'spirit' of a sanguine and jovial disposition, grateful at having escaped from terrestrial bondage, and animated with a strong desire to reach a 'higher sphere.'"[28]

The appearance of spirit manifestations, a spiritualist pointed out, could be explained by "the law of sympathy": the channel of communication with the beyond existed through the same invisible ties that unite two friends or two brothers.[29] Spirits were often family relations or acquaintances of some of the persons present or identified themselves as famous personalities of the past, such as Joan of Arc or Benjamin Franklin, who were well known to sitters. They were willing to consent to the sitters' demands: following a pattern found in many séance reports, the sitters asked the spirits to provide evidence of their spiritual identity, such as the name of a close relative or friend who was unknown to the other sitters, or to produce a particular manifestation. In a book published in London in 1862, for instance, the author reported that sitters at one séance had asked a spirit to write on an open book, to raise the table, and then to raise it again while one of the sitters, who was still skeptical, placed his fingers underneath its edge; the entity accomplished every single feat they requested.[30] In 1878, an article in the London spiritualist magazine *Medium and Daybreak* described a communication with a spirit in the following way: "Yes, a *pleasant* physical seance! . . . [The spirit] gently talked and reasoned with us, and made us feel that he was like ourselves, a responsible moral being, endowed with self-respect, a sense of propriety and consideration for the feelings of others. . . . Indeed it was a spiritual seance, the influence pervading the room being of a high order, and leaving a satisfaction on the minds of the sitters which no mere manifestations could produce."[31]

Victorian spiritualist séances were fueled by emotions and feelings similar to those excited by literature, theater, and film, such as an emotional high, amusement, and fascination with the unknown.[32] Sittings were ruled by a recurring dramaturgy, which, no different from a theatrical sketch, manipulated the attention and the reactions of sitters. The contact with spirits elicited a climax of excitation that was similar in many ways to what, in overtly spectacular contexts, we call "suspense."[33] If one compares the experience of spirit communication in nineteenth- and early twentieth-century spiritualism with the representation of ghosts in fictional texts and representations, however, one key difference is evident: while in the gothic literary tradition, in spectral apparitions on the theatrical stage, and in horror movies, ghosts most often appear as evil presences, the specters of spiritualism were usually benevolent to séance sitters. Joy and happiness—not fear—were the sentiments that these events kindled in sitters and spectators. Antagonistic spirits are very rare in reports of spiritualist séances, and the interaction between sitters and spirits was usually described as one of sympathy and community.[34] The good temperament of the spirits was frequently emphasized as evidence of the uplifting character of the spiritualist enterprise and of the benevolence of the spirit world toward both believers and skeptics. Thus, Emma Hardinge, one of the most popular mediums of the nineteenth century in Britain and the United States, referred to the spirits with whom she was in contact as a "tender, loving, wonderful presence."[35] This is particularly interesting given the prevalence of fearful ghosts in fictional representations.[36] Indeed, the evilness of fictional ghosts and the loving nature of the ghosts of spiritualism is perhaps the most evident discrepancy between them.[37]

The semipublic character of private séances was further enhanced by the fact that they were described in detail in periodicals and books. Scholars in media history have shown that the telegraph was one of the main metaphors that spiritualists used to describe the act of communicating with the beyond.[38] Less attention, however, has been given to spiritualists' references to broadcasting—a term that, in its metaphorical and literal sense, resonates widely in twentieth-century media culture.[39] Many believed that spreading (broadcasting) the messages of spirits was one of the main goals of the spiritualist faith. They stressed that spirits were eager to have their words heard by the widest public possible and described interactions with spirits using a one-to-many model of communication, based on print media and on the idea of religious preaching.[40] A leaflet entitled "Seed Corn," published in London in 1872, for instance, suggested the best strategies for disseminating spirit messages through journals and other publications on spiritualism.[41] Likewise, the Ohio spiritualist entrepreneur Hudson Tuttle praised the movement's ability to disseminate its periodicals across the land and suggested that its astounding success in spreading spiritualist truth could not be explained "unless the myriad spirits of the departed, standing behind the scenes of their invisibility, push on the work."[42] By circulating séance reports and transcripts of spirit communications, spiritualists hoped to turn their private explorations into a public and collective agency that would extend the impact of their interactions with the spirit world. They believed that the accumulation of knowledge about the spirit world, similar to scientific knowledge, could only be possible if séance experiences and experiments were publicized as widely as possible.[43]

In broadcasting reports of séance phenomena, private séances had much in common with other scientific experiments performed within domestic settings in the Victorian era, which were reported in scientific and popular periodicals.[44] Since the introduction of mesmeric practices in

Britain and the United States in the first decades of the nineteenth century, demonstrations of trance phenomena had garnered wide public attention, and experiments in trance were a popular subject in the press. For instance, trance performances developed by the O'Key sisters under the scrutiny of John Elliotson, one of the first British physicians to experiment with mesmerism, were widely discussed in medical journals such as the *Lancet* in the 1830s. At the lecture theater of the University College London Hospital, the girls sang and danced under the condition of trance, entertaining an audience of spectators interested in the novel mesmeric method and its effects. This resulted in the establishment of what Amy Lehman has called the "medical theatre" of mesmerism: "Although the context for the event was scientific, the goal to study the physical effects of mesmerism, . . . the demonstrations were clearly a variant of Victorian theatre."[45]

In summary, opening the house to sitters and spirits, séances gathered small groups of people for exciting journeys into the supernatural, within the domestic environment. The porosity of these domestic spaces suggests that the difference between the "private" and "public" séance was less relevant than it might seem. For the spiritualist movement, participation in séances meant investing in community relations that focused on shared experience, sympathy, and a blurring of the boundary between private and public spaces. The publication of reports and news about séance experiences, moreover, further contributed to disseminating spirit communications beyond the domestic walls. Private séances were therefore semipublic events in which friends and strangers joined the medium under the reassuring shield of the spiritualist faith. As I discuss in the next section, the blurring of public and private environments also helped establish private séances as spaces for social activities of a playful nature. Elements such as the séance table and musical instruments, which maintained a central function in spiritualist sittings throughout the nineteenth century, suggest that séances, as Molly McGarry put it, "played with and in the contemporary genres of entertainment and belief."[46] The private séance can thus be regarded as a kind of domestic pastime, similar to other distractions that were customary in nineteenth-century households, such as table games, amateur prestidigitation tricks, and philosophical toys.

THE RATIONAL AMUSEMENT OF THE SPIRIT SÉANCE

The role of the "spirit table" in séances is perhaps one of the most eccentric aspects of the spiritualist faith. While the use of objects such as musical instruments, automatic-writing devices, and spirit cabinets depended on the skills and the habits of the medium, tables were apparently a necessary precondition for spiritualist sittings. As Daniel Cottom put it, soon after the Fox sisters' rapping initiated the spiritualist craze, "tables took on a new and controversial life."[47] This apparently insignificant piece of furniture was suddenly the subject of scientific commissions, press reports, and pamphlets attempting to disclose the secrets of the miraculous, or fraudulent, *danse des tables*.[48] Especially in their first decade, before more complex manifestations were developed, table turning and table walking were widely regarded, by spiritualists and critics alike, as the most significant spirit manifestations.[49] The collection of evidence supporting the spiritualist claims commonly relied on devices purportedly designed to record any movement of the table.[50] Tables were sometimes equated with living beings, as if the phenomena were delivered directly from them. The noise of a tapping on the table could have a profound emotional impact on believers in spirit communication, producing the feeling that the soul of the dead was embodied in this object.[51] The American Joseph Hartman related how the table responded "quite energetically and intelligently" to his incitements, beating in time when anyone played the piano, answering mental questions, moving about through the rooms, and turning upside down when it was touched with the ends of the fingers.[52] Popular illustrations of spiritualist séances assigned this item a central role in the formation of the spirit circle. In an engraving published in 1882, for instance, the table appears to have forced the sitters to stand up, directing through its movement and levitation the actions of the participants and the functioning of the séance (fig. 6). Indeed, the disposition of the "magnetic rope" created by the combined psychical powers of the sitters was regulated by the presence of the table; after all, the basic arrangement of a sitting—the spirit circle—replicated the circular form of the séance table.[53]

How can we explain this religious and symbolic function that tables appropriated? Why were tables so important to believers in communication with the otherworld? Historians of spiritualism have scarcely addressed these questions. Cottom, however, has perceptively noted that the use of tables in spirit séances is symptomatic of the way spiritualism vulgarized the supernatural, "making the most trivial objects resound with portentous significance."[54] In fact, the triviality of this item was frequently acknowledged by the opponents as well as the supporters of the movement. For instance, in making excuses for the presumably unscientific nature of this object, the author of a treatise translated from French

FIG. 6
The table played a central role in the functioning of spiritualist séances. This illustration depicts a table levitation, a common spirit manifestation in nineteenth-century spiritualism. From *Confessions of a Medium* (London: Griffith and Farran, 1882), 109.

in 1857 appropriately conceded that "tables they were, and tables they shall remain."[55]

Yet Cottom's argument provides only a partial explanation for the role of tables in spiritualism. The fact that mediums often employed objects of common use to establish communication with the spirits, and that the material culture of spiritualism was closely linked to its religious component, does not completely clarify why mediums relied on tables, instead of other objects, to raise the dead. A possible interpretation of this practice is that spiritualist sittings were social and entertaining events. The table is one of the structural elements of domestic spaces—such as the living and dining rooms—that are private and public at the same time, as they are used in private households to receive visitors and host social meetings. In explaining the symbolism of spirit communication, one spiritualist reasoned that "the table is the center around which friends and kindred meet, to feast and commune in friendship and love in earthlife, so angels and spirits make the table the center around which we meet and hold communion with the spirits of our departed friends."[56] Another insider observed that the tipping of tables particularly resounded with the heart of the civilized man, who saw in this object an irreplaceable element of every human dwelling and valued "the social meetings which take place around it."[57]

The use of the table, in this regard, is linked to the entertaining nature of spirit séances. As a domestic object frequently employed to receive visitors, engage in conversation, and play cards, the table associates spiritualism with the activities of leisure time. Private séances might thus be considered a kind of highly regulated table game that followed a set of shared rules and contributed not only to the spiritual life but also—and perhaps even more—to the amusement of the sitters.

As Margaret Hofer observed in her history of board games, the games that entertained people on both sides of the Atlantic during the Victorian age offer an extraordinary window onto the social and cultural transformations of the time.[58] Especially in the middle class, as the spheres of home and workplace became more distinct, families increasingly practiced leisure activities in the domestic environment. In a parallel manner, the production of cards and other popular table games was increasingly mechanized during the nineteenth century, and improvements in paper and printing enabled the large-scale commercialization of board games.[59] As a consequence, the table around which spiritualists gathered to summon the spirits of the dead was, in the middle of the nineteenth century, a piece of furniture whose social and entertaining function went far beyond dining and traditional social rituals such as meeting for tea.

In *Homo Ludens*, Johan Huizinga stressed both the ritual significance of play and the presence of elements of playfulness in religious and magic ceremonies.[60] By integrating leisure and entertainment activities, séances contributed to spiritualism's underlying playful nature. Music, for instance, played a significant role in sittings (fig. 7). Private séances were often introduced by an intermezzo, such as singing or piano music. In one report, a medium was said to have incited sitters to sing before the beginning of a séance; they performed some "pretty, cheerful little hymns, such as 'Hand in Hand with Angels,' 'The Beautiful River,' and Longfellow's 'Footsteps of Angels.'"[61] In 1853, a spiritualist from Philadelphia went so far as to publish a volume of songs for use in spirit circles.[62]

Spirit manifestations frequently consisted of noises and sounds. The darkness of séance rooms forced spirits and mediums to rely on nonvisual experiences. As Steven Connor has argued, "The members of the séance

FIG. 7
Music played an important role in Victorian séances. In this illustration, a musical instrument levitates over the séance table. From *Confessions of a Medium* (London: Griffith and Farran, 1882), 95.

would see much less than they would touch, taste, smell and, most importantly, *hear*."[63] One of the most widespread spiritualist manifestations was the playing of musical instruments by the spirits. As one spiritualist reported, spirits "rang the bells and played the music, they swung the guitar about over our heads, and knocked the ceiling itself."[64] The medium Georgiana Houghton, in a book whose title, *Evenings at Home in Spiritual Séance*, seems to suggest the social and leisure aspects of séance sitting, recalled that on one occasion the sitters laid some instruments on the séance table, "among them one composed of eight metal cups (forming the scale)."[65] After the séance started, the spirits played a well-known song, "The Last Rose of Summer," and performed a little musical concert: "They then struck one single note, and carried the instrument round and round the room until the sound had faded away, and so on with each note:—after which they produced the most harmonious effect I ever heard; they struck the deepest note, carrying it *once* round, above our heads, so that the room was filled with the vibrations, then the second in the same way, until at last we heard the vibrations of the whole eight, softened and blended into one another, forming, if I may so express it, a perfect *rainbow* of sound."[66]

Spirit music often involved the use of the piano, an instrument that was present in many middle-class houses where private séances were held. In a sitting described by Emma Hardinge, the piano was played by two young girls "who had scarcely reached their teens, both of whom were unacquainted with music, yet acted upon by spirits in a way to play the most exquisite tunes upon the piano."[67] The use of music not only established a pleasing environment at a spiritualist gathering, but also evoked activities of leisure and social life in the domestic house. The study of music, and especially of piano, was common among young middle-class women in Europe and North America during the nineteenth century. Young ladies demonstrated their musical skills for evening guests, and piano playing was an important activity in the process of courting.

The range and variability of spirit manifestations were instrumental in ensuring the entertaining quality of séances, too. Although the first séances relied solely on spirit rapping and table turning, spiritualist phenomena soon became more varied. Already in the 1870s, Catherine Berry, citing instances of spiritual phenomena, listed manifestations as diverse as the painting of faces; the apparition of flowers, fruits, birds, butterflies, and flour; the physical manifestation of spirits; the cutting of fruit; the disappearance of objects; the movement of pictures and carrying of objects by spirits; the drinking of ale by a spirit; spirit music, voices, and touches; levitation of the medium or the sitters; and a shower of feathers.[68] She described the latter as "a wonderful manifestation, although not one of my liking, and I would much have preferred a shower of flowers, which my spirit friends generally give me."[69] "Wonderful" manifestations could also include dance mediumship, eccentric movements performed by mediums who were "possessed" by spirits,[70] spirit painting or drawing in trance,[71] and spirit photography.[72]

The reaction of sitters to these phenomena was often described as joyful. Mediums welcomed manifestations of happiness and delight from sitters. Such emotions were considered to be the fuel that nourished spirit communication and a prerequisite for the successful functioning of the spirit circle. Even reactions of laughter were well received, and some mediums viewed mirth as one of the main symbolic and emotional displays of the bond between sitters and spirits.[73] The spiritualist Joseph Hartman reported that a session of spirit drawing—a phenomenon that involved the sketching of drawings by a medium in trance—was watched by the sitters with a mixture of wonder and enjoyment: "No words can express our astonishment and delight, for the entertainment seemed to come as the result of association with youthful spirits, who were glad to have found an open avenue by which they could 'come' and manifest their presence and tell of their happiness." The spirits drew forty or fifty cartoons within an hour and a half, explaining each design and explicitly saying that they had "fun."[74] Spirits frequently asserted that they received as much pleasure from séances as did the sitters. When Robert Dale Owen, who converted to spiritualism in 1854 and subsequently authored two successful books on this topic, expressed his gratification at having been allowed to witness some spectacular manifestations, the spirits responded, "Don't you know that we are as much gratified to give them as you to receive them?"[75] According to another report, spirits were drawn to a wide array of popular entertainments: they played cards; frequently organized parties, balls, and other forms of recreation in the otherworld; and celebrated whenever a spirit rose "to the higher sphere" with "a grand entertainment of music and dancing."[76]

As Peter Lamont noted, spiritualist phenomena appear to bear relations to prestidigitation, an art that was performed as evening domestic entertainment in the late nineteenth century by middle-class amateur magicians.[77] In fact, many manifestations observed at spiritualist séances resembled these sleights of hand. Georgiana Houghton, for instance, described a séance in which the spirits gently withdrew a handkerchief from the hands of a sitter, knotted it into the form of a figure, and tucked it into the front of her dress.[78] In a séance recorded in 1867 by William Lloyd Garrison, a basket containing artificial oranges and lemons was emptied, its contents distributed around the circle, and the basket successfully put upon the head of everyone present in a grotesque manner.[79] These phenomena were unmistakably similar to customary tricks from the tradition of prestidigitation.[80] Such feats performed by the spirits were instrumental in arousing the wonder of the sitters, suggesting that séances were a kind of domestic spectacle that played with audience members' taste for sensation as much as with their religious belief.[81]

Spiritualist séances also have much in common with popular games and toys marketed for use in domestic environments during the Victorian era. Throughout the nineteenth century, for instance, American and British publishers offered a great variety of "oracles"—books that promised to predict players' fortunes and, at the same time, provided groups of men and women with a possible means of interaction during social occasions.[82] The most famous of them was Henrietta Dumont's *The Lady's Oracle*. The book's introduction explained that the oracle was meant to prevent those times in an evening's enjoyment when conversation flagged, "and every one feels the necessity of some movement which shall dissipate the awkwardness and restraint of the moment, and afford the means of active and interesting amusement."[83] The oracle books provided a simple game and a pattern for social interaction based on a series of questions and responses. Answers to questions were randomly chosen by the person whose fortune was to be read, and then read aloud by the person acting as the oracle. Spiritualist séances could sometimes function similarly to the oracle books, providing sitters with a preestablished set of interaction dynamics to follow. Sitters

FIG. 8 The spiritoscope, designed by Robert Hare, provided experimental evidence of spirit contact. From Robert Hare, *Experimental Investigation of the Spirit Manifestations, Demonstrating the Existence of Spirits and Their Communion with Mortals* (New York: Partridge and Brittan, 1856).

might ask the spirits to give them insight into the future, reproducing quite accurately the tradition of oracle games.

Devices purportedly designed to ensure the clarity and authenticity of spirit messages, which were frequently employed in séances, bore relations to popular toys of the time, too. Particularly famous were those designed by Robert Hare, a chemistry professor at the University of Pennsylvania, whose conversion to spiritualism had warranted front-page coverage in the *New York Times* in 1855.[84] He created as many as six versions of his mechanized instrument, called the "spiritoscope," which aimed at preventing the possibility of trickery and manipulation during sittings. Hare's most effective idea was to place a disk bearing the letters of the alphabet, which spirits might use to communicate with sitters, in a position that hid it from the eyes of the medium (fig. 8). In this way, Hare reasoned, mediums had no control over the message delivered, "even clairvoyance being nullified,"[85] and the experimenter could collect empirical, unabridged evidence of spirit communication.

The spiritoscope was meant to make all spirit communications performed through the "bare" table obsolete, replacing table rapping with a more mediated signal. If the table were to cease to be at the center of the spiritualist enterprise, the playfulness of the experience would not be lost; on the contrary, it would possibly be enhanced. The passion for knowledge that led Hare to design increasingly complex devices for testing the authenticity of spirit communication reveals the convergence of spiritualist practices with the tradition of scientific demonstrations and pastimes.[86] Hare incessantly employed his devices in spiritualist séances and with different mediums, giving practical demonstrations of their functions and marveling at the revelations that the spirits sent through them.[87] He was neither the first nor the last in the history of spiritualism to design, employ, and demonstrate devices for registering spirit messages and phenomena. For instance, the British engineer Cromwell Fleetwood Varley, who was involved in the laying of the successful transatlantic telegraph cables of the 1860s and converted to spiritualism at the end of that decade, used electrical apparatuses to establish whether spirit contact involved the discharge of electric and magnetic streams.[88]

Several of these instruments employed in séances were commercialized as popular games throughout the nineteenth century, inaugurating a tradition of toys inspired by spiritualism and mediumship that reaches to the present day. Companies such as Sears Roebuck in the United States and the Two Worlds Publishing Company in Britain marketed several models of "spirit boards" in the last decades of the century, turning spirit communication into a popular game that was advertised as such.[89] Inspired by the likes of the spiritoscope and the planchette—a simple instrument that facilitated written communication with spirits[90]—numerous devices were patented with different names, including the "toy fortune-telling device," the "dial planchette," and the "talking board."[91] While maintaining their designation as popular games, toy companies openly invoked the tradition of instruments designed for the investigation of spiritualism.[92]

The most successful spiritualism-related instrument and toy is undoubtedly the Ouija board. The first version of this board was patented in 1891 in the United States and originally commercialized by the Kennard Novelty Company in Baltimore.[93] The patent described it as "a toy or game by which two or more persons can amuse themselves by asking questions of any kind and having them answered by the device used and operated by the touch of the hand, so that the answers are designated by letters on the board."[94] Advertisements for this "wonderful talking board" began to appear as early as February 1891 in the popular press.[95] The Ouija board was so successful that in the following years the Kennard Novelty Company opened new factories in New York, Chicago, and London and registered several patents for improvements on this instrument.[96] Despite being marketed as a toy, it was also widely employed by spiritualists at séances; domestic entertainment was thus combined with religious practice and the investigation of spirit phenomena. Ethnographic studies confirm that the Ouija board is still used today as both an instrument of inquiry into the supernatural and a game. Jean M. Myrick conducted interviews with people who used the Ouija board; interviewees compared it to playing cards and Monopoly, a popular table game, while contending that there was also something "more serious" about it.[97] In 2014, the board lent its name to a successful horror film, *Ouija*, distributed by Universal Pictures. The launching of the movie coincided with the marketing of a table game, inviting playful as well as realistic interpretations of the Ouija's functioning.[98]

The use of instruments to facilitate spirit communication suggests that séances had something in common with the "rational amusement" of popular nineteenth-century philosophical toys, such as the phenakistoscope and the stereoscope. These devices were designed to demonstrate the achievements of rational sciences, especially optics, and at the same time to arouse curiosity and to serve as entertainment for private use. As David Brewster, who invented the kaleidoscope and popularized the application of the stereoscope for photography, put it, "The toy that amuses the child will instruct the sage, and many an eminent discoverer and inventor can trace the pursuits which immortalize them to some experiment or instrument which amused them at school."[99] Likewise, the use of spiritualist devices such as the spiritoscope and the Ouija board coupled leisure with spiritualist inquiry, arousing curiosity and a thirst for knowledge.

Marketed simultaneously as instruments for spiritualist circles and domestic entertainment, spirit boards provided users with standardized practices for conducting spiritualist séances as religious inquiries and as domestic games, allowing for a flexible interpretation of these events. Instruments conceived for the investigation of spiritualism were redesigned as parlor and table games, participating in the tradition of rational amusements in the nineteenth century. The application of scientific principles for the purpose of amusement, in fact, was based on a mixture of curiosity, wonder, and desire for knowledge that characterized the experience of spiritualists at séances. Private séances shared with philosophical toys, as well as with popular scientific experiments performed in domestic settings, the constant appeal to the senses, which resulted in the wonder and excitement felt by many sitters.[100] The attempt to establish communication with the beyond mingled with the hope to gain further awareness of the mysteries of the otherworld and with the thrill of witnessing spectacular spirit manifestations.

Despite strong evidence supporting such an analogy, the link between philosophical toys and spiritualist séances has been commonly dismissed, due to the fact that rational entertainments explicitly refused any contact with the supernatural. In *Letters on Natural Magic*, Brewster firmly underlined their distance from superstition and magical beliefs, carefully explaining the illusory nature of supernatural phenomena.[101] Similarly, as Simon During claims, prestidigitation profited from the fascination with the supernatural but nonetheless explicitly opposed spiritualism, denouncing the trickery of fraudulent mediums.[102] Such analysis, however, does not take into account the fact that spiritualists also claimed to oppose superstition; they explicitly refused the concept of the supernatural by arguing that spiritualism was based on the objective and scientific discovery that the living are able to communicate with the dead. They considered spiritualist séances to be a rational and uplifting activity, a journey into the realms of rationality rather than mystery and the occult. As one spiritualist put it, those who believed in spirit communication "hold convictions and cherish aspirations of which no rational, pure-minded or devout man need be ashamed, but which are worthy the serious regard of all thoughtful people."[103]

The analogy with the philosophical toys can shed light on how spiritualism, as Daniel Herman appropriately claimed, "offered entertainment by encouraging believers and non-believers to test its truth."[104] Nicolas Dulac and André Gaudreault have suggested that philosophical toys such as the phenakistoscope—which gave the illusion of movement through a spinning disc around whose edge a dozen figures were arranged in a circle, and was used to explain the optical theories of afterimage and persistence of vision—functioned according to a logic of circularity and repetition.[105] Their appeal was thus based on the principle of the loop. Although spiritualist séances did not loop, they also entailed the repetition of a well-established pattern, by which the expectations of the sitters were manipulated toward the symbolic fulfillment of the event—the manifestation of the spirit. The ritualism of this pattern was highly standardized and regulated, requiring sitters to act accordingly within a recognized mold. Waiting was an inherent part of this process, since spirit manifestation "required time and patience to arrive at."[106] A spiritualist suggested that this was the reason why little progress was made toward the conversion of determined skeptics, since "men who say 'show me that yonder table can be made to jump up to the ceiling in broad daylight and I will believe your trash!' . . . are not likely to have the patience to sit quietly at a table."[107]

The sense of wonder stimulated through philosophical toys was closely connected to forms of commerce. As Susan Horton aptly emphasizes, devices such as zoetropes and phenakistoscopes were marketed and purchased, and people bought tickets to attend visual attractions such as panoramas and dioramas.¹⁰⁸ Rational amusements, in other words, were a commercial enterprise that interacted in many ways with the nineteenth-century consumer culture, as well as with show business. Likewise, instruments such as the psychograph, the planchette, and the Ouija board were industrially produced and marketed in Britain and the United States. A strong commercial component was also present in private spiritualist séances, which usually required the payment of a fee or some other kind of compensation to the medium, making the search for the unknown a profitable business.

As a private "rational game," spiritualist sittings contributed to opening Victorian parlors to novel forms of domestic entertainment. The house was, for nineteenth-century spiritualists, not only the "true locus of religiosity," but an increasingly permeable space that allowed for the introduction of social gathering and play into the private and familial sphere. Media historian Joshua Meyrowitz noted that, from the end of the nineteenth century, the introduction of media such as the telephone reshaped the definition of the private sphere, opening the domestic environment to new channels of communication with the outside world.¹⁰⁹ In a similar way, séances broke the alleged inviolability of Victorian houses with their promise of communication with an external entity—the spirits of the dead. But what is perhaps most revealing in the analysis of private spiritualist séances, as discussed in this chapter, is that séances opened the house to novel forms of domestic entertainment. Similar to philosophical toys, séances set up the house as the principal theater for a rational game that succeeded in acquiring the dedicated and excited attention of the tenants and guests who sat together at the spirit table. Private spiritualist sittings, therefore, pertain to the history of the introduction of entertainment practices within the domestic space. If philosophical toys are examined in film studies as one of the most direct antecedents to audiovisual media such as cinema and television,¹¹⁰ séances should be integrated into the prehistory and the archaeology of domestic entertainment media.¹¹¹

In the next two chapters, we will move away from the performance of spiritualist séances to question more specifically how these events were marketed and advertised. As I will show, mediums and spiritualists employed several of the techniques and strategies that were customary in show business, such as the stimulation of controversies in the press and the fabrication of celebrity status.

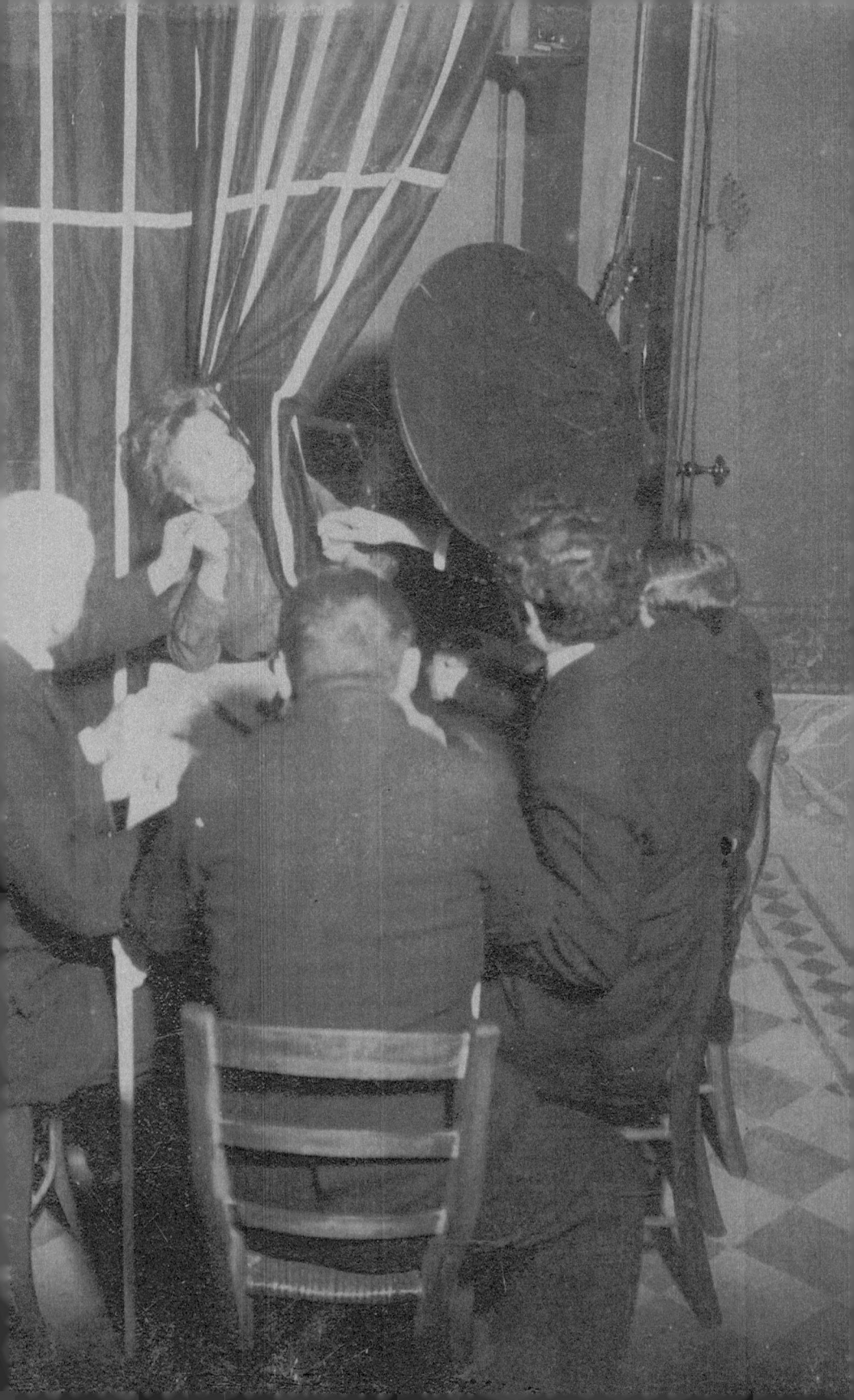

PART TWO

HOW TO SELL A SPIRIT

3

BREAKING THE NEWS

CONTROVERSY, SENSATION, AND

THE POPULAR PRESS

On 17 February 1851, a joint letter signed by three professors at the University of Buffalo and published in the *Commercial Adviser* claimed to disclose the secret behind the legendary Fox sisters' spirit phenomena. The authors—Dr. Flint, Dr. Lee, and Dr. Coventry—had visited one of the sisters' public exhibitions, and they declared that the mysterious rappings were produced by movements of the knee joints. They also affirmed that a lady of their acquaintance had produced similar sounds by that means.[1] Leah, the older sister of Kate and Margaret Fox, promptly responded with a public statement that invited the professors to demonstrate their theory. "As there seems to be much interest manifested by the public on that subject," she wrote, "we would suggest that as early an investigation as is convenient would be acceptable to the undersigned."[2] Yet, despite the Fox sisters' eagerness in calling for further inspections, the investigation that followed did not lead to a withdrawal of the professors' claims; it rather prompted a second report, published in the *New York Tribune*, confirming all allegations. This time, the professors' argument was supported by the observation that every time the girls' knees were seized, the manifestations came to an abrupt end. Although the editor of the *Tribune*, Horace Greeley, published a note in response that called for "another version of the matter,"[3] news of the exposure of the Fox sisters' trickery spread through the national press.

Those who expected the newly born spiritualist movement to be short-lived, however, were wrong. As Eliab Wilkinson Capron—a former journalist who assisted the adolescent mediums in their public appearances—observed,

"The report soon called forth replies and criticisms, and, instead of allaying the excitement in Buffalo and other places, it was greatly increased by the efforts of the professors."[4] Rather than signaling a setback for the newfangled séance craze, the emergence of criticism spurred curiosity across an American society where popular newspapers such as the *New York Tribune* and the *New York Sun* dictated the issues of public debate. "The rooms of the ladies," Capron wrote, "were crowded with visitors, many of whom went to confirm the theory of the University doctors, and many from a wish to make a candid examination themselves."[5]

As James W. Cook convincingly demonstrated, one of the most innovative marketing schemes that accompanied the rise of modern show business came with the discovery that a degree of uncertainty about the authenticity of an attraction contributed to an arousal of interest in the public and the popular press.[6] In Victorian America and England, showmen such as P. T. Barnum understood that doubts about the authenticity of their spectacular feats only added to their appeal. As a well-established motto in the entertainment sector goes, "There's no such thing as bad publicity." This chapter argues that the spiritualist movement profited from this strategy as well. Controversy and skepticism were never overlooked by mediums and leaders of the movement, who regularly responded with an endless play of exposure and counter-exposure that grabbed the attention of the press and stimulated the curiosity of audiences at spiritualist demonstrations.

THE POWER OF CONTROVERSY: AMERICAN AND BRITISH SHOW BUSINESS AROUND 1850

In order to comprehend how spiritualists transformed controversies into opportunities for promotion, it is important to consider the extent to which similar strategies were employed within the broader field of American and British show business, and how this was closely linked to the mass circulation of the press, which provided a new vehicle for publicity. During the first half of the nineteenth century, attitudes toward diversions and commercial entertainments underwent a striking change. Long before the era of film and television, live performances were largely responsible for the astounding growth of the entertainment sector.[7] The new opportunities offered by commercial advertising were particularly pivotal in the advent of a golden age for theater, freak shows, anthropological exhibits, dime museums, stage magic, and many other forms of popular entertainment.[8]

Spectacular attractions gained a new capacity to draw large audiences, as a growing number of professional showmen competed to offer the most sensational feats and experimented with new ways of advertising to attract the attention of the press.

Given the need to appeal to the interest of the public, exaggerations, deceptions, and fraud became a staple of the trade. Frequently, successful attractions were artful fabrications of clever impresarios who strove to conform to their audience's taste.[9] Showmen and promoters constantly manipulated the public presentation of their exhibits. Whether it was a magic show, a feat of funambulism, or a theatrical sketch, every attraction required some degree of fabrication to make it more appealing to the audience. Exaggeration and embellishment came to be the true essence of the most popular attractions in the nineteenth century.[10] In the case of spiritualism, too, a high degree of hyperbole and sensationalism characterized public presentations and press reports of the alleged powers of famous mediums, such as Daniel Dunglas Home and the Davenport brothers.[11] The rise of popular journalism accelerated this tendency, providing performers and impresarios with unprecedented opportunities for marketing their attractions and shows. As the first periodicals to rely on the commercialization of news, the American penny press signaled, in the 1830s, the transformation of newspapers from small-circulation dailies and weeklies closely tied to political parties and interest groups to large-circulation dailies that usually avoided any political affiliation and found their primary source of funding in advertisements.[12]

If not the first American showman, P. T. Barnum was certainly one of the most acute in his understanding that publicity was the key to success in show business. Barnum demonstrated an ability to make his attractions appealing to a wide potential audience, spreading propaganda about both these feats and his own public image. As Eric Fretz put it, he "made a name for himself by stylizing the lives of others and packaging them for public consumption."[13] Historians of the American show trade agree that Barnum's development of promotional and publicity techniques was instrumental in making show business a permanent part of American life.[14] One of the main strategies employed by Barnum was the stimulation of public controversies that, by spreading through the press, provided extraordinary advertising opportunities.[15] In this way, the showman's attractions became the topic of press reports and news items in magazines and papers, which served as a much more powerful engine for publicity than paid commercial advertisements. The penny press, in fact, frequently used controversies to heighten sales.[16]

By turning public controversy into an advertising opportunity, Barnum became involved in what James Cook called "artful deception," a particular mode of popular culture that pervaded urban entertainment in America throughout the nineteenth century. This included attractions such as automatons, panoramas, trompe l'oeil paintings, and stage magic, all of which appealed to spectators by challenging them to inquire about the truth of their perceptions.[17] The strategy adopted by Barnum to promote his first attraction, the allegedly 161-year-old woman Joice Heth, was exemplary of this approach. In the effort to stimulate popular interest, the showman was clever enough not to defend too inflexibly the authenticity of Joice's age. On at least one occasion, Barnum went so far as to send a newspaper an anonymous notice that claimed that she was nothing but a "curiously constructed automaton, made up of whalebone, india-rubber, and numberless springs ingeniously put together, and made to move at the slightest touch, according to the will of the operator."[18] By planting this story, he ensured that his show would be widely reported and discussed in the popular press. As Barnum recalled, "Hundreds who had not visited Joice Heth were now anxious to see the curious automaton; while many who had seen her were equally desirous of a second look, in order to determine whether or not they had been deceived."[19]

The strategy of using controversy as a marketing opportunity also characterized the rise of spiritualism. In fact, mediums and spiritualist leaders often benefited from the hype kindled by controversies surrounding their claims. It was not by chance that Barnum was drawn toward the case of spiritualism, given his interest in deceptive and fraudulent practices. In *The Humbugs of the World*, a book intended to expose deceptions in several fields, including science, literature, and medicine, Barnum dedicated much space to the exposure of spiritualist séances. After explaining how spiritualism had artfully started with the Fox family's lucrative humbug, Barnum pointed out that "an aptitude for deception is all the capital that a person requires in order to become a 'spirit-medium'; or, at least, to gain the reputation of being one."[20] Notwithstanding his firm condemnation of spiritualism, Barnum apparently considered it to be a valid attraction for his American Museum. Opened in 1841 at the corner of Broadway and Ann Street in New York City, the museum offered freak shows alongside exhibits of natural history, encouraging its patrons to be skeptical of institutional authority. It was a place, by Barnum's own design, where laypeople could take on the experts and win.[21] The museum's collection included samples of William Mumler's spirit photographs,[22] and its lecture rooms featured demonstrations with mesmerized subjects.[23]

Barnum was not the only figure in nineteenth-century show business to manipulate public debate for the sake of advertising. The American clown Dan Rice, one of the most famous circus performers and entrepreneurs in mid-nineteenth-century America, also realized the lucrative applications of controversy in advertising. Like Barnum, he made public admissions of this strategy, declaring that he found "no advertising more profitable than that obtained by one of [his] circuses being attacked from the pulpit."[24] Likewise, stoking doubts about the authenticity of an attraction helped many showmen publicize their exhibitions of freak shows and human oddities. This, as Robert Bogdan noted, was particularly relevant in the case of bearded women, whose popularity depended on challenging the established boundaries of gender.[25] Challenges and imitations were a staple of the show trade: performers presented their rivals as mere imitators or shams and responded to challenges that were frequently staged in order to kindle the curiosity of the public.[26]

While P. T. Barnum and other American showmen frequently crossed the ocean, adapting their attractions and commercial strategies to the British context,[27] the use of sensation and controversy to arouse the interest of the press was a strategy that developed independently in Britain. As Michael Diamond aptly shows, if it is true that restraint and decorum were highly valued in nineteenth-century British society and that many sensational subjects were taboo, this does not mean that British Victorians did not enjoy sensation as much as Americans did.[28] The development of a popular press did much to facilitate public debates and controversies. In the middle of the nineteenth century, the removal of taxes on newspaper advertising (1853), as well as the repeal of stamp duty on newspapers (1855) and of paper duty (1861), made newspapers affordable for the first time to a large mass of people in Britain.[29] Papers such as the *London Journal*, *Reynolds's Miscellany*, and *Cassell's Illustrated Family Paper* adapted, for the British context, some of the strategies that made the American penny press popular. They promoted an editorial approach that combined popular entertainment with literature and culture, featuring stories, essays, fashion news, humorous items, poetry, and pictures.[30] British showmen made confident use of the new opportunities for publicity provided by the mass circulation of newspapers and took advantage of advertising strategies similar to those employed by P. T. Barnum.[31] As Diamond notes, "In all branches of entertainment, including literature but above all in the performing arts, great efforts were made, as they are now, to create sensations."[32] Journalists received free and discounted tickets to shows, and some entrepreneurs in theater and live entertainment went so far as to offer them refreshment and dinner in conjunction with their previews.[33]

The appeal of public controversies helps explain the popular success of public lectures on technological and scientific subjects. It is difficult to overestimate the relevance of this cultural form throughout the nineteenth century. According to one estimation, between 1840 and 1860 more than three thousand advertised lectures took place in New York City alone; in Britain, they were at least equally successful.[34] Lectures were a public ritual and an intellectual event designed to entertain as well as to educate, and to make knowledge accessible to the common person. Popularizers of science such as John Henry Pepper, who enriched his lectures at London's Royal Polytechnic with illusionistic tricks that could have easily been found in the cabinet of a stage magician, understood that they had to satisfy the public's craving for visual images and effects—one of the hallmarks of Victorian mass culture.[35] However, the divulgation of scientific knowledge and the quality of visual effects were neither the only nor the main reasons for the lectures' appeal. Definitions of what counted as a scientific lecture were malleable: the quasi-magical status held by phenomena such as electricity and magnetism in the public imagination benefited those lecturers who performed demonstrations of more controversial bodies of knowledge.[36] Lecturers reporting on subjects such as mesmerism, mediumship, and spiritualism often mingled with those who turned science and technology into spectacular attractions.[37] The presentation of science and spiritualism to the public thus proceeded along parallel lines, with debates on controversial scientific issues such as mesmerism and hypnotic states coinciding with the moments of greatest public visibility for the spiritualist movement.[38]

Like impresarios in show business, spiritualists invited newspapermen to public séances, often stimulating rather than avoiding the criticism that might arise.[39] If they did not—like P. T. Barnum and other nineteenth-century showmen—actually fabricate evidence against their own claims, they nonetheless benefited from public controversy regarding the authenticity of spirit phenomena and actively encouraged skeptical scientists, magicians, and journalists to undertake public investigations of mediumship. As séance sitting evolved from a local sensation in a small New York town to a popular activity that reached large masses of people in North America and Europe, spiritualist mediums and promoters employed some of the very same strategies that had been successfully used by American and British showmen to promote their trade. Similar to entertainers and performers in show business, spiritualists never feared skepticism or controversies. On the contrary, they constantly made reference to the polemics of those who questioned their claims, conceiving of mediumship as an unending play of exposures and counter-exposures.[40]

THE ROLE OF CONTROVERSIES IN THE RISE OF AMERICAN SPIRITUALISM

The use of controversy as a marketing device within the spiritualist movement is evident if one takes a closer look at the Fox sisters' public exhibitions organized in the years 1849–50. As Arthur Conan Doyle reported in his history of the movement, the first demonstration of spiritualism at the Corinthian Hall in Rochester did not convince all of the audience members, but rather increased their skepticism.[41] In the days that followed, there was a lively debate in the local press, with Rochester's *Daily News* and *Daily Democrat* taking conflicting positions on the matter.[42] The controversy soon spread to national newspapers, so that the Fox sisters' "weak imposture"—as one publication put it—brought "a certain notoriety" to the city of Rochester.[43] This pattern was invariably repeated in the following years, as the Fox sisters demonstrated their mediumship in several large towns and before considerable audiences. Constantly challenged by disbelief and accusations of fraud, the adolescent mediums became a hot item in the penny press. In this regard, skepticism was not an enemy but an ally for the early leaders of spiritualism. No less than articles authored by advocates of spirit phenomena, newspaper reports exposing the Fox sisters' trickery contributed to their status as national celebrities. As Leah Fox stated, the harshest criticism coincided with their greatest successes, even from a financial point of view: the challenges levied by the three professors at the University of Buffalo, for instance, prompted their supporters to send them monetary gifts "as tribute of sympathy for what we had to bear."[44]

The Fox sisters benefited from the assistance of counselors who supervised both their public performances and their contact with the press. The first and most important of these was the professional journalist Eliab Wilkinson Capron, editor of the *Daily Mirror* in Providence, Rhode Island, who met the Fox sisters as early as 1848 in Rochester. Capron's involvement in their career was quite similar to that of agents and managers in show business.[45] Besides giving the Fox sisters valuable publicity in his paper, he introduced their shows with lectures at the Corinthian Hall and on many other occasions.[46] Like every good theatrical agent, he took great care in his relationship with the press; as he stated in the preface to a pamphlet about the Fox sisters that was reprinted twice in 1850, he often had to deal with newspaper editors.[47] When public controversy about the sisters' mediumship erupted, Capron made use of his professional experience to respond effectively to the attacks. For instance, on 17 April 1851, after a Mrs. Norman Culver publicly declared that Kate Fox had revealed to her the secret of how the raps were artificially produced, Capron reacted with the readiness of an accustomed impresario, publishing a crushing response.[48]

With their séances in New York City in 1850, the Fox sisters definitively succeeded in making themselves known throughout the United States. Capron paved the way for their arrival in the metropolis, writing and ensuring the publication of a long letter in the *New York Tribune*, which was presented as the first detailed account of the rappings in a newspaper of national circulation. Capron's piece subsequently launched a deluge of articles and letters published in the *Tribune* and other New York newspapers, heightening anticipation of the arrival of the mediums.[49] On 4 June 1850, Mrs. Fox and her three daughters—Margaret, Kate, and Leah, who had joined the family venture—arrived in New York and occupied a room at Barnum's Hotel, where their public sittings were to take place.[50] Although this establishment had nothing to do with Barnum the showman, its location at the corner of Broadway and Maiden Lane—right in the center of a district that was quickly becoming the hub of the entertainment industry in the United States—was hardly a coincidence.

Feeling the rush of attention from a booming midcentury New York was certainly a singular experience for the two adolescent mediums from Hydesville. Several decades later, Leah described what it felt like to be an attraction for the press and the public: "The editors of the Tribune and many other papers were in our rooms daily. Mr. Ripley used to say to us: 'Ladies, you are the lions of New York.' Mary Taylor, in a Broadway theatre, sweetly sang 'The Rochester Knockings at Barnum's Hotel,' as a popular topic of the day. Many things in stores, on sidewalks, and newspaper advertisements, were paraded and labeled with the words 'Rochester Knockings.' What a time, to be sure, we had of it during that first visit, of nearly three months, to the great metropolis!"[51] When the Fox family left New York two months later, the exhibition of their astounding mediumship had grossed, on average, one hundred dollars a day.[52] Returning to Rochester to plan their subsequent tours, they left behind several circles of sitters who were ready to start their own investigations into the mysteries of spiritualism.[53]

Capron served as the Fox sisters' adviser during their New York séances. He provided the advertisements that were published in the local papers and supervised visits with the public. As he later recalled, "no day passed without some comments on the strange phenomena" appearing in the New York press.⁵⁴ While most papers proved skeptical toward the spiritualist claims, Capron gained the collaboration of one of New York's most influential journalists: Horace Greeley. An advocate of free labor and the abolition of slavery, Greeley was the editor of the *New York Tribune*, the newspaper with the largest circulation in the United States.⁵⁵ He reported in the *Tribune* on the Fox sisters' arrival and, according to the testimony of one of the girls, gave the family several suggestions, including how much to charge for admission to their séances.⁵⁶ Authoring numerous boastful columns in his paper, Greeley became one of the architects of the Fox family's success on the New York tour. When the sisters were finished giving demonstrations at Barnum's Hotel, Greeley hosted them for several weeks at his residence at Turtle Bay in upstate New York, where they performed séances for him and his wife.⁵⁷ The loss of his son in the cholera epidemic of 1849 possibly contributed to his confidence that the Fox sisters were capable of communicating with the dead.⁵⁸ Greeley's belief in spiritualism also intersected with his faith in the power of the press: according to a spiritualist source, he offered to give 2,500 dollars a year to any medium who could provide him with fresh news from London on a daily basis, anticipating the benefits brought about some years later by the introduction of the Atlantic telegraphic line.⁵⁹ Greeley later retracted his endorsement of spiritualism, attributing his own involvement to his wife's hope to contact their dead child.⁶⁰ He also reported to have exposed the trickery of the Fox sisters by 1850. Yet his account is contradicted by numerous sources, suggesting that his involvement in spiritualism was longer and deeper than he admitted.⁶¹

Albeit in different ways, Horace Greeley is remembered as a pioneer of both spiritualism and modern advertisement. In the same year that he was promoting the Fox sisters' New York séances, Greeley published an essay entitled "The Philosophy of Advertising" in *Hunt's Merchants' Magazine and Commercial Review*, an early advertising trade journal. The essay observed that American businessmen were mostly unaware of the enormous power that the press had attained, with the circulation of newspapers having multiplied several times in the span of just a few years. Neglecting to use the press as a marketing opportunity, Greeley pointed out, was equivalent to "resolving never to travel by steam nor to communicate by telegraph."⁶² Some lines of the essay have remained entrenched in the history of advertising in the United States, as Greeley urged promoters to acquire more legitimacy by using the straightforward language of business: "Leave the clown's jests to the circus," he exhorted, "and let sober men speak as they act, with directness and decision. The fewest words that will convey the advertiser's ideas are the right ones."[63] Decades later, after he had passed away, Greeley's "spirit" made a brief appearance in an American séance, delivering a message that he requested be sent to the *Tribune*.[64] The posthumous appearance of famous mediums and prominent figures in the history of the movement was a common trope in spiritualist sittings. In this sense, the apparition of Greeley's spirit signaled his insertion into the historical legacy not just of advertisement but of spiritualism, too.[65]

PUBLIC CONTROVERSIES, SENSATIONALISM, AND THE EMERGENCE OF BRITISH SPIRITUALISM

In England, the emergence of the spiritualist movement followed a pattern similar to the Fox sisters' first American séances. Although news concerning the Hydesville case was reported in the British press and a few British mediums became active soon afterward, the dawn of the spiritualist craze in old Europe is usually identified with the October 1852 arrival in England of an American medium, Maria Hayden. Like the Fox sisters, she benefited from the services of a counselor—her husband—who managed her relations with the press. Mr. Hayden was a respected New England journalist and the former editor of the *Star Spangled Banner*. He provided the advertisements for the demonstrations of his wife's mediumship. These were published in several newspapers, but, he reported, they were not always welcome; the *Times*, for instance, refused to run one of his ads.[66] Reviews of Maria Hayden's performances were mostly negative, and most newspapers and magazines that published accounts of her séances ridiculed them. As Arthur Conan Doyle put it, "The ignorant British Press treated Mrs. Hayden as a common American adventuress."[67]

Yet the "explosion" of the spiritualist craze was imminent. It coincided with a letter on "table-turning" authored by the great English chemist and physicist Michael Faraday, published in the *Times* on 23 June 1853. Although the letter was a public condemnation of spiritualism, the relevance of the person who signed it turned spiritualism into a popular topic of discussion. Faraday argued that mediumistic phenomena had nothing to do with spirit agency and could instead be explained as the result of unconscious muscular action.[68] This was only the first of a series of famous controversies concerning spiritualism that were heralded by the British press, with the intervention of eminent scientists. Such polemics often signal the periods of maximal momentum in the history of the British spiritualist movement. In the 1870s, for instance, the conversion of the prominent chemist William Crookes to spiritualism initiated a revival of the debates on spiritualism in the British press.[69]

The thirst for sensationalism in the popular press certainly enhanced spiritualism's public visibility during the Victorian age. It is perhaps not a coincidence that one of the most famous figures in British nineteenth-century sensationalist journalism, W. T. Stead, became one of the main advocates of spiritualism and belief in telepathy at the end of the century.[70] Stead, who edited influential papers such as the *Pall Mall Gazette* and the *Review of Reviews*, is considered the founder of the "New Journalism," a name coined by journalist Matthew Arnold in 1887 to designate a new style of reports that played strongly upon sensationalism and popular emotions.[71] From 1893 to 1897, Stead served as the founder and editor of *Borderland*, a journal consecrated to the study of spiritualism and psychical research. He did not consider his career as a spiritualist publicist to be essentially different from his activities as a mainstream journalist. *Borderland*'s organization and editorial strategy followed quite closely the model of his main publishing enterprise of the 1890s, the *Review of Reviews*: each quarterly issue contained a biographical sketch of a medium or a person with psychical gifts, a monograph on a particular branch of psychical research and occult beliefs, and reviews of relevant publications and periodicals.[72] Years later, in 1912, Stead lost his life in the sinking of the Titanic and began some sort of new career in ghost form, as his spirit allegedly contacted several spiritualist circles in the twentieth century.[73]

SKEPTICISM AND THE PERFORMANCE OF VICTORIAN SÉANCES

As discussed above, the issue of authenticity and fraud was brought to the forefront of public debates on such numerous occasions throughout the nineteenth century that the history of Victorian spiritualism can be regarded as a continuous interplay between its supporters and its opponents.[74] The importance of maintaining a skeptical perspective was evoked again and again by the opponents of the movement as well as by the spiritualists themselves. Popular periodicals and books reported, discussed, and often questioned the reliability of spiritualist claims.[75] Attempts to debunk spiritualism as a fraud kindled public debates, drawing the attention of the press and the public toward the spiritualist movement.[76]

To what extent, however, did the dispute between spiritualists and skeptics influence the performance of séances? Skepticism and investigation were encouraged not only by published reports about spiritualism but also by the performances of mediums. For instance, the Fox sisters' spiritualist demonstrations incorporated onstage attempts by skeptics to debunk them as frauds.[77] Even when skeptics pointed to naturalistic explanations that contrasted with the spiritualists' claims, their investigations excited the interest of viewers, strengthening the spectacularism of the show rather than spoiling it.[78] Skepticism played a strong role in the performance of séances not only for the Fox sisters but also in the later history of spiritualism. The possibility of fraud was instrumental for the functioning and the success of public séances. As David Walker notes, spiritualist demonstrations created a participatory environment that "invited discussion of what it might look like if communication were achieved, what it might look like if communication were faked, and what might be the social significances of connecting with unseen knowledge."[79] The appeal to controversy and skepticism, therefore, shaped the performance of Victorian spiritualist séances as much as it informed the mediums' advertising strategy.

Throughout the nineteenth century, spiritualist exposés—as antispiritualist exposures were often called—were frequently performed by magicians on the theatrical stage (fig. 9). Under the influence of the French clockmaker Robert-Houdin—the greatest magician of all time, according to many popular historians of magic—conjuring had become a popular entertainment in the second half of the nineteenth century. Magicians of this kind were technically skilled stage performers whose sketches included the use of optical illusions, magic lanterns, automata, mechanical effects, electricity, and, later, early films.[80] John Henry Anderson, who, in addition to Robert-Houdin, is considered one of the founders of modern magic, started to expose spiritualist humbugs as early as 1855. It was due to the growing success of the Davenport brothers, who explicitly presented their spirit séances to large audiences as a kind of stage show, that spiritualist exposés became ubiquitous. The Davenports' performances held a great fascination for stage conjurers. John Nevil Maskelyne, probably the leading stage magician in late nineteenth-century Britain, began his career with an exposé of the Davenport brothers' spirit cabinet. Recalling his first contact with spiritualism, Maskelyne wrote in 1891 that he had been able "to reproduce every item of the Davenports' cabinet and dark séance." So close was the resemblance to the original performance, he claimed, that the spiritualists would have no alternative "but to claim us as most powerful spirit

FIG. 9   Exposés of spiritualist mediums were often attempted by magicians and skeptics. In this illustration, a fake spirit is grabbed by a skeptical sitter at a séance. From Lionel A. Weatherly, *The Supernatural?* (Bristol: Arrowsmith, 1891), 198.

mediums, who found it more profitable to deny the assistance of spirits."[81] Maskelyne's 1876 book *Modern Spiritualism* explained in detail how the Davenports' séance effects were produced.[82] American magician Harry Kellar was also influenced by the two mediums. He was hired by them as an assistant in 1868 and acquired much of his illusionist skill during this employment. After breaking his association with the Davenports, he specialized in onstage exposés of spiritualist séance tricks, which set attendance records in New York, Cincinnati, and Chicago.[83] As cultural historian Simon During pointed out, "What was magic show one night could (without technical changes) be presented as a spiritualist séance on the next night."[84]

By the turn of the century, antispiritualist performances had become a regular part of magic shows. Harry Houdini, the most popular American conjurer of the early twentieth century, claimed in his 1924 book *A Magician Among the Spirits* that he considered the exposure of spiritualist tricksters to be a moral duty.[85] Three years later, he donated to the Library of Congress what he described as "one of the largest libraries in the world on psychic phenomena, Spiritualism, magic, witchcraft, demonology, evil spirits, etc., some of the material going back as far as 1489."[86] This large collection was suggestive of how antispiritualist activities not only played a part in his shows but were a sort of obsession for him. As vaudeville historian Albert McLean suggested, even Houdini's celebrated escape art may have originated in the Davenports' spiritualist shows.[87] In fact, the Davenport brothers would tie themselves up at the beginning of their séances in order to ensure the "spontaneity" of the subsequent phenomena, and Maskelyne's exposures of their tricks already involved some kind of escape show.[88]

Historians have offered different interpretations of the involvement of magicians in spiritualist exposés. According to During, in this way, magicians could establish an implicit link with the supernatural, profiting from the nineteenth-century fascination with the world of the occult.[89] Others have observed that exposures of spiritualism gave stage magic an aura of scientific respectability, supporting the claim that such spectacles should be considered within a rationalizing framework.[90] Yet the link between stage magic and spiritualism was probably also related to the strategy of using controversy to stimulate the interest of the public. In their spectacular exposés, end-of-the-century magicians such as Maskelyne, Kellar, and Houdini played with the contrast between skepticism and credulity. They bound their audiences in a relationship of complicity, joining their more skeptical spectators in opposing the spiritualists. Arguably, they understood better than anyone else the advertising potential of spiritualism's investigation of the otherworld.

Additionally, one might wonder whether spiritualists benefited from the publicity deriving from these exposés. While most scholarship on stage magic has tended to draw a rigid distinction between stage magic (viewed within a spectacular frame in which the use of tricks was openly acknowledged) and spiritualist séances (set in a religious frame in which the authenticity of the phenomena was stressed), it is also true that these two fields had much in common. Fred Nadis notes that, despite their public conflicts, spiritualists and magicians purchased their tricks and cabinets from the same catalogues, and "the decision to define oneself as Spiritualist, anti-Spiritualist, or in between often had less to do with ethics than with box office concerns."[91] Moreover, in the scholarly discussion of the relationship between spiritualists and magicians, little attention has been given to the role that skepticism played in the development of the spiritualist movement. As shown above, the effects of skepticism were not only negative but also productive: it contributed to spiritualism's proliferation in the public arena. This was stated, for instance, in a publication instructing spiritualist believers in the best strategies for disseminating their faith; it noted that tracts and pamphlets should be prepared "to be given away at the exhibitions of conjurers professing to expose Spiritualism, at Secularist lectures, or at the meetings of Educationalists, religious or social reformers." The author indicated that exposés provided key opportunities to widen the reach of spiritualism, stating that they should "be carefully saturated with appropriate Spiritual information."[92]

Although stage magic and spiritualist séances were based on different frameworks,[93] their relationship was probably more complex and multifaceted than is usually acknowledged. Through an unending interplay of exposures and counter-exposures, stage magicians and spiritualists created not two contrasting discourses but rather a fundamentally coherent one that mutually reinforced their public visibility. The case of Martin Van Buren Bly, who simultaneously performed as a spiritualist trance lecturer and as a debunker of spiritualist mediumship, is particularly revealing of the mingling of faith with skepticism in nineteenth-century spiritualism.[94] Bly's performances sometimes defied definition as séances or exposés, inviting audiences to decide for themselves whether the phenomena were the result of supernatural powers or mere trickery. A spiritualist magazine reported that he gave séances only to confess at the end that he was not a medium but a conjuror, and that he had developed all of the phenomena by the means of mere tricks. Yet Bly still contended that he allowed people to form their own conclusions.[95]

Neil Harris argues in his influential biography of Barnum that the success of scientific lectures in the nineteenth century was rooted in the "aesthetic of the operational"—the delight in the observational process and examination for literal truth that characterized other contemporary forms of spectacle.[96] According to this perspective, technical and scientific explanations were made recreational by appealing to the same popular taste that Barnum and other showmen cleverly exploited. Audiences were just as curious to learn about genuine curiosities as to question and discuss potential deceptions and frauds. As Harris put it, "It was a form of intellectual exercise, stimulating even when literal truth could not be determined."[97] The ambiguity between skepticism and faith, brought to its apex in Bly's séances, shaped the environment of spiritualist séances, which participated in this same aesthetic.[98] Spiritualist mediums, as David Walker observes, invited everyone to "come and investigate," in order to "generate discussion about their performances and their methods and about the source and meaning of their rappings."[99] The appeal of such demonstrations was based on the delight of examining them for truth and humbug, which attracted spectators to scientific lectures, freak shows, and other attractions. Controversies were domesticated and incorporated into the spiritualist ritual, rather than excluded from it.

The uncertainty between authenticity and fraud characterized not only public demonstrations but also the functioning of private séances. Séance sitting entailed and emphasized the possibility of skepticism and exposure. Séances were often held under deception-proof conditions, and spiritualist mediums welcomed to their tables those who were skeptical about spiritualism but willing to make inquiries. The skeptical sitter, who does not yet believe in spiritualism but is open to conversion, is so readily found in séance reports that she appears to play an instrumental role in the functioning of the ritual. There was always, or almost always, someone who needed to be convinced of the truth of spiritualism, to whom the spirits had to provide evidence, to whose questions they had to respond, and to whose attention the manifestations—or the tricks—were ultimately directed.[100]

As many have noted, the spiritualist faith required no affiliation of any kind, and spiritualists seemed mostly unconcerned with establishing an institutional form—a necessity felt by most religious groups.[101] This apparently unshakable resistance to building a regulated system of membership was instrumental in the spread of belief in spirit communication during the nineteenth century. Curiosity was the only quality required to join a circle that was investigating spiritualist phenomena. Welcoming skeptics as well as committed believers, mediums offered those who attended their séances different possible interpretations of the events. Sitters were not forced to embrace the spiritualist faith, but were allowed a flexible interpretation of their role. The skeptic, the believer, the curious—for any of them, there was a reason to attend a séance in a private household or to watch a medium's trance performance on the stage. In this, spiritualism was similar to the show trade, which counted on a similar flexibility of interpretation to attract diverse audiences. This is particularly evident, as this chapter has attempted to demonstrate, in the way that both popular showmen and spirit mediums exploited the public's taste for exposure and controversy. Just as Barnum encouraged skepticism toward spiritualist attractions, mediums eagerly invited the participation of those who were willing to investigate—with a skeptical eye—the mysteries of spirit communication.

Examining shamanistic healing practices, anthropologist Michael Taussig argues that religious faith not only coexists with skepticism but may even require it. Taussig notes that shamanistic practitioners did not exclude skepticism from their rituals; on the contrary, they demanded and actively encouraged participants to engage in a skeptical inquiry. Magic is efficacious not despite the trick but on account of the act of its exposure: "The mystery is heightened, not dissipated, by unmasking, and in various ways, direct and oblique, ritual serves as a stage for so many unmaskings."[102] In spiritualist rituals, as in the shamanistic practices examined by Taussig, controversy was an element of structural relevance, widening the reach of spiritualist claims within the public and the popular press and shaping séances as environments for skeptical inquiry. As a consequence, skepticism should be considered an essential part of the cultural discourse of nineteenth-century spiritualism, rather than only its adversary. Instead of being merely an obstacle to the advancement of belief in spiritualism, skepticism on many occasions played a positive role in the history of the movement. The voice of spiritualism was not a monologue; it was a dialogue composed of the reciprocal claims and responses of supporters and opponents. It was through this dialectic that the movement progressed.

4

MEDIUMS AND STARS

RELIGION, CONSUMERISM, AND

CELEBRITY CULTURE

In *Le interviste impossibili* (The impossible interviews), Italian writer Giorgio Manganelli imagined dialogues with illustrious personalities of the past, such as Dickens, Tutankhamen, Casanova, and Marco Polo. These imaginary discussions, however, also include an interview with a lesser-known character: the Italian spiritualist medium Eusapia Palladino. Although readers might wonder why such significance is given to a medium, Manganelli's work is reminiscent of the fact that Palladino was elevated to the status of an international celebrity in the 1890s and early 1900s.[1]

From its origins, spiritualism was a highly personalized field. This is evident, for instance, in that a large part of the public discourse on spiritualism focused on the role played by spirit mediums and that their biographies were among the most successful spiritualist literature.[2] By opening one of the most widely read histories of the spiritualist movement, one would ascertain that this history is largely composed of a gallery of eminent personalities, most of whom are spirit mediums.[3] Frequently, it was the appeal of famous mediums that made spiritualism "breaking news" in the popular press, grabbing the attention of a public that went beyond just believers in spiritualism.

Scholars in celebrity studies have posited a similarity between forms of celebrity and the formation of religious and magical beliefs about the powers of spiritual leaders. Steve Nolan, for instance, claimed that both film and liturgy invite their constituents to identify with one another: just as audiences tend to build a relationship of identification with the main character of a film, Christian believers might identify with the priest.⁴ Following this line of thinking, this chapter argues that celebrity studies can be employed to interpret and understand the role played by mediums and spiritualist leaders, providing useful insights into both celebrity theory and the history of spiritualism. It argues that celebrity functioned as a mechanism that contributed to the spread of the movement's fame. While the assumption that celebrity is a product of the twentieth century has been dominant for decades, scholars have recently argued for a more broadly historicized approach in celebrity studies. As Simon Morgan points out, celebrity was one of the key drivers of modernization in the late eighteenth and nineteenth centuries: "By stimulating the production of consumer goods, printed images and periodical literature, celebrity played a crucial role in the growth of the public sphere, the emergence of consumer society and the global expansion of western culture."⁵ Thus, studying the impact that forms of celebrity culture specific to the Victorian age had on spiritualism might provide further evidence of how the movement developed in connection to show business, consumerism, and commodity culture.

The chapter is organized into three sections. In the first section, I address the role of celebrity culture in the formation of a culture of consumerism in nineteenth-century American and British societies, showing how celebrity functioned as a vehicle for publicity in both show business and the spiritualist movement. Rather than emphasizing the role of single personalities, this section examines celebrity as a mechanism that contributed to spreading spiritualist claims. The second section, in contrast, addresses the topic from the perspective of celebrity as persona, focusing on the case study of Eusapia Palladino, who was arguably the most famous spiritualist medium of the late nineteenth and early twentieth centuries. Although Palladino was born in Italy and spent much of her career in Italy and France, her renown went far beyond these two countries, testifying to the international character of spiritualist celebrity. Her career, more than that of any other spiritualist medium, demonstrates how mechanisms of celebrity and publicity that were typical of show business were also at play within the spiritualist movement. Finally, the third section addresses the uniqueness of the spiritualist celebrity in the nineteenth century and questions how an examination of the case of spiritualism may contribute to ongoing debates regarding nineteenth-century celebrity culture.

CELEBRITY AS MECHANISM: THE SPIRITUALIST MOVEMENT AND THE CULTURE OF RENOWN

In his study of Victorian commodity culture, Thomas Richards notes that cultural historians usually underestimate how the nineteenth century left its mark on twentieth-century consumer culture in areas such as show business, advertisement, and popular culture.[6] A similar consideration applies to the field of celebrity studies. In this field, scholars have almost exclusively focused on the era following the rise of so-called classical cinema. Yet it was in the late eighteenth and nineteenth centuries, long before the advent of Hollywood stardom, that forms of highly mediatized fame became influential; this is where phenomena such as fandom and stardom find their origin.[7]

While Leo Braudy's monumental history of renown, published in 1986, refused to posit a firm distinction between premodern and modern fame, claiming that "societies *always* generate a number of people willing to live at least part of their lives in the public eye,"[8] more recent scholarship has eagerly considered modern celebrity as qualitatively different from previous forms of fame. In his book *A Short History of Celebrity*, Fred Inglis distinguished between two terms designating different forms of notoriety and reputation throughout history. While the first one, "renown," refers to the consideration of personalities as filling prominent and clearly defined roles (for example, a soldier, jurist, or scholar) and recognizes their accomplishments, the second one, "celebrity," refers to a specifically modern phenomenon. According to this view, celebrity was a particular, historical form of fame that appeared in the middle of the eighteenth century and was based on the artful construction of a public personality through the use of different media.[9] Over the following two and a half centuries, popularity has been constantly fabricated in an organized effort to display personality as a public spectacle. Although it is tempting to regard celebrity as roughly corresponding to the lives of the specific women and men who became widely known, celebrity can also be approached as a mechanism—a "representational technology" that functioned as an agent of modernization.[10] In this regard, the history of celebrity overlaps with the rise of modern consumerism and popular culture. In contrast to earlier forms of reputation, in fact, celebrity shifted the focus from the public recognition of personal achievements to forms of consumption in which the famous character functioned as a trigger for the public's desire.[11]

Despite continuities between the mechanism of Victorian celebrity and contemporary stardom, the celebrity culture of the nineteenth century also had a distinctive character. As Braudy noted, during this period, a growing consumer society melded with an environment in which traditional and legal authorities were still very strong. As a result, resistance to new modes of presenting public personalities was particularly common, and the commercialization of celebrities was regarded by many with suspicion or skepticism.[12] Moreover, although nineteenth-century celebrity was highly mediatized, it is important to recall that the main vehicles through which such mediatization occurred were different from the ones that characterize contemporary forms of celebrity. Among the "new" media of the nineteenth century, the cheaper, industrially produced newspapers figured most prominently.[13] This means that the construction of celebrity in the nineteenth century, in fields such as show business and in spiritualism, was strongly shaped by print media. Newspaper reports, biographies and autobiographies, and magazines and journals formed the main stage on which celebrity was constructed. Moreover, during the second half of the century, photographic reproductions increasingly played a key role in the representation of celebrity. They interacted with older graphic media, such as engraving, etching, and lithography, to allow for new modes of circulating the likenesses of famous persons.[14]

The show trade was certainly one of the main contexts for the development of novel forms of celebrity. Showmen constantly took advantage of the advertising opportunities connected to fame, stimulating media hype and struggling to fabricate celebrities *ex novo*. Many of them understood that appearance, personal history, and even aspects that would hardly be considered personal achievements, such as the involvement in sexual scandals, could foster celebrity, if manipulated correctly. The mechanism of celebrity culture was also at play in the nineteenth-century lecture circuit. In 1862, *Harper's Magazine* pointed out that major lecturers were "personally more widely known than any other class of public men in this country."[15] Although this claim might be exaggerated, audiences certainly preferred speakers who had been in the public eye, and successful lecturers counted on their fame and reputation as much as on their performance skills to ensure the widest possible attendance at their public talks.[16]

Nineteenth-century celebrity culture was an eminently transatlantic phenomenon.[17] In the United States, theatrical, literary, and show-business celebrities benefited from the reputation they had acquired in Britain—or, conversely, they successfully made a name for themselves in the Old World after having become famous in America. In the United Kingdom, from at least the early nineteenth century, impresarios commonly used the fame of performers as a means of increasing ticket revenue.[18] While the world of theater provided the model of celebrity and stardom that would later be employed in other spectacular contexts, Victorian celebrity culture also encompassed literary, political, and scientific figures.[19] One of the seminal figures to stimulate mechanisms of celebrity and fandom in Britain, for instance, was Lord Byron, whose literary accomplishments, coupled with titillating scandals and rumors about his affairs and excesses, piqued the curiosity of the British public at the beginning of the nineteenth century.[20] Modern celebrity culture quickly developed in nineteenth-century America, too.[21] The person who probably most contributed to its formation was, again, P. T. Barnum. He became one of the most acclaimed American celebrities and, at the same time, was among the most skillful impresarios in creating popular crazes centered on fabricated celebrities, such as General Tom Thumb, the Swedish "songbird" Jenny Lind, and the allegedly 161-year-old Joice Heth.[22] Barnum actively manufactured his own reputation and the fame of his performers, using all possible means to get the public talking about him and his attractions.[23]

Spiritualists participated in transatlantic celebrity culture, too. The most famous mediums were known on both sides of the Atlantic. When they traveled from one side to the other, they could count on their reputations to ensure attendance at their séances.[24] Mediums' celebrity convinced both spiritualists and nonspiritualists to sit at the séance table. While spiritualists were eager to take part in séances and to see stage performances by mediums they had heard or read about, nonbelievers were often drawn by curiosity or a desire to test mediums who were presented as giving the most robust demonstrations of the authenticity of spirit communication.[25]

Marvin Carlson, Joseph Roach, and Heather McPherson have employed the concept of "ghosting" to explain the phenomenon of theatrical afterlife, by which a performer lives on in collective memory and remains associated with the role she played, whether she is still alive or not.[26] According to Carlson, ghosting is a mechanism at play in virtually every theatrical performance and closely follows the mechanism of celebrity. Audiences, in fact, are constantly "affected by the operations of celebrity itself to view and experience a famous actor through an aura of expectations that masks failings that would be troubling in someone less celebrated."[27] This applies not only to theater but to the functioning of celebrity culture as a whole. Being famous, in fact, is commonly related to the capacity to "survive" death in the memory of others; as Braudy pointed out, the great ones of the past are "dead as bodies, undying as images."[28]

FIG. 10
Sometimes a medium's spirit guide could become even more famous than the medium herself. This portrait of Katie King, the spirit guide of medium Florence Cook, was reproduced from a woodcut in the *Spiritualist* of 15 May 1873. From E. E. Fournier d'Albe, *New Light on Immortality* (London: Longmans, Green, 1908), 222.

The concept of ghosting is particularly apt for describing the relationship between mediumship and celebrity culture. During spiritualist séances, famous personalities of the past were literally resuscitated, communicating with the sitters and the medium in trance.[29] The most famous mediums haunted subsequent generations of spiritualists for decades after they passed away. Their afterlife as celebrities was manifest in two different, complementary ways. First, they were kept alive in the memory of spiritualists, who often dedicated much attention to the history of past mediums. Second, they resurfaced through the messages they sent from the spirit world through the intermediation of other mediums.[30]

A medium's celebrity status could, in certain cases, be "extended" to her spirit guide. This was the case, for instance, with the spirit Katie King, who was summoned by medium Florence Cook in London in the 1870s and later appeared in many séances led by other mediums. She was believed to be the daughter of John King, who had been the spirit guide of several mediums since the 1850s. When Katie or John was evoked, the spirit's renown, apart from that of the medium, gave added appeal to the séance. The publication of photographs and drawings depicting Katie's likeness (fig. 10) certainly contributed to her celebrity. The scientist William Crookes, who took several pictures of the spirit and was a strenuous supporter of Florence Cook, pointed out that "photography is as inadequate to depict

FIG. 11
Photographic portraits of well-known mediums were published and commercialized within the spiritualist movement. This photograph features the famous Victorian medium Georgiana Houghton. From Georgiana Houghton, *Evenings at Home in Spiritual Séance* (London: Trübner, 1881).

the perfect beauty of Katie's face, as words are powerless to describe her charms of manners."[31] Controversies ensued over whether Katie was, in reality, none other than Florence Cook, who would disguise herself during séances in order to impersonate the spirit. This lively debate heightened the celebrity of both the spirit and the medium, mirroring the way in which an actress's career is epitomized by her most successful roles on the stage.[32] Indeed, the concept of ghosting has also been employed with regard to the theatrical representation of historical and legendary figures, who are resurrected onstage by the interpretation of performers.[33] In this sense, the role-playing of mediums such as Cook and those who later raised the spirit of Katie resembles the way in which theatrical performers gain allure and visibility by enacting celebrities of the past. The public image of the spirit and that of the medium followed similar paths: for instance, Katie King's libertine behavior during séances was the subject of controversy, while critics accused Florence Cook of being involved in a romantic liaison with William Crookes, which would have clouded the scientist's judgment.[34]

Evidence of spiritualism's celebrity culture can be found in the different ways in which the careers and the personalities of mediums were appraised. The fabrication of celebrity is always, to a certain extent, mediated, and media representation is therefore one of the key factors facilitating the development of celebrity culture.[35] This was the case with spiritualism's celebrity culture, which strongly relied on print and other media technologies and forms. Just as newspapers and magazines began dedicating more and more space to notable lives and personalities, so spiritualist journals welcomed into their pages narratives about mediums' lives.[36] Biographical accounts and news about spiritualist personalities were frequently illustrated with their portraits. As Patrizia Di Bello aptly shows, photography played a key role in the formation of nineteenth-century celebrity culture: photographic prints and cartes de visite functioned as reproducible, increasingly inexpensive commodities that stimulated the circulation of effigies of famous personas and, ultimately, the functioning of celebrity culture itself.[37] Likewise, photographic portraits of famous mediums provided a crucial link between the representation of the medium as a public personality, on the one hand, and material culture and consumerism, on the other (fig. 11).[38]

The public image of theatrical celebrities (as well as film celebrities) is often built upon a combination of their private lives and their fictional characters—or, in other words, of the spectacular and the everyday.[39] Stars have an existence that endures beyond their appearance on the stage: their behaviors, personalities, and marriages decisively contribute to their relationship with the public.[40] Celebrities, then, are often a more or less schizophrenic combination of two different identities of the same person.[41] Often, the depiction of famous mediums followed a similar pattern, with the medium being described as a combination of her trance performance at the séance table and her everyday identity—two faces of the same person that were clearly separated yet mutually enforced. The relationship between private life and public performance played a significant role, for instance, in the careers of Kate and Margaret Fox. The two sisters, who "discovered" spirit rappings when they were in their teens, benefited for decades from their status as founders of the movement.[42] This, however, was as much a burden as an honor for them. During their career, which covered almost the entire second half of the nineteenth century, the sisters went through exposures and admissions of trickery, tormented emotional lives, and a pathological addiction to alcohol.[43] Kate Fox, who had been praised for decades as the most famous medium in the world, was arrested in Rochester in August 1886 for drunkenness; in May 1888, she was again arrested and her boys taken from her by the Society for the Prevention of Cruelty to Children. As Arthur Conan Doyle noted, "It is natural that those who speak of the danger of mediumship and especially of physical mediumship should point to the Fox sisters as an example."[44]

The irregular and libertine conduct of the Fox sisters was the subject of much attention from the spiritualist press, which added, eventually, to their celebrity status. In June 1885, the *Medium and Daybreak* commented on the return of Kate Fox to the United States after a short series of séances held in Britain:

> The love which we all bore her would not permit of an open acknowledgement of faults; but it must be said that Mrs. Fox-Jencken was found extremely difficult to manage. Even her best and most devoted friends got exhausted in their patience and assiduity on her behalf. How painful it is to write this we alone can know. It is not said to reproach: the love of truth and of the unhappy sufferer compels it. Whether hereditary or acquired, the influence of alcohol had assumed far too much control, and the paroxysm increased in frequency and intensity.... Such cases enforce the consideration that public mediumship, as now carried on, is utterly bad, alike for the Cause and the mediums.... All mediums should seek an independent position, based on industrial considerations, and thus be free to sit or refuse, as their enlightened impulses may direct. The sit-for-all-comers course is the rapidly-declining scale, that end in all that is deplorable.[45]

As this account shows, a medium's private behavior was a topic of public debate, enforcing her characterization—common to all celebrities—as a combination of her public and her private self.

Reports about private life were instrumental for the fame of not only the Fox sisters but other mediums as well. This is a typical dynamic in contexts beyond spiritualism, too, as fans' emotional ties to a celebrity make them eager for information about her personality and private life.[46] The star is often an ambivalent figure who alternates between achievements and signs of ruinous decadence. In the show trade, impresarios and managers soon realized that controversies regarding the sentimental and sexual life of stars from the theater or other entertainment sectors could easily be breaking news and result in consistent gains at the box office.[47] This is perhaps connected to the fact that the relationship between celebrities and fans, as Reni Celeste points out, benefits from "anything that will bring closer the realism or vulnerability of the body of the star."[48] The careers of many theatrical and show-business celebrities have been marked by scandals, divorces, and addictions to drugs or alcohol, all of which have molded the link between them and their fans. Scandals and addictions marked the lives and careers of many mediums: as Marlene Tromp shows, spiritualist mediums were frequently associated with libertine behaviors as well as the abuse of drugs and alcohol. The séances of mediums Catherine Wood and Annie Fairlamb, for instance, mixed the uplifting character of spiritualism with strong sexual connotations.[49] The two mediums began to give séances in their hometown of Newcastle upon Tyne in England in 1873, when Wood was eighteen and Fairlamb seventeen years old. Their sittings, conducted under the auspices of the Newcastle Spiritualist Society, featured materializations and the appearance of strongly racialized child spirits. The consistent gains connected to their spiritualist activities, however, resulted in financial litigations between the mediums and the society in 1876. This public controversy revealed more particulars about the private lives of the two mediums, especially with regard to the relationship between Fairlamb and her fiancé, James Mellon, who was deemed responsible for some of the troubles.[50] Reports in spiritualist journals were sometimes quite harsh: an open letter published by the *Medium and Daybreak*, for instance, hinted at the conflict between spiritual endeavors and monetary interests, and it underlined the "alcoholic element introduced into the promiscuous séances of the Society."[51] Yet the controversy contributed to the spread of Wood and Fairlamb's renown beyond the local context of Newcastle, signaling not their demise but the beginning of longer careers. On numerous occasions after their partnership ended, Wood was again at the center of public debate due to her unconventional behavior and the sexually charged character of her séances.[52] Although her repeated exposures eventually diminished the respect that spiritualists had felt for her, her libertine conduct benefited her celebrity status within the spiritualist field. Indeed, as Mary Louise Roberts has argued, famous theater actresses in the nineteenth century used their eccentric behavior to attract the attention of the public and the press; a similar strategy also worked for spiritualist mediums.[53]

The influence of celebrity culture on spiritualism is also suggested by the fact that mediums were often supported by assistants, who functioned similarly to agents and managers in show business. If fame is considered a commodity—with its intrinsic, albeit ungraspable and evanescent, value—the fabrication of celebrity is understood as the marketing of this commodity. This marketing is usually accomplished through those whom Chris Rojek calls "cultural intermediaries"—such as impresarios, agents, promoters, photographers, and personal assistants—who manage the presence and the representation of celebrities in the public sphere.[54] In spiritualism, mediums such as the Davenport brothers, who specialized in public events, openly hired managers to organize their performances, handle their relationship with the press, and collect revenues.⁵⁵ Mediums who worked within a less overtly spectacular frame employed assistants to perform similar duties. The difference was that, among the latter, the existence of a financial agreement between the assistant and medium usually went unacknowledged, for fear that this might raise doubts about the good faith of the medium and the authenticity of the phenomena involved.⁵⁶

Addressing celebrity as a cultural mechanism helps us comprehend how celebrity culture was instrumental in spiritualism's capacity to reach increasingly large masses of people. In the following section, this argument will be further supported through the examination of the career of Italian medium Eusapia Palladino. Palladino became an international celebrity in the context of turn-of-the-century spiritualism and psychical research and traveled to both Britain and the United States to perform séances. Her case is particularly apt in reflecting the international character of celebrity culture within the spiritualist movement.

CELEBRITY AS PERSONA: THE INTERNATIONAL CAREER OF EUSAPIA PALLADINO

Eusapia Palladino, probably more than any other medium, has "ghosted" the collective memory of spiritualism and psychical research. In 1908, Italian psychical researcher Filippo Bottazzi estimated that she had been mentioned several thousands of times in articles on psychic topics—enough to assemble an entire library of work written about her.⁵⁷ Certainly, Bottazzi's figure must be multiplied numerous times if we wish to account for the references to Palladino that appeared in the following century—up to the present day.⁵⁸ Such an astounding volume of reports and references reflects the fame and the honor that she experienced in life. While there are many famous mediums in the history of spiritualism, in fact, probably no other had the celebrity status that Eusapia Palladino did in the 1890s and 1900s. Heralded by historians of spiritualism as one of the few mediums who "left their mark in history,"⁵⁹ she toured Europe and America incessantly, like a theatrical star, performing séances in Italy, France, England, Poland, Germany, Russia, and the United States. She drew the attention of eminent personalities—including the world-famous Italian psychiatrist Cesare Lombroso and the Nobel Prize laureates Charles Richet and Marie and Pierre Curie—and served as a constant pole of attraction for the popular press.

More than any other spiritualist medium of her time, Palladino displayed on numerous occasions throughout her career the ability to manipulate the attention of the public and the popular press. She and her agents invited journalists to participate in séances and constantly encouraged public controversies about her phenomena, aware that this would kindle the interest of the press and ultimately benefit her celebrity status, if not her reputation. Yet the use of elaborate and self-aware marketing strategies and the careful staging of her séance demonstrations do not mean that she was not committed in her beliefs or that she was undoubtedly a fraud. By looking at the case of Palladino, I would like to give a specific example of how the celebrity culture of spiritualism was fabricated and how it affected the public discourse on spiritualist mediumship; however, it is important to reinvigorate my claim that issues such as celebrity, marketing, entertainment, and spectacle do not contrast with genuine endeavors or with religious practice. As mentioned below, Palladino's mediumship was exposed as trickery many times during her career. Yet the question of authenticity or deceit is not at stake here, as the construction of Palladino's celebrity followed paths that may well be independent of the authenticity or the fakery of her mediumship.

Palladino's spirit guide, John King, had already been in contact with several other mediums from the history of spiritualism.[60] King embodied Palladino's privileged relationship with the movement and was widely known to all committed spiritualists. He not only represented a kind of homage to spiritualist history, but also, since King claimed to have been Palladino's father in another life, symbolically inserted the Neapolitan medium into the lineage of the most important mediums of the Victorian age.[61]

Like many other historical mediums, Eusapia Palladino demonstrated her mediumship before the paying public in theaters and public halls. Her séances also took place on the stage before much larger crowds than could fit into a room in a private house.[62] But even when she was holding private or experimental séances, Palladino's success was largely attributed to the fact that she was an accomplished performer. As a journalist once put it, she "would have been an excellent actress or mime," if destiny had not "brought her toward other paths."[63]

The theatrical character of Palladino's trance phenomena was conjectured by her detractors. At the end of her career, rumors that she had once been married to a professional stage magician began to circulate and were stressed by those who believed that her mediumship was mere trickery.[64] When asked about this, she replied indignantly that the story was false. Her defense, however, was quite ambiguous: despite denying that her first husband was a professional conjurer, Palladino admitted that he had been "connected with theatricals" and that "he also knew a few tricks, and took a delight in exhibiting them to his fellow workers."[65] Sometimes even Palladino's supporters seemed to realize that her mediumship might be a theatrical display. The Italian psychiatrist Enrico Morselli, who published two monumental volumes about her in 1908, sensed a hint of quasi-dramaturgical planning in her séances, observing that "the program of every evening seems pre-arranged, as it is also the case of the program of a series of sittings, when Palladino proceeds carefully from simple to more complex phenomena."[66]

Séance reports often underlined the spectacular character of spirit manifestations developed by Palladino. Her sittings featured both acoustic and visual manifestations, including the sudden appearance of lights and ectoplasms and the playing of musical instruments.[67] She was a "physical medium," which means that her trance phenomena were mainly of a material nature, such as movements of the table and the levitation of objects (fig. 12). Hereward Carrington delightedly reported how "tables and chairs move around the room of their own accord, untouched by visible hands; the table around which the sitters are seated, rocks violently, and finally goes completely into the air, contrary to the law of gravitation."[68]

Among the sitters at Palladino's séances were scientists, journalists, psychical researchers, and important representatives of the European aristocracy and bourgeoisie.[69] As Cesare Lombroso's daughter Paola Carrara wrote, the "saleswoman" of Naples appeared in "the most elegant drawing-rooms of the aristocracy of Europe."[70] Her humble origins and simple manners were frequently emphasized to suggest that she was too naive to be a trickster.[71] One writer, for instance, claimed that "Eusapia, poor woman without any culture, does not deceive anyone: she really has in herself the energy needed for the production of her phenomena."[72] Many noted the contrast between her humble appearance and her celebrity status; as an article in the Italian magazine *L'Italia del Popolo* pointed out in 1892, a person who looked at Eusapia Palladino "would not certainly realize that she is a celebrity."[73] This contrast turned her career into a story of social and economic redemption—a pattern found in the careers of many early film and theater stars. A rising star herself, Palladino was a simple woman from southern Italy who had achieved social promotion.

The popular depiction of Palladino followed a pattern similar to that of theatrical celebrities whose personas, as noted above, consisted of a combination of private life and public performance. Her reputation was not

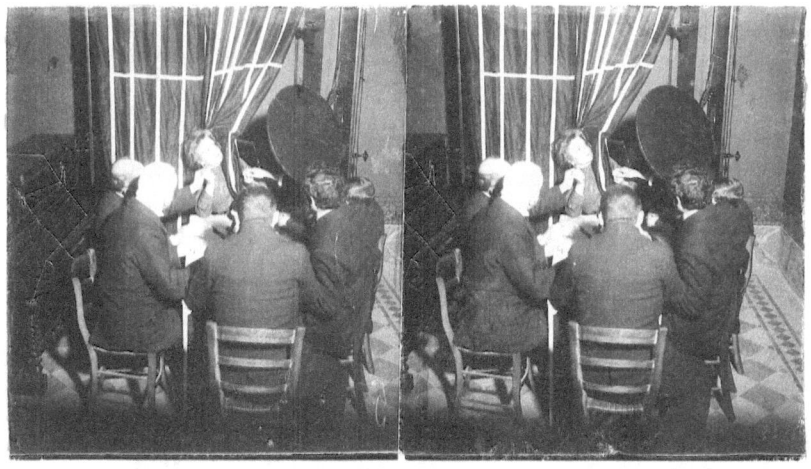

FIG. 12 A stereoscopic photograph of a séance with Eusapia Palladino. Note the table levitating on her left—one of the most spectacular phenomena observed at her sittings. The photograph was taken with a camera with two lenses and intended to be viewed through a stereoscope, which causes photographs and illustrations to appear as three-dimensional images. This suggests that the image was produced not only for evidentiary reasons, but also to be displayed as a curiosity and visual attraction. "Cesare Lombroso" Photographic Archives, Cesare Lombroso Museum of Criminal Anthropology, item 346. Courtesy of the Cesare Lombroso Museum of Criminal Anthropology at the University of Turin, Italy.

solely the result of the phenomena she produced in trance. The extraordinary medium and the emotional Italian peasant were two faces of the same person, which mutually conspired to build her public image. Details about Palladino's life and personality were used to reinforce her credibility as a medium. Morselli argued, for instance, that her character helped explain the physical and monotonous quality of her mediumistic phenomena. According to him, it was due to her poor culture and scarce imagination: she was, after all, a woman of the Neapolitan lower class.[74] Another aspect of Palladino's personality that was frequently linked to her mediumistic powers was her sensitive temperament—a disposition that many believed was common to all psychic mediums. Palladino was described as very easily frightened and impressed. She was a somnambulist, extremely vulnerable to hypnosis, and demonstrated a stunning sensitivity to the characteristics of her environment and to the emotional state of the persons she encountered.[75] She had mood swings, passing very easily from happiness to sadness, from quietness to rage, from cries of devotion to bursts of laughter.[76] According to various reports, Palladino's sensitive character and lighthearted temperament were a central factor in the development of spirit manifestations. If she was in a bad humor, sitters had to wait much longer than usual for the phenomena to take place. As her American manager noted, "She enjoys all such diversions in the childlike manners of all true Neapolitans, and is easily amused by trifles."[77] As a consequence, the investigators of her psychic phenomena encouraged her social manner in hopes of pleasing her and thereby providing the best conditions for a séance. Attempting to create a sociable atmosphere at her séances, they also facilitated a playful interpretation of these events.

As was often the case with professional mediums, Palladino was paid a generous fee for giving sittings. During her American tour in 1909, the *New York Times* reported that her rate was fixed at the respectable sum of 250 to 300 dollars.[78] She always had someone who, although often hidden behind the guise of "assistant" or "adviser," acted as her manager, organizing the sittings and making contact with those who wished to attend her séances.

Palladino's longest-lasting and most important adviser was Ercole Chiaia, who assisted her during the period that saw her definitive rise—from 1888 until his death in 1905. A physician by profession, Chiaia was one of the most active and influential Italian psychical researchers at the turn of the century. Arthur Conan Doyle later remembered him as "an ardent worker and propagandist to whom many distinguished men of European reputation owed their first knowledge of psychic phenomena."[79] Chiaia demonstrated a unique ability to manage Palladino's interests, promoting her mediumship not only within the boundaries of the spiritualist movement, but also in the popular press and through contact with eminent intellectuals, aristocrats, and scientists. He facilitated Palladino's rise to the rank of international celebrity through a combination of several strategies. Soon after he became involved with Palladino, Chiaia started to support her cause through the network of contacts provided by spiritualism and by the field of psychical research. He realized that the spiritualist movement was capable of transcending national boundaries and worked to establish contacts outside Italy, particularly in France. At the end of the 1880s, his propagandist activities at spiritualist conferences and meetings prepared the field for the standing that Palladino would achieve internationally in the following decade.[80] Chiaia also contributed to her ascent by using the press as a vehicle for promotion. He demonstrated an uncommon sensitivity to the interests of the public and the demands of the popular press: journalists were always welcome to participate in Palladino's séances, giving her mediumship greater publicity.[81]

Chiaia's most successful strategy was his use of the authority of science. He understood that the encounter between scientific frameworks and supernatural beliefs could make a sensational attraction for the press and the public. His crowning achievement was the conversion of the internationally celebrated Italian psychiatrist and sociologist Cesare Lombroso.[82] This provoked much sensation and interest and was greeted as a historical triumph by psychical researchers throughout all of Europe.[83] Chiaia skillfully orchestrated Lombroso's conversion, proving his proficiency as a manager and contributing to the fabrication of Palladino's international celebrity.[84] In 1888, in order to convince the famous scientist to sit at the medium's table, Chiaia addressed an open letter challenging Lombroso and arranged to have it published in *La Fanfulla*, an influential Italian magazine that counted Lombroso among its collaborators. Chiaia referred to an article previously published by Lombroso, in which he had pointed out that every age is resistant to new discoveries challenging previous knowledge and theories, and that claims ridiculed today as mere fantasies might one day be proven true. As a consequence, Chiaia could reasonably argue that if Lombroso was really committed to science—unbiased and free of prejudgments, as he proclaimed to be in that article—he would not hesitate to accept the challenge.[85] This strategy ultimately worked. Although the first negotiations following the letter's publication in 1888 failed because of Chiaia's refusal to fulfill some of Lombroso's demands—particularly his request that the séances be held in full light—it was only a matter of time before the scientist accepted. Three years later, Lombroso finally attended one of Palladino's sittings and was convinced by her powers.

On many other occasions, Chiaia encouraged scientists of national and international repute to investigate spiritualism and was ready to profit from the resulting publicity. Between 1890 and 1909, Palladino engaged in what Christine Blondel called "a veritable campaign of collective experimentation," comprising hundreds of recorded experiences.[86] As numerous reports demonstrate, Chiaia was personally involved in the organization of many of Palladino's "experimental séances."[87] Scientists who participated in these investigations included Pierre and Marie Curie, the world-famous physicists who had been awarded the Nobel Prize in 1903 for their contributions to the discovery of radioactivity.[88] A factor that certainly contributed to Palladino's fortune in the scientific world was that both she and her mentor maintained a substantial openness regarding the interpretation of séance phenomena. Especially when they were dealing with nonspiritualists, Chiaia and Palladino never pointed too explicitly to spirit communication, granting sitters the opportunity to devise other explanations, such as telekinesis and other kinds of psychic energies emanated by the medium's brain. Lombroso, for instance, was initially cautious about giving credit to the spiritualist claims, preferring other theories that were more consistent with contemporary research in psychology and physiology.[89] Similarly, Charles Richet attributed Palladino's phenomenon of table levitation to "facts of objective *metapsychique*," which he defined as "a science that focuses on mechanical or psychological phenomena that are due to forces that seem intelligent, or unknown powers that are latent in human intelligence."[90] Others, such as the Italian Pier Francesco Arullani, ventured to link Palladino's manifestations with radioactivity, perhaps in an attempt to profit from the scientific credit that this area of research was granted at the end of the nineteenth century, following the discoveries of the X-ray and the principle of radioactivity.[91]

Scientists such as Camille Flammarion, Richet, and Lombroso greatly contributed to the reputation of Palladino's mediumistic phenomena. Their confidence in her did not recede even given the numerous exposures and accusations of trickery that she suffered throughout her career. As Richet wrote, such was his trust in her mediumship that "even if Eusapia Palladino had been the only medium in the world, it would be still enough for telekinesis and ectoplasm to be scientifically proved."[92] He strenuously defended her good faith before the most unmistakable evidences of trickery. When a committee of the Society for Psychical Research in England issued a negative report about her mediumship, for instance, Richet explained that it was due to the ineptitude of the investigators, who "almost provoked the fraudulence." He claimed that all who experimented with Palladino under a rigid scientific framework had been convinced that her manifestations were authentic.[93]

Chiaia was Palladino's manager until 1905, the year of his death.[94] But the disappearance of her most faithful agent, the man who had made the most successful efforts to fabricate her celebrity, did not end Palladino's career as a medium. She attempted one of her most ambitious enterprises some years later, in 1909, visiting the United States for a series of spirit séances.

It is interesting to examine how Palladino's arrival in America was prepared by the careful orchestration of press reports, following a well-established tradition in show business when a performer engaged in international tours.[95] The person who acted as Palladino's manager during her American tour was Hereward Carrington, a member of the American Society for Psychical Research.[96] Palladino's arrival in New York was a skillfully organized media event. Carrington arranged for the publication of several articles in the American press in order to elicit sympathy from the American public and build anticipation of her coming.[97] The news that she was giving séances onboard the steamboat *Prinzess Irene* kindled the curiosity of the public.[98] As soon as she reached American soil, Carrington organized a press conference in his apartment, where Palladino was visited by a dozen or more reporters.[99] During the meeting, a man informed the reporters that his employer, a theatrical manager, was negotiating with Carrington to obtain the services of Eusapia and her spirit guide, John.[100] Palladino also gave a public demonstration of her mediumistic powers for the benefit of newspapermen. This was set in the Lincoln Square Theater, on whose stage the séance table was placed. The participation of local celebrities added to the sensational character of the event: the Broadway actress Grace George and her husband, William A. Brady, also a theater actor, sat around the table with Palladino, Carrington, and three journalists.[101] Reports emphasized the presence of "persons connected with theatricals" among the audience, strengthening the impression that the séance demonstration had as much to do with spiritualism as with show business.[102]

Newspaper reports and press conferences were only the start of a wider publicity campaign that established Palladino as a celebrity in the American public sphere. This included the publication of her autobiographical sketch in the *Cosmopolitan Magazine*, which was, at the time, a key publication in the media empire of William Randolph Hearst (fig. 13).[103] As historian of psychical research Carlos S. Alvarado put it, autobiographies of mediums illuminate "the strategies, as well as the realities and fictions with which these unique individuals choose to represent themselves."[104] Palladino's account was no exception, adding much color and personality to the medium's character. Her Italian origins were particularly emphasized, giving her a definite exotic charm.[105] The story of how she suffered the loss of her parents, refused to enter a convent, and slowly discovered her powers highlighted the struggle that she had endured before becoming a famous and celebrated medium, and it offered a positive view of Palladino to the American public. Similar to autobiographies of theatrical actresses published in the same period, Palladino's autobiographical sketch presented her life as a journey marked by personal struggle and leading to the climax of celebrity.[106]

Throughout her American tour, Palladino's public image was strongly informed by her Italian origins. She was openly associated with her fellow nationals who immigrated from Italy to America: the *New York Tribune*, for instance, mentioned the immigration procedures that Italian immigrants had to undergo upon their arrival, ironically suggesting that Palladino "brought over foreign spirits that could neither be searched by Collector

EUSAPIA PALLADINO'S REMARKABLE EYES

My Own Story
By Eusapia Palladino

Editor's Note.—For more than twenty years Mme. Palladino has been importuned by noted journalists and editors of important publications, in all parts of the world, to tell or write something about herself and her marvelous psychic powers, but until now she has steadfastly declined either to reveal personal facts or to make any statement concerning the source of her mystic gifts. Several alleged "interviews" have been printed, but none of these has been sanctioned, endorsed, or even read, before publication, by Palladino or her sponsors. It has remained for the Cosmopolitan Magazine to give the real life story of this extraordinary woman in her own words.

FIG. 13   The *Cosmopolitan Magazine* published an autobiography of the medium Eusapia Palladino in 1910. The first page of the piece, shown here, presented the "remarkable eyes" of the Italian medium, whose mesmerizing gaze was directed at the reader. From Eusapia Palladino, "My Own Story," *Cosmopolitan Magazine* 48 (1910): 292–300.

Lee nor detained at Ellis Island by Commissioner Williams."[107] American newspapers often quoted her own words in Italian: the *New York Times* cited her remark "'Sono molto, molto nervosa,' (I am very nervous)," and commented that Italian is a language in which "you can talk more and say less than any other [language] in the world."[108] Sometimes nicknamed "the signora,"[109] Palladino came from "the land of fine arts, sunny skies and spaghetti"; [110] many of her compatriots reportedly remembered her "cooking supper for her husband on the sidewalk of one of the principal streets of Naples and publicly dishing up the macaroni for both him and herself."[111]

Despite Carrington's efforts, Palladino's appearances in the United States did not conclude in triumph, but rather in an episode that signaled the beginning of her decline. During a series of séances held in Boston, she experienced what was probably the most shameful exposure of her entire career. The Boston sittings were highlighted by the presence of Hugo Münsterberg, director of the psychological laboratory at Harvard and probably the most influential psychologist in the United States at the time. Münsterberg had never attended a spiritualist séance before sitting at

Palladino's table in 1909.¹¹² In his first writing on spiritualism, "Psychology and Mysticism," published in 1899, he had explained his strict avoidance of séances: he considered it "undignified to visit such performances, as one attends a variety show, for amusement only, without attempting to explain them."¹¹³ But he managed to keep his resolve for only ten years, until the arrival of Eusapia Palladino in America convinced him that it was finally time to enter the spirit room.

Today, Münsterberg is mostly known for his pioneering contribution to film theory as the author of *The Photoplay: A Psychological Study*, a book originally published in 1916; it was rediscovered in the 1960s and 1970s and is today considered a classic in film studies.¹¹⁴ Publishing both academic works and more popular writings that targeted a broader public, Münsterberg was regarded by his contemporaries as the "father of applied psychology."¹¹⁵ He was extremely attentive to opportunities to apply psychology to issues of popular interest. For instance, in *American Problems from the Point of View of a Psychologist*, he concentrated his attention on broad social questions such as the choice of a professional vocation and what he called the "intemperance" of women.¹¹⁶ He thereby stressed the practical importance of this young science. Consequently, Münsterberg did not refuse to participate in debates on subjects that might be considered "trivial" by some of his contemporaries, such as spiritualism. Unlike Cesare Lombroso, however, Münsterberg was not about to be convinced by Palladino's mediumship. At the sittings in Boston, he managed to bring a collaborator; they had an agreement of which Palladino and all the other sitters at the séance were unaware. Münsterberg's accomplice succeeded in catching the medium's foot in his hands as she was trying, with a contortionist move, to lift the séance table. Palladino responded with a scream, indicating her realization that, at last, her glory was shattered. As Münsterberg wrote, "Her greatest wonders are absolutely nothing but fraud and humbug; this is no longer a theory but a proven fact."¹¹⁷

Although it was certainly not the first time that Palladino's trickery had been revealed,¹¹⁸ this exposure had particular consequence for her, perhaps, in part, due to the high expectations of her American audiences. Münsterberg's report was summarized in several newspapers, including the *New York Times*, and it was taken by many to be the final word on spiritualism in general and on Palladino's mediumship in particular.¹¹⁹ She suffered another shameful debunking during a séance organized in New York by a professor at Columbia University, Dickinson S. Miller.¹²⁰ Three stage magicians—James L. Kellogg, John W. Sargent, and Joseph F. Rinn—were among the sitters; they were supposed to use their knowledge of legerdemain and stage magic to design a means of unveiling Palladino's trickery. At the beginning of the séance, Miller proposed a test of Palladino's alleged powers through an electroscope, a device with which Palladino was already familiar. This was, however, only a diversion. It was meant to distract Palladino while Rinn, who had specialized in the exposure of mediums, and Warner Pyne, a student at Columbia, wriggled along the floor to position themselves beside the séance table (fig. 14). Meanwhile, the other sitters played their part, trying to appear friendly and sympathetic toward the medium in hopes of making her more comfortable and less careful. When the manifestations began, Rinn and Pyne, from under the table, could see how she was using her feet to make the table move and levitate and to perform the alleged "spirit phenomena." When Palladino realized that she had been framed, she reportedly lost control and, "in very rapid Italian, yelled so loud that the noise was heard in the street."[121]

In the course of the polemics that followed Palladino's exposures, Carrington admitted in a public letter that she had cheated, but claimed that this proved nothing, as "Eusapia herself says that she will cheat if allowed to, and begs her sitters to prevent her from cheating."[122] According to Carrington's argument, the exposures were due to the fact that the investigators had "allowed" Palladino to cheat, thereby failing to notice that, behind her tendency to add some more color to her exhibitions, lay authentic phenomena.[123] But Carrington's call for a new series of tests went unheard, and Palladino's American tour signaled the definitive decline of the woman who had been, for decades, the most famous medium in the world. If her arrival in the United States had been heralded by the popular press, her return to Italy went mostly unnoticed. Her reputation never fully recovered. A diabetic, Palladino's physical condition had worsened by May 1911.[124] She continued to hold séances, but not as many aristocrats, scientists, and journalists sat at her table as before. She died of nephritis some years later, in 1918.

THE MEDIUM AND THE STAR

This chapter's examination of how celebrity culture worked as a mechanism to enhance the popularity of the spiritualist movement and the subsequent case study of the international career of the medium Eusapia Palladino serve as further evidence for the connection between nineteenth-century spiritualism and the rise of the media entertainment

FIG. 14 Dickinson S. Miller, a professor at Columbia University in New York, set up a committee to investigate Eusapia Palladino's mediumship, which included several professors and lecturers at Columbia. What took place, however, was no ordinary séance; it was a trap. This illustration, published in *Collier's Weekly*, depicts the exposure suffered by Palladino in this séance. From Joseph Jastrow, "The Unmasking of Palladino: An Actual Observation of the Complete Machinery of the Famous Italian Medium," *Collier's Weekly* 45, no. 8 (1910): 21–22.

industry. Additionally, pointing to the case of spiritualism may make a contribution to scholarship in celebrity studies. It is useful in this regard to underline not only similar elements, but also the uniqueness of the spiritualist celebrity in comparison with other forms of celebrity.

The first distinctive characteristic of spiritualist celebrity concerns the issue of gender. As scholars addressing celebrity in the nineteenth century observe, "Though women could be famous in the nineteenth century, it was difficult for them to enjoy celebrity. This was, after all, the era of separate spheres, the time when the prevailing gender order frowned on women in public life."[125] It is not surprising, in this sense, that many of the female celebrities who emerged during this period were actresses and performers from the world of theater and spectacular entertainments. As Mary Louise Roberts points out, female celebrities from show business were able to assume different roles, defying established representations of gender, and they used their eccentric behavior as a strategy and a posture that helped them manage their fame.[126] In addition to theater and show business, the spiritualist movement provided an environment in which women could attain celebrity status at least as often as men throughout the nineteenth century. Women found in spiritualism a space where they could express their opinions and personalities with more freedom than they could in other contexts.[127] As Ann Braude points out, because the agency in their trance lectures and communications was attributed to the spirits, "mediumship gave women a public leadership role that allowed them to remain compliant with the complex of values of the period."[128] Spiritualist women celebrities, moreover, often resembled the celebrities of show business. Take, for instance, Eusapia Palladino. As Angela Dalle Vacche observes in her examination of the earliest stars of Italian cinema, Italian divas were characterized as exhibiting hysteria, reflecting established representations of femininity at the time.[129] Likewise, Palladino was depicted as a "bundle of nerves" who displayed "an air of vitality and of nervous strain about her."[130]

A second element characterizing spiritualism's celebrity culture regards the extent to which celebrity status was acknowledged or denied. In contrast with show-business stars, spiritualist mediums did not openly acknowledge their status, at least not in relation to the market. Performativity, celebrity strategies, and the use of managers and agents were, for spiritualists, extremely problematic issues, since they could spark doubts about the good faith of the medium. In this sense, celebrity mediums were marketed commodities who struggled to demonstrate that they did not pertain to the market. Paradoxically, their attempt to deny the market, as proof of their honesty, was one of the foundations for their success as mediums and, consequently, for their celebrity status. Recalling a pilgrimage site, where everything is marketed but, at the same time, this commercial approach is never openly acknowledged, the medium needed to deny the market in order to become the market's hero.[131] In this sense, celebrity studies might employ the case of spiritualist mediums, and of other religious leaders raised to celebrity status, to gain insights into the way that processes of fabrication and marketing involved in the construction of a celebrity are subject to forms of denial that make them more easily accepted by the public.

A third element unique to spiritualist celebrity is its relationship with the world of science. In numerous cases throughout the history of spiritualism, the involvement of famous scientists in séances and demonstrations provided mediums with a valuable opportunity to become widely known beyond the boundaries of the movement. As noted above, for instance, the conversion of Cesare Lombroso and other respected scientists was a key factor in Eusapia Palladino's celebrity, and probably for this reason, her agents and assistants arranged for experimental séances to be conducted with famous psychologists and physicists, such as Marie and Pierre Curie. Likewise, the committed involvement of chemist William Crookes in Florence Cook's séances was of paramount importance in achieving her celebrity status in England during the 1870s.[132] The case of spiritualism, therefore, provides further ground for the examination of how the popularization of science interacted with nineteenth-century celebrity culture, and it suggests that debates on supernatural phenomena might have contributed—not unlike reports of scientific inventions and novelties—to the celebrity of scientists, too.[133]

By examining the process of fabrication involved in celebrity culture, this chapter has shown how spiritualist mediums were turned into objects of consumption. In the third and last part of this book, we will turn to more traditional forms of commodities—such as books, photographic prints, and other material objects—that circulated within the spiritualist movement.

PART THREE

SPIRIT AND MATTER

5

STRANGER THAN FICTION

PRINT MEDIA, AUTOMATIC WRITING,

AND POPULAR CULTURE

In 1872, spiritualist journalist and publisher James Burns initiated the publication of a series of short, inexpensive tracts entitled "Seed Corn." The first tract explained the idea behind the title, advising believers in spirit communication on how to spread their faith and promote spiritualism. Spiritualists, he reasoned, needed to work together to broadcast information about their beliefs, and the best way to do this was to devote their efforts, time, and money to the circulation of tracts, papers, and other publications. Burns cited the arguments of a writer who had called for a "new programme" in the spiritualist enterprise:

> 1st, Circulate tracts by millions. Let them be short, and to the point, such as can be afforded for sixpence a hundred. Each hundred, judiciously circulated, would secure at least one subscriber to a Spiritual paper.
>
> 2ndly, Circulate Spiritual papers. Let each subscriber take two where he or she now takes one, and give away to all who can be induced to read or circulate them.
>
> 3rdly, Free circles—public and private; also local, county, state, and national mass meetings, where spirits and their mediums shall not be trammelled by would-be leaders, who fear erratic, striking, and comical manifestations, which are just the thing to draw the thoughtless crowd, and enable wise Spiritualists to scatter in tracts, papers, and publications, the seed which will, in due time, produce a bountiful harvest.

Carry out the above programme, and tracts, papers, and converts will increase tenfold faster than by patronising leaders, creeds, and expensive organisations.[1]

Equating the new program with a publication strategy, Burns encouraged spiritualists to spread their faith by contributing to the diffusion of spiritualist print media. It was for this purpose, in fact, that the "Seed Corn" tracts had been prepared—"to scatter broadcast over the land."[2] In Burns's view, spiritualist periodicals, books, and tracts were the chief means by which the spiritualist message would reach the widest audience possible.

Although the invention of the printing press dates back to the fifteenth century, it was not until the nineteenth century that print commodities ceased to be based on an artisanal mode of production and began to adopt industrial techniques.[3] By the 1850s, books had largely become an industrial commodity in both Britain and the United States. Growth in the volume of sales was stimulated by improvements in the manufacture of books and in the mode of production, as well as by the expansion of the potential market due to the spread of literacy and a rising population. While at the beginning of the nineteenth century American publishers considered 6,500 copies to be the sales limit for a popular book, around the 1850s editions of 10,000 were normal, and the most successful works could sell up to 300,000 copies.[4] A similar process was at play in the British context, where the printed text became the center of a mass market during the first decades of the nineteenth century.[5] In addition to the growing number of copies published, changes included the character of print products: while books and magazines were mainly addressed to clergymen and gentlemen in the eighteenth century, the publications that flooded the market in the first decades of the nineteenth century were cheap books and periodicals aimed to appeal to the masses.[6]

The history of the book and print media is closely linked to the history of religion: it might suffice to recall that the first major print project completed by Gutenberg with his new technology of movable type was the Bible. In the Victorian age, improvements in print technologies and the consumer revolution stimulated the rise of religious publications as products of mass consumption. During this period, readerships targeted by the book market became increasingly transatlantic, a change that informed the market of popular religious publications, too.[7] As with other religious communities in Britain and America, the spiritualist movement flooded the book market with books, pamphlets, and journals, contributing to the development of spiritualism's material culture. Moreover, the publication of exhibition pamphlets that were sold at lectures on spiritualism, mesmerism, and mediumship—and the presence of news and reports on public séances in both spiritualist journals and the popular press—shows that print media were employed to support the performances of mediums as well. In this regard, spiritualism's print and performance cultures were strongly interconnected: by setting séances in a spectacular framework and by promoting the sale of print commodities, mediums and spiritualist leaders turned spiritualism into something that could be marketed and consumed.

This chapter examines British and American spiritualist publications, in which entertainment merged with the inquiry of spirit communication, in order to argue that the publication of books and journals within the spiritualist movement became part of the newly established mass market of books. After taking into account the role of publishing companies within spiritualism, focusing in particular on the case of James Burns and the Progressive Library and Spiritual Institution, the chapter examines the content of spiritualist publications, linking them to genres of popular literature that were successful at the time. It then emphasizes a type of writing specific to the spiritualist field—works that were authored, according to their publishers and editors, by the spirits themselves. These were often the most entertaining spiritualist publications, featuring adventurous lives and explorations into the spirit world by departed authors. The analysis of these texts introduces what is apparently one of the greatest contradictions to be found in nineteenth-century spiritualist publications: although the spirits could communicate metaphysical and religious truths, they often decided to offer their readers something comparable to popular literature of the time.

PRINT MEDIA AND THE BROADENING OF THE SPIRITUALIST FAITH

Several scholars have addressed the question of how the rise of spiritualism influenced literature in the nineteenth century and beyond. Jennifer Bann, for instance, argues that after the Hydesville rappings, literary spirits appearing in gothic narratives started to seem empowered rather than constrained by their deaths: "They were as varied and as psychologically complex as they had been in life, their ability to act within a physical sphere evidence of both their individuality and their liberation from the restrictions of mortality."[8] Others have focused on the relations between spiritualism and narratives of mourning,[9] or on how literary fiction reflected the scientific claims of spiritualism, shifting from the character of the priest—in early nineteenth-century gothic literature, the man who confronts the supernatural menace—to that of the scientist, such as Van Helsing in Bram Stoker's *Dracula*.[10] These, however, are not the only ways in which spiritualism dialogued with the world of popular literature. Spiritualists not only influenced contemporary narrative texts but produced a considerable volume of literature themselves. The number of books, pamphlets, and magazines that they published during the nineteenth century is astonishing. In 1871, the *American Bookseller's Guide* advised its readers, "The sale of [spiritualist] books is as steady as of books in any other department of the trade, and they should not be overlooked by the bookseller."[11] The same source reported that spiritualist publications accounted for the sale of fifty thousand books and fifty thousand pamphlets every year. These included successful treatises such as Andrew Jackson Davis's speculative works,[12] personal testimonies of conversion by spiritualists,[13] and popular pamphlets reporting the "miracles" of table tipping.[14] Books and periodicals filled the gap left by the spiritualist movement's lack of organization: as Ann Braude put it, "Spiritualists did not join organizations, but they did read and write."[15]

Spiritualist periodicals played a particularly significant role in the diffusion of spiritualist print media. Functioning as a place where spiritualist writings were advertised and reviewed, they made an essential contribution to broadening the circulation of texts and creating a community of spiritualist readers. In this context, the British spiritualist journal *Medium and Daybreak* is a particularly interesting case because it was connected to the book publishing activity of its editor, the British spiritualist James Burns, who produced successful titles such as *Hafed Prince of Persia* and Catherine Berry's *Experiences in Spiritualism*. After buying out the provincial monthly *Daybreak* in 1869, Burns founded the *Medium and Daybreak* in 1870, described in its subtitle as "a weekly journal devoted to the history, phenomena, philosophy, and teachings of spiritualism." It ran for more than three decades, ending publication in 1895, the year after Burns's death. According to Frank Podmore, a member of the Society for Psychical Research and author of one of the earliest and most informative histories of the movement, the *Medium and Daybreak* was by far the leading spiritualist periodical in Britain, based on its number of subscribers.[16] While other spiritualist periodicals mainly targeted a readership of erudite spiritualists, Burns regarded the simplicity of language as a duty and a matter of pride, seeking to make his journal accessible to the broadest possible public.[17] Featuring a wide range of columns and memoirs authored by correspondents or communicated by the spirits through mediums, the *Medium and Daybreak* was particularly open to those contributions that appealed as much to serious inquirers as to curious and passionate readers.

Burns's publishing activities were conducted under the auspices of his Progressive Library and Spiritual Institution, located in Southampton Row in Holborn, London. His marketing strategies were well synthesized in the "Seed Corn" tracts mentioned at the beginning of this chapter. There, Burns argued that the best way to broadcast the spiritualist faith was to circulate the *Medium and Daybreak*. He also suggested that tracts and publications could be given away when traveling, left in waiting rooms at railway stations and in railway carriages, and distributed at special meetings and congregations; in fact, the spiritualist promoter should always carry a supply with her. Other ways to contribute to the cause included distributing the tracts in private houses or to passersby on the street. For this purpose, nothing was cheaper or better than the "Seed Corn" tracts, which were specially designed to appeal "to all classes of minds."[18] Moreover, "special publications should be carefully selected, and sent per post, neatly addressed, to clergymen and others occupying influential and professional positions," as well as to personal friends.[19] Spiritualists were also encouraged to present the most successful works published by the Progressive Library and Spiritual Institution, such as Emma Hardinge's history of spiritualism, at events organized at public libraries and other institutions. The first "Seed Corn" tract contained a list of available titles with prices, and everything could be ordered by post.

Illustrations and engravings were given particular attention in Burns's publishing efforts. The *Medium and Daybreak* was known for its beautiful graphic design, and Burns employed a well-known spiritualist artist and illustrator, Henry Bielfeld, to create its new header in 1872. Bielfeld had contributed work to other spiritualist publications, including the frontispiece for Hardinge's *Modern American Spiritualism*, which was taken from a painting that he executed specifically for this purpose.[20] His illustrations were sometimes created under the influence of the spirits, as in the case of *The Ten Spiritual Commandments*. Reproduced by lithography in several tints and advertised as having been "given by the spirits through [the mediumship of] Emma Hardinge," this picture was sold through correspondence to the readers of the *Medium and Daybreak*.[21] Bielfeld also engaged in portraiture of spirit forms, as in an oil painting of the celebrity spirit Katie King, which reportedly was very much appreciated by the spirit herself.[22]

Like other periodicals being marketed at the time, the *Medium and Daybreak* used a burgeoning postal service to boost sales, offering discount prices to subscribers in the United States, as well as in European countries and in the colonies.[23] It also played a leading role in promoting the books published or distributed by Burns and the Progressive Library and Spiritual Institution. Every issue featured advertisements for publications and for the services of mediums and other practitioners, in addition to other commodities and goods. In an attempt to attract potential advertisers, the journal employed the language of advertising by using the slogan "If you wish to succeed, advertise in the 'Medium.'"[24]

Considering the strong role played by therapy and alternative medical practices throughout the history of spiritualism,[25] it is not surprising that advertisements for natural salts, essences, medications, and treatments were among the most common items in the journal's pages. As historian of advertising Jackson Lears emphasizes, therapeutic remedies and panaceas played a leading role in the development of modern advertising culture, featuring among the most sensational and common announcements that targeted consumers in the nineteenth century.[26] In this sense, spiritualist journals such as the *Medium and Daybreak* fully participated in the broader process of the development of a modern advertising culture. Advertisements filled not only periodicals but also spiritualist books. For instance, *The Next World*, a book that featured spirit communications channeled by medium Susan Horn, contained more than thirty pages of advertisements for other publications that were available by post through Burns's Progressive Library and Spiritual Institution.[27] Goods that were promoted in spiritualist journals and books also included instruments for spiritualist inquiries that, like the Ouija board, were widely marketed as popular toys,[28] as well as merchandise such as copies of spirit photographs.[29] The relationship of the spiritualist movement with consumer culture, therefore, not only concerned the way in which spiritualism dialogued with show business, but also emerged in the production, marketing, and advertisement of material commodities.

Burns's Progressive Library and Spiritual Institution was one of many similar enterprises that mingled spiritualist inquiry with the successful commercialization of print media in the nineteenth century. Virtually all spiritualist associations and societies of some standing in Britain and the United States published or promoted periodicals and books.[30] While relatively little is known about sales figures, the volume of texts produced within the movement and the number of reprints and new editions of successful books and pamphlets show that spiritualist publications constituted a flourishing enterprise within the nineteenth-century print market.[31]

What role did such an astounding range of print media play in Victorian spiritualism? Historian of American spiritualism Ann Braude points out that spiritualist periodicals contributed to the building of community within the spiritualist movement. In the nineteenth century, the press provided an arena where people from different geographical areas, but with common interests, could learn about one another's lives and make contact through the columns of periodicals.[32] Because spiritualists believed that each individual should find her own path toward the acquisition of spiritual knowledge, spiritualist communities usually lacked institutional integration and a fixed hierarchy. Spiritualist journals provided a means to fill this gap, linking isolated spiritualist believers across America and Britain.[33] The spiritualist movement was, therefore, more a community of readers unified by print media than an institutionalized religion. Indeed, the high degree of transatlantic integration between the spiritualist movement in Britain and that in the United States was largely due to the agency of the press and print media in forming transnational communities of readers. The ambivalent reception of spiritualism by the scientific and religious establishments prompted spiritualists to search for collaborations and exchanges beyond their own specific national contexts.[34] As a result of periodicals and book publications, news, opinions, and reports about spiritualist mediums and phenomena circulated widely through channels that transcended national boundaries, allowing British and American spiritualists to feel that they belonged to a larger, transatlantic community.[35]

Spiritualist periodicals played another key role in the movement: they provided spiritualists with news about spiritualist séances, demonstrations, events, and meetings. The history of print in the nineteenth century is closely related to the commercial development of the show trade. In Britain and the United States, impresarios and managers relied on the press to publish advertisements and to incite curiosity about their shows. Publications often accompanied the display of attractions, too. Exhibition pamphlets, for instance, consisted of short essays that provided discussion and background information about the exhibited sensation; they could be sold for a small price to spectators at a lecture or a show.[36] Spiritualist print culture supported the performance of spiritualist mediums and leaders in similar ways: the press was used to market and advertise séances and events, and exhibition pamphlets were sold during lectures on spiritualism and during public séances.[37] Journals advertised the activities of mediums, included information on how to contact them about organizing private séances, published lists of public demonstrations and events, and reported on local and national meetings organized by spiritualist associations and societies. In short, they provided an essential support for spiritualism's performance and spectacular culture.

In her book on print media in antebellum America, Isabelle Lehuu argued that there was a deep resemblance between print culture and spectacular shows in the nineteenth century. As Lehuu noted, newspapers covered a miscellany of curiosities and attractions that resembled the exhibitionary culture of dime museums and fairs. Theatrical publishing was paramount and corresponded to the popular practice of reading melodrama; writers and publishers shared with performers and theatrical managers a common knowledge of what piqued the interest of the public.[38] A similar alliance between print and show culture is evident in spiritualism, in the way that both spiritualist performances and publications played as much on entertainment and leisure as on the religious beliefs of sitters and readers. Just as spiritualist séances were simultaneously a ritual and an entertaining event, spiritualist writings had a twofold purpose: to spread the spiritualist faith and to function as a commercial enterprise. For this reason, as the next section will show, they were designed to discuss spiritualist issues but also to amuse the reader.

THE POPULAR LITERATURE OF VICTORIAN SPIRITUALISM

The Victorian age signaled the rise not only of belief in spiritualism but also of several forms of popular literature, such as the gothic novel, that relied on the themes of the ghost and the supernatural.[39] Following the introduction of cinema in the late nineteenth century, moreover, ghosts became an integral part of the cinematic imagination.[40] Ghosts were thus part of a burgeoning popular culture in two distinctive ways: through the inclusion of spiritualism in a broader array of popular attractions, and through their inclusion in fictional narratives popularized by theater, literature, and film. Yet scholarship addressing the presence of occult fantasies in popular culture has mainly focused on fictional uses of supernatural beliefs, without fully acknowledging the inherent playfulness of spiritualists' religious experience.[41] This is probably due to how issues regarding belief and disbelief are approached in discussions on the reception of literary, theatrical, and cinematic texts. These discussions often imply that the consumption of fiction invites a substantially different attitude than participation in an event such as a spiritualist séance—where the text is offered as an authentic transcription of spirit messages and audience members may believe in what they see, smell, hear, and touch.[42]

While I still contend that such distinctions are useful in many regards, I also believe that the spiritualist case examined in this book provides a relevant contribution to the development of a more nuanced approach to the relationship between fiction and belief. Let us take, for instance, the notion of the "willing suspension of disbelief," often used in discussions of cinematic spectatorship. This is the widespread idea that consuming a product of fiction involves a momentary removal of our normal level of skepticism, allowing us to participate emotionally in events and stories that we would usually not accept as realistic. Although the concept of suspension of disbelief can be useful in the examination of genres such as the horror movie or the gothic novel, scholars have criticized some of its assumptions, especially concerning the relationship between belief and emotional response.[43] In this regard, the mingling of religion with entertainment in spiritualist séances reminds us that the suspension of disbelief is not needed to engage in entertainment activities; in other words, we can also be entertained by something we believe in.[44]

This becomes particularly evident if one looks at the content of spiritualist texts published throughout the nineteenth and early twentieth centuries. The dramatic increase in the sale of books, periodicals, and other print media during the nineteenth century also extended to the emergence of literary genres, such as the popular novel, that were consumed by a growing mass of readers in Britain and the United States. In terms of content, spiritualist publications often replicated the patterns and strategies of the works of popular literature that were successful in this period. Many spiritualist works bore similarities to successful literary genres of the time, presenting texts authored by spirits, mediums, and spiritual leaders in a way that responded to the interests, expectations, and habits of Victorian readers.

A good example of the spiritualist imitation of a popular genre is biographical accounts of spiritualist mediums, which reached a high level of standardization during the second half of the nineteenth century. Autobiographies and biographies were an important staple of the new literary market of the period: works such as Benjamin Franklin's autobiography, *The Narrative and Life of Frederick Douglass*, and *The Life of P. T. Barnum, Written by Himself* were highly successful and contributed to establishing a recognized literary genre.[45] As the frequency of their appearance in the spiritualist field shows, biographies were a popular genre

FIG. 15
Biographies of mediums were a popular genre in spiritualism, and spiritualist journals, such as the *Medium and Daybreak*, sometimes dedicated their cover pages to them. From *Medium and Daybreak* 16, no. 770–71 (1885): 1.

among spiritualist readers, too. The *Medium and Daybreak* often published accounts of the lives of spiritualist mediums and in some cases dedicated its cover page to them (fig. 15).[46] Similar works were frequently published in book form. If a medium was particularly famous, her biography could be authored by a recognized publicist or writer: Thomas Low Nichols, who had previously published novels such as *Ellen Ramsay* in 1843 and the two-volume *Forty Years of American Life* in 1864, wrote a biography of the Davenport brothers.[47] In other cases, mediums authored their own personal narratives. The publication of these memoirs was intended to demonstrate their devotion to the goal of spreading the spiritualist faith, along with their understanding of mediumship as a public role. As Sidonie Smith points out, moreover, autobiographies have a performative character, as the author produces a particular representation of herself.[48] In this regard, autobiographies of mediums shed light on the strategies they used to represent their own identity as well as their role within the spiritualist enterprise.⁴⁹

Biographies of mediums can be regarded as a kind of literary subgenre with recurring conventions and patterns. The story of the medium's childhood, for instance, followed unspoken but rather established rules. The death of a close relative, such as the medium's father, was often the subject of particular attention, leading to his reappearance as a spirit guide after the discovery of mediumistic gifts.⁵⁰ Frequently, the powers of the medium were revealed in early childhood, without being recognized as such. In George Redman's *Mystic Hours*, for instance, on the night of his father's death, the young medium, having somnambulist tendencies, got up in his sleep and climbed out a two-story window before being miraculously saved by the intervention of spirits.⁵¹ These recurring elements were connected with established beliefs about mediumship. At the same time, they framed the works within the biographical genre and furnished further evidence of the reality and coherence of spiritualist claims. For example, the existence of relatives with special sensibilities or powers was frequently stressed, implying, as one medium put it, "that the mediumistic temperament is hereditary and transmissible."⁵² Doctrinal questions were directly addressed and discussed as well, and the religious background of the medium was thoroughly described.

Invariably, one of the pivotal moments in a medium's life was the revelation of mediumistic gifts. The narrative of this discovery usually moved from a sudden breakthrough, in which the medium's powers spontaneously revealed themselves, to gradual training and continual development in the phenomena of spirit communications. Following this path, advances in mediumship could continue through the medium's entire life. For example, the medium Joseph Armitage reported that, after discovering his mediumship, he deepened his knowledge of spiritualism, which led him to develop the ability of trance lecturing. Later, when he tried to help a person who had his arm crushed in a wheel, he discovered that he was a healing medium, too.⁵³

In contrast to other spiritualist writings that dedicated much attention to metaphysical and religious speculations, biographies of mediums mostly relied on anecdotes. This characteristic gave those publications an entertaining character. Redman's autobiography, for instance, was full of adventurous episodes. One time, before leaving New York City for a journey to Buffalo, Redman was compelled by his spirit guardian to walk down Broadway toward Battery Park. Upon reaching Cortland Street, he was suddenly turned into a store, where he was made to take a box lying on the counter and hand the attendant a twenty-dollar bill from his pocket. Later, when Redman discovered the box contained a Colt revolver, he received instructions from his father's spirit to load the weapon in order to save his life. "Here," thought Redman, "is a pretty specimen of a spiritual teacher: on one side of my breast I am carrying sentiments of peace, progress, happiness, and good will; on the other a loaded revolver."[54] One night soon thereafter, he had the opportunity to use it when he was assaulted by two bandits on his way home:

> At this moment I felt a stunning sensation as if struck by some heavy instrument, and fell staggering against a door nearby. I now perceived my hand jerk suddenly, and though partially stupefied, I had sufficient perception to see the ruffians backing from me with their hands before their faces; then dodging into a by-way, they disappeared. By this time I knew all; my arm was still raised, and in my hand the revolver. . . . On retiring to bed that night, I felt I should rest ever after secure from harm, and truly appreciated the guardianship of him, who was happy to call me child.[55]

On another occasion, Redman could again thank his spirit friends for helping him survive a tragic and thrilling train accident.[56]

The use of narrative strategies such as colorful anecdotes, which also characterize the most popular works of the biographical genre,[57] exemplifies the close resemblance of nineteenth-century spiritualist publications to popular literature of the time. Moreover, it reveals how spiritualism found legitimization not only by mimicking the experimental patterns of positivist science, but also by using the strategies employed within the realm of popular culture. As David Turley emphasized, anecdotes have both a narrative and an important rhetorical function: they make a statement about the character's nature, profession, and agency.[58] In other words, anecdotes in popular biographies function as narrative patterns that give legitimacy to the protagonist, as well as to the class of individuals that the protagonist represents. In biographies of artists, for instance, as Ernst Kris and Otto Kurz famously claimed, anecdotes support widespread claims about the act of artistic creation and confirm well-established ideas about the "artistic" temperament;[59] in biographies of inventors, they follow established representations of the process of innovation and the role of inventors in scientific and technological progress.[60] Likewise, the establishment of a tradition of biographies and autobiographies of mediums in the nineteenth century supported spiritualism's claims regarding spirit communication, mediumship, and the medium's role in the formation of knowledge about the otherworld. Corroboration of these claims was offered to the public through the entertaining and accessible formula of colorful anecdotes, such as those featured in Redman's autobiography.

The entertaining and popular approach employed in biographies of spiritualist mediums demonstrates spiritualist print culture's repetition of broader literary genres and strategies that signaled the formation of popular culture and mass readership. This is also evident in a genre of publications that were specific to the spiritualist movement: those that had been allegedly dictated by spirits to mediums. Like spiritualist performances at séances, these publications were based on a successful combination of claims of authenticity and the pursuit of entertainment. In fact, while pointing to trance mediumship as evidence of mechanical and objective agency, spirit writings also employed strategies and genres that were typical of popular literature of the time.[61] In these texts, readers could find not only a confirmation of their belief in spirit communication but also an enjoyable pastime.

In May 1882, an article in the *Medium and Daybreak* acknowledged spiritualism's relationship to literature. The author hinted at the role played by trance and direct writing in the work of great masters of the past, such as Shakespeare and Milton. It was reported, in fact, that Dickens once declared that every word his characters said "was distinctly heard by him."[62] The article also mentioned the writings of a much less famous author, the young Florentine medium Gino Fanciullacci; he published a volume in Dantesque meter entitled *A Pilgrimage in the Heavens*, which had been dictated to him by his spirit guide.[63]

Spirit writings, however, were usually much more frivolous than the verses delivered by Fanciullacci. Designed to appeal to a large public, some of them enjoyed popular success that went far beyond the boundaries of spiritualism. Their editorial strategy was frequently based on the mingling of religion with leisure, providing readers not only a spiritual uplift but also an opportunity for diversion and recreation. Several genres, such as historical novels, autobiographies, war correspondence, and poetry, were composed through the authorship of spirits. The most common works of this kind were the memoirs of spirits, who were in a privileged position to describe their existence on earth and in the afterlife. Although these were usually presented as accounts of real events, many of them clearly show a reliance on literary motifs and conventions, as well as some traces of the medium's education and knowledge. Just as many mediums had theatrical experience, a number of those who practiced direct writing and published books authored by spirits had literary backgrounds.[64] Discourses on philosophical and religious matters that came directly from the otherworld, following in the tradition of trance lecturing, were frequently published.[65] Compositions of spirit poetry appeared as early as 1853, when four thousand rhymed lines were delivered through the American medium Thomas Lake Harris.[66] The next year, a volume of verses "spoken and written in obedience to superior influences by one who, in a normal condition, possesses no such power of utterance" was published in New York.[67] According to the publisher, the medium through whom the spirit versified had never displayed any tendency or capacity for literary creation: poetry was, to him, "as verily an unknown tongue as was ever given to prophet or apostle."[68]

Journalistic correspondence and news reports also found a spiritualist analogue. The *Medium and Daybreak* published a regular column entitled "The Spirit-Messenger," featuring articles authored by spirits of the dead, submitted to the magazine by spiritualist mediums.[69] Some of them could have easily appeared, if not for the claims of spiritual agency, in a popular newspaper. In February 1885, for instance, the magazine published an article about the British mission in Sudan dictated by the spirit of the seventeenth-century architect and mathematician Sir Christopher Wren, implying that spirits in the afterlife were aware of current political and international events. The events described in the article had acquired much attention in British nonspiritualist newspapers of the 1880s.[70] Another popular literary genre, historical fiction, was reflected in the magazine's column "Historical Controls."[71]

One spirit author acknowledged the complex mixture of fiction and spiritualism, pointing out at the beginning of a piece that continued through several editions of the magazine, "This is not a novel, and yet to the majority of the readers, certainly to the bulk of those who are not Spiritualists, this little story will seem a romance."[72] The narrative was, indeed, quite dramatic. The spirit was Italian, and his story seems to follow patterns that could easily be found in popular depictions of his countrymen in the English-speaking world. An artist from Tuscany, he drowned while rowing a little boat in a neighborhood of Venice. His national character was described in conventional ways: "The entire duration of my earthly life was only twenty-three years, but we Italians mature early, under the genial influence of a southern sky. We soon ripen intellectually as well as physically. We are a receptive as well as an emotional people."[73] The moment of death was, as in many other spirit stories, the turning point of the entire narrative, a climax in which the spirit experienced "a charming sense of freedom," his earthly life passing before him "with marvellous distinction."[74]

The celebrity status of spirit authors could turn the attention of the public toward these cultural products. For this reason, spirit writings were sometimes used in advertising. At the beginning of the twentieth century, a cosmetic firm in Germany claimed to receive the recipes for its miraculous products from the spirit of the Renaissance physician and alchemist Paracelsus. The name of the firm, Bombastuswerke, was a tribute to Paracelsus, whose complete name was Theophrastus Bombastus von Hohenheim. The business had started when the director of the enterprise, a Mr. B., discovered that he was a trance medium. However, his powers were not to bring him luck, as he was subsequently convicted of fraud by a German tribunal.[75] In other cases, the profitability of spirit writings was ensured by the fact that the spirit had been a famous writer in life. The history of spiritualism is full of posthumous works dictated from the beyond, such as the book that Oscar Wilde supposedly wrote twenty-six years after his death. Entitled *Oscar Wilde from Purgatory: Psychic Messages* and edited by the medium Hester Travers Smith, who received Wilde's spiritual communications, this book was highly regarded in the spiritualist community. Arthur Conan Doyle intervened in the dispute about Wilde's authorship, claiming that the communications should be accepted as genuine since they corresponded to Wilde's style.[76] In his *History of Spiritualism*, Doyle explained that "the verity of any particular specimen of such writing must depend not upon mere assertion, but upon corroborative details and the general dissimilarity from the mind of the writer, and similarity to that of the alleged inspirer."[77] Posthumous works were also authored by the stars of other cultural worlds, such as cinema: in the late 1920s, the popular press reported rumors that the spirit of Rudolph Valentino was dictating a screenplay to the medium Carla McKinstry. The movie that Valentino proposed from the spirit world was a love story set in the desert, to be produced under the title *The Warning of Time*. Both the medium and the spirit were sure that this work was destined to be a great popular success.[78]

One of the most interesting examples of spirit writing that recalls popular fiction is *Hafed Prince of Persia*, delivered through the Scottish medium David Duguid and published by James Burns. Hafed was one of Duguid's main spirit guides. Appearing in forty-six sittings between 1870 and 1871, he presented himself as the spirit of a prince and warrior who lived in Persia almost two thousand years earlier. *Hafed* was incessantly reviewed and advertised in the *Medium and Daybreak* as "a book written and illustrated by spirits."[79] According to these ads, Hafed dictated the book through the lips of Duguid and sketched the pictures through the hands of Duguid, who was in an unconscious trance. The authenticity of these spirit drawings was demonstrated through the automatism of the act; the magazine review stressed that "it matters not to him whether he works in darkness or in light."[80] Despite this evidence in favor of his mediumship, the spirit drawings published in *Hafed* raised many doubts within the spiritualist world, especially when some of Duguid's sketches were discovered to have been copied from Cassell's illustrated *Family Bible*.

Hafed's illustrated story was a consistent success in nineteenth-century spiritualism, going through several editions and reprints in the decades after 1876. The illustrations enhanced its appeal, functioning as further proof of the automatism of Duguid's trance and as a visual element familiar to the readers of illustrated novels. The story was a mélange of Orientalist and biblical literature. In the first sittings—the book is, in fact, organized into sittings instead of chapters—Hafed described his early life, from his birth in "a lovely spot of earth's surface, situated on the eastern shores of the Persian sea,"[81] to his marriage and the birth of his first son, when Hafed was thirty-three. The decisive turn in the plot came in the sixth sitting, when Hafed, returning home from a war campaign, discovered that his family had been brutally murdered by a barbarian tribe that plundered his town. When the Holy Spirit appeared to him, Hafed asked why he did not save their lives; the Holy Spirit answered that henceforth Hafed's existence "was to be devoted to something higher and better than war."[82] Hafed then decided to leave on a long journey toward the land of Judea. The story climaxed when Hafed revealed to the readers that he was one of the biblical magi, the three wise men who visited Jesus after his birth. The book reported how Hafed became Jesus's instructor and mentor, traveling with him to distant lands such as Greece, Persia, and even India.

The plot of *Hafed Prince of Persia* exploited widespread reinterpretations of historical and religious events, as well as episodes in Jesus's youth from the apocryphal gospels, which are not included in the New Testament. Following a well-established narrative in the spiritualist field, Jesus was presented as a powerful medium who communicated not only with God but also with the spirits of the dead; the appearance of angels was depicted as

FIG. 16
Hafed Prince of Persia, a text delivered through the mediumship of David Duguid, featured illustrations that he supposedly sketched in trance under the influence of spirits. This illustration depicts a séance in ancient Egypt. From David Duguid, *Hafed Prince of Persia: His Experiences in Earth-Life and Spirit-Life, Being Spirit Communications Received Through Mr. David Duguid, the Glasgow Trance-Painting Medium* (London: James Burns, 1876), 113.

an early example of spirit communication.[83] Such spiritualist readings of historical and religious events went so far as to describe a séance attended by Hafed in an Egyptian temple—an episode that was illustrated by Duguid in trance. Egyptian priests of the first century, Hafed explained, organized séances and communicated with the spirits of the dead. Hafed's illustration of one of these Egyptian séances contributed to the appeal of his narrative to spiritualist readers of the time (fig. 16). Moreover, the episode placed the book in the context of the British interest in Near Eastern archaeology, resulting in a variety of stage spectacles on Assyrian, Persian, and Egyptian themes during the nineteenth century.[84]

As the case of *Hafed* shows, spirits could offer readers literary products with the potential to be widely appealing. Works such as Duguid's book, in this sense, exemplify the complex links between books authored by spirits and popular literature of the day. The illustrated *Hafed* was a kind of spirit novel, hardly distinguishable from a work of fiction. Referring to Oriental realms, furnishing incredible revelations about religious history, and enriching the narrative with a number of illustrations, it was a book that could be successfully commercialized by spiritualist editors and publishers.

The popular success of spirit writings as a literary form was grounded in specific techniques of spirit communication that relied on the written word. Such processes involved issues of mediumship and trance, by which the deliverer claimed to function as a channel of communication without being directly involved in the intellectual creation of the text. In chapter 1, I examined the role of trance in the performances of spiritualist mediums: it constructed a theatrical environment while at the same time providing grounds for the claims of authenticity of these events. Here, I would like to show that spirit-authored texts were based on similar dynamics. The fact that mediums wrote spirit messages in trance, completely disconnected from their own will, was meant to demonstrate that these texts were authentic manifestations of spirits' presence. Such claims of authenticity, however, were combined with the use of literary strategies and conventions that made spirit writings pleasurable to read, too. Entertainment and belief, as a result, harmoniously coexisted in this form of spirit communication, as they did in spiritualist séances and demonstrations.

As Helen Sword notes, written spirit messages tended to undermine the notion of authorship: copyright laws and library catalogues, which legitimize the boundaries of authorship, were troubled by spirit authors.[85] It was only in 1941 that the American Library Association provided specific instructions for cataloguing "mediumistic writings": the correct procedure was to "enter a work received through a medium (automatic writing, table rapping, Ouija board, etc.) under the medium with added entry for the purported author."[86] Earlier, in 1926, an article in the *Virginia Law Review* underlined the contradictions raised by a dispute on copyright claims about a book supposedly authored by spirits; it pointed to the fact that if the spirit was really a dead man, he could not own property, since the law vests a dead man's estate in living persons.[87]

Spirit-authored texts could be delivered in several ways. A common procedure was automatic writing, in which the medium fell into a trance and wrote under the influence of spirits. To demonstrate that automatic writing conveyed spirit messages and was not a conscious act of the medium, spiritualists often emphasized the difference with the medium's usual calligraphy. Spirit agency could also be proven through devices such as the planchette, "a capricious little wooden machine which runs on wheels with a pencil attachment, on which if a hand is placed, it immediately proceeds to write legible and intelligent communications."[88]

In the psychological field, automatic writing was interpreted as a manifestation of unconscious movements. While she was still studying psychology under the direction of William James,[89] the American writer Gertrude Stein coauthored with a Harvard graduate student, Leon M. Solomons, an article on automatic writing for the third volume of the *Psychological Review*. Using themselves as experimental subjects, Stein and Solomons employed the planchette and other spiritualist techniques for automatic writing, coming to the conclusion that "a large number of acts ordinarily called intelligent, such as reading, writing, etc., can go on quite automatically in ordinary people."[90] Two years later, Stein published another article on the same subject. Testing automatic writing with subjects other than herself, Stein provided evidence of how a movement could be "cultivated" by the experimenter, by rhythmically moving the planchette while the subject's eyes were shut and the subject was distracted. This "training" often resulted in the subject's unconsciously repeating the movement taught.[91]

Another common technique used to produce spirit-authored texts was called direct writing. It required the spirit to produce the inscription without visible physical contact with the medium or, in certain cases, without even employing writing materials. Although messages delivered through the planchette were often listed under the categories of automatic or direct writing, the most specific instances of this technique involved writing magically appearing, for instance, on a sheet of paper that had been closed in a box. A particularly famous version of this phenomenon was the "slate writing" performed by mediums such as William Eglinton and Henry Slade. In a general meeting report of the Society for Psychical Research, an experiment with slate writing conducted by a member, Dr. Wyld, was described in detail:

> Slade sat about four feet from Dr. Wyld at the opposite side of a table, but some distance from the table, and Dr. Wyld having first examined both sides of the slate, and found it a new dusty slate, placed a crumb of pencil on the table; he then covered the pencil with the slate and pressed the slate to the table with his elbow, while he seized Slade's two feet with his two feet, and his two hands with his two hands, and then said "Now write."
>
> Immediately the sound of writing occurred, and this having ceased, Dr. Wyld ... found a message written in dusty slate pencil writing, containing five Christian family names and a message concerning a family matter of importance.[92]

In comparison to automatic writing, this and other forms of direct writing were reputed to possess a greater evidentiary value, since the phenomenon was performed without any apparent intervention of the human hand, though it usually resulted in shorter and less elaborate messages.

A third technique of spirit authorship involved spirit dictation through trance lecturing by the medium. This required the participation of a third person, who acted as a kind of secretary, transcribing the memoirs of the spirit. The agency of authorship was then ideally attributed to three—the spirit, the medium, and the transcriber—since all were involved in the process of delivery. This was the case, for instance, with *Hafed Prince of Persia*, which was delivered through trance lecturing by David Duguid and transcribed by H. Nisbet, who declared in the introduction that he recorded "nothing beyond what was spoken by the medium in his trance state."[93]

The challenge to the issue of authorship brought on by spirit writing has been linked by scholars such as Lisa Gitelman and Friedrich Kittler to the development of techniques such as stenography and to the technologies that mechanized writing, such as the typewriter, typography, and telegraphic inscription.[94] This argument is enhanced by the fact that these spiritualist processes required the medium to operate as a kind of communication channel, speaking or writing for someone else. During the nineteenth century, and especially with the development of telegraphic and, later, telephonic communication, media technologies introduced the presence of a person, the operator, whose duty was to register and to communicate messages to others. The operator spoke the language of the machine and was supposed to disappear, at least symbolically, in the process of delivering the message. Although mediums often defended the importance of their profession by describing themselves as secretaries taking dictation from dead authors,[95] their resemblance to telegraph operators was occasionally acknowledged, too.[96]

The process that guided spirit writing was frequently attributed to unspecified ethereal or electrical forces that might be able to control, or galvanize, the medium's movement. A book discussing spirits' influence on mediums under trance reported the following anecdote: "A young man, sitting in a circle, had his arm shaken with irresistible violence, making innumerable curves and lines. When this had gone on some time, a very intelligent person in the party, who had been observing all that passed, said, 'I am sure that all this is some action of electricity.' Instantly the hand wrote, with exceeding rapidity, and no spaces between the words, '*Youarerightitiselectricitythatmovesthehandbutthereisaspiritthatguidestheelectricity.*'"[97]

FIG. 17 (LEFT) "The good spirit above is throwing the influence through the higher portions of the brain, namely, the organs of veneration, benevolence, ideality, and the intellectual portion. The evil spirit, nearer to earth, is trying to mesmerize the base of the brain." From Sophia Elizabeth De Morgan and Augustus De Morgan, *From Matter to Spirit: The Result of Ten Years' Experience in Spirit Manifestations* (London: Longman, Roberts, and Green, 1863), 54.

FIG. 18 (RIGHT) "I asked [the spirits] for a drawing of the process, when two persons' hands were joined, and the drawing No. 2 was made." From Sophia Elizabeth De Morgan and Augustus De Morgan, *From Matter to Spirit: The Result of Ten Years' Experience in Spirit Manifestations* (London: Longman, Roberts, and Green, 1863), 55.

The spirit who "guides the electricity," and consequently the medium's hand, was represented in two drawings printed some pages later as a spiritual presence that exercised its influence on the brain and the muscles of the medium (figs. 17–18).[98] The medium acted as a truly mechanical device that was activated, like the telegraph, by electricity. A similar process seems to be at play in Rudyard Kipling's short story "Wireless," in which a character goes into a trance to write some verses from Keats while an experiment with wireless telegraphy is taking place in a nearby room.[99]

In the spiritualist field, the medium was regularly likened to a kind of typing machine operated by the remote control of spirit agency. An early writing debunking spirit communication as fraudulent mentioned how the spirit of Benjamin Franklin had delivered to the medium Edward P. Fowler some written samples, after Fowler saw him "with a large box of electrical apparatus (galvanic we suppose)"; the spirit later revealed that he sent the messages "by the aid of the battery."[100] The same author listed a number of processes employed by writing mediums (figs. 19–20). The "electrical process" (fig. 20) involved the spirit commanding the medium's hand at a distance of about two miles, thus establishing "a complete chain of spiritual substance . . . between the directing spirit and the system of the

FIG. 19 Spiritualists distinguished between several kinds of automatic and direct writing techniques. In this illustration, the "direct process" is depicted as the direct influence of the spirit on the medium's hand. From Hiram Mattison, *Spirit Rapping Unveiled!* (New York: Mason Brothers, 1853), 62.

medium, by which chain a perfect connection is formed from one to the other."[101] The connection of spiritualist theories with telegraphic machinery—which, as Jeffrey Sconce documented, was often recalled in accounts of spirit communication[102]—was strongly influenced by the nature of communication media as mechanized systems of inscription.

This link between spirit writing and the world of mechanized writing responded to the development of printing technologies that made literature and the book market increasingly industrialized and commercialized. The spirits seemed to be perfectly conscious of how to succeed in the rising realm of popular culture. Like professional editors, spirits gave precise indications of how a publication could be successfully marketed. Following their directions was a way to confirm faith in the spirits and, at the same time, to ensure the success of a publishing enterprise. Samuel Watson, a Methodist priest who converted to spiritualism, reported that the spirits had agreed to suspend the publication of the *Spiritual Magazine* so that the *Voice of Truth*, a weekly, might be a success; at the same time, they had assigned him the task of preparing and publishing a new book. When Watson finished this work, the spirits claimed their authorship and declared that they were "anxious to see the work appear."[103] Another example of spirits

FIG. 20   Another kind of spirit writing was the "electrical process," by which the spirit used the force of electricity to guide the medium's hand. From Hiram Mattison, *Spirit Rapping Unveiled!* (New York: Mason Brothers, 1853), 62.

providing advice on publishing strategies can be found in the career of Allan Kardec, who succeeded in founding a strong spiritualist organization in France. Kardec's *Le livre des esprits* (Book of spirits), first published in 1857, went through twenty-two editions by 1875 in France alone and was translated into multiple foreign languages, including English. By early 1866, his journal, the *Revue Spirit*, counted as many as 1,800 subscribers. Before starting publication of this journal, Kardec reportedly asked the spirits what approach he should follow. As John Warne Monroe noted, the answer revealed "an acute sense of what made publications on spirit phenomena appealing":[104] the spirits suggested that the journal appeal to curiosity, containing both the serious and the entertaining, in order to attract men of science as well as the ordinary reader.

Practices of automatic and direct writing also contributed to the interaction of spiritualist print culture with spectacle and performance. In fact, mediums produced these forms of writing at private and public séances, before the sometimes stupefied, sometimes skeptical gaze of sitters and spectators. In this sense, spiritualist manifestations that resulted in the production of texts provide a further link between spiritualism's print and performance cultures. Employing trance writing as a performance, mediums delivered a dramatized representation of the activities of writing and publishing in a mechanized age.

While writing is usually regarded as an act of human creation rather than a means of objective knowledge, spiritualist techniques of direct and automatic writing linked it to mechanical objectivity.[105] In Victorian spiritualism, trance lecturers were presented to the public as a spectacular show as well as a neutral channel of communication with the otherworld. Likewise, spirit writing allowed for the production of texts that functioned simultaneously as entertaining pieces of literature and as evidences of the spiritualist claims. The standardization of specific patterns by which spirit messages were recorded on paper contributed to the emergence of a spiritualist literature that amused readers while at the same time providing them with authentic manifestations of spirit agency.

THE SPIRIT AND THE BOOKSELLER

The way in which spiritualist publications took up strategies of popular literature and circulated in the marketplace is meaningful to this work for three main reasons. First, as shown by the commercialization of pamphlets accompanying spiritualist lectures and public events, the importance of the press as a vehicle for publicity, and the performative character of automatic writing, spiritualist publications were connected to the performances of mediums in private and public séances. Second, spiritualist publications were located at the same intersection of religious beliefs with entertainment and leisure that, as I argue, characterized spiritualism as a whole. Third, the circulation of spiritualist books and journals as cultural commodities was part of the process by which the movement took on elements of nineteenth-century consumerism and material culture.

The history of the planchette, the device commonly employed in automatic writing, epitomizes the link between spiritualism and the book market that has been explored in this chapter. Invented by a French spiritualist in 1853, it consisted of a small board supported by wheels, to which a pencil was attached to write signs or letters that were interpreted as spirit messages.[106] This "mysterious toy," as the Bostonian spiritualist Epes Sargent called it, became "a puzzle and a study to thousands of intelligent inquirers, for whom the great problems of psychology and physiology have a not irrational interest."[107] Although it was soon disseminated in Europe and America, the planchette was not widely used in the spiritualist movement until the end of the 1860s. Sargent confessed that "why so sudden a demand for it should have sprung up, nobody could explain," since the "planchette was nothing new."[108] An answer to this question, however, can easily be found in the marketing history of this device. As Sargent himself documented, the production of planchettes was taken over in 1868 by a firm of American toy makers, who flooded the market with a great number of them.[109] The place chosen for the commercialization of the planchette was the bookseller's shop, where other forms of this device had been available since the 1850s.[110] Booksellers—the commercial venue of a rising book industry—turned this instrument of spiritualist inquiry into a popular toy.

Manufacturers such as Kirby and Co., Gilman Moulton, Jaques and Son, N. Bangs Williams, and G. W. Cottrell competed to produce and distribute different models of the planchette. The "Boston Planchette," for one, was advertised in spiritualist publications as well as in popular magazines, where it was described as "full of fun, puzzle and mystery, and a pleasant companion in the house."[111] The functioning of these devices was discussed in periodicals such as the *Scientific American* and *Once a Week*; the latter published a letter signed by "an anxious mamma," who reported to have "a family of sons and daughters, ranging from ten to twenty-three, . . . who must be amused," and asked where a planchette could be bought. The editor provided the address of a retailer, Messrs. Elliots Brothers.[112] The popular craze for planchettes also inspired popular songs. In 1868 alone, as the planchette was being introduced to the American market, two sheet-music publishers launched popular songs celebrating the marvels of this device: Lee and Walker in Philadelphia marketed *Planchette: Song and Chorus*, while C. Y. Fonda from Cincinnati published the *Planchette Polka*.[113]

In Britain, as in the United States, the history of the planchette intersected with the history of the book market. Companies such as Two Worlds Publishing marketed this device alongside spiritualist books and periodicals. Founded in Manchester in 1887, the company promoted a periodical entitled *The Two Worlds*, which was edited by celebrity medium Emma Hardinge. By the turn of the century, Two Worlds Publishing had added to its portfolio of spiritualist publications several versions of popular devices for spiritualist séances, such as planchettes, crystal balls, and dial boards.[114] James Burns, too, advertised and marketed the planchette alongside other "appliances" employed in the study of spiritualist and occult phenomena.[115]

The planchette, originally created to give more credibility to the claims of spirit authorship, was made part of a commercialized literary world increasingly haunted by fantasies and apprehensions about the manufacturing of written texts. With the introduction of this device in bookshops, spirit manifestations were symbolically launched into the book market, a system of production and distribution that in the nineteenth century widened the consumption of popular literature. Mirroring the successful marketing history of the planchette, spirit-authored texts were also introduced into the market of print media. They became one of the most successful products of spiritualist publishing enterprises. Electricity drove the medium's hand toward the production of books that were almost indistinguishable from works of fiction. Ultimately, spirits had joined the commercial ventures of popular literature.

6

THE MARVELS OF SUPERIMPOSITION

SPIRIT PHOTOGRAPHY AND SPIRITUALISM'S

VISUAL CULTURE

In 1946, French film critic and theorist André Bazin published an essay entitled "The Life and Death of Superimposition." This short critical piece, based on an analysis of the special effects employed in three American films—Alexander Hall's *Here Comes Mr. Jordan* (1941), Sam Wood's *Our Town* (1940), and Garson Kanin's *Tom, Dick, and Harry* (1941)—sketched a history of the use of superimposition in cinema, from Méliès's trick movies to the filmic production of Bazin's time.[1] In this chapter, I undertake a similar task. Unlike Bazin's analysis, however, this history of superimposition will start before Méliès, and even before the invention of cinema. The visual device that involved superimposing ghostly apparitions on a given background cannot be understood by looking at the history of photography or at cinema alone. This history demands what Lynda Nead has called "an integrated approach to visual media,"[2] which moves beyond the use of an interdisciplinary framework to focus on the connections and spaces *across* media.

In the 1860s, a new genre of spirit manifestations was established in the spiritualist movement: spirit photography. This phenomenon was based not on the capacity of photography to document what was visible to the human eye; on the contrary, it was presented as the result of photography's purported unsettling and uncanny faculty to detect the images of spirits who were among the living but went undetected by human senses. Like trance mediums, the visual medium of photography was able to access the spirit world, offering spiritualist believers the possibility of obtaining a portrait of a loved one from the otherworld.

As expert photographers and other skeptics soon pointed out, this apparently extraordinary phenomenon could be explained as the product of a simple photographic trick or accident. Most notably, critics pointed to multiple exposure and other superimposition techniques that were commonly used in photography. Fake "spirit" photographs were produced to demonstrate the trickery that had been employed in spiritualism. During the second half of the nineteenth century, photographic images that featured a superimposed element were at times believed to be real manifestations of spirits and ghosts, at times debunked as a photographic trick, and at times used for their entertaining and spectacular effect. Following the emergence of film, multiple-exposure imagery became a common way to render onscreen the apparition of ghosts and the occurrence of dreams and visions. This chapter explores the circulation of a photographic technique—multiple exposure—and a visual effect—superimposition—in spiritualism, stage magic, magic-lantern projection, photography, and cinema. The underlying argument is that the circulation of superimposition in multiple technological and cultural contexts framed it as a body of technologies and knowledge that wavered between realism and fantasy, stasis and movement, fiction and belief.

Since Tom Gunning's pioneering essay "Phantom Images and Modern Manifestations," spirit photography has been examined within film studies as a key to understanding the relationship among cinema, the uncanny, and the supernatural.[3] Scholars such as François Jost, Matthew Solomon, Karen Beckman, and Lynda Nead have recognized the debts of early cinema, and of the trick-movie genre in particular, to the iconography of spirit photography.[4] Despite the extent of this literature, however, the relations between spiritualism and the world of the still and moving image raise questions that have been left largely unanswered. How can we connect spirit photography, regarded by many spiritualists as an object of belief, with the motion picture, which from its very beginning was presented as a spectacle and maintained strong ties to the realm of fiction? As many have noted, there was never a "spirit cinema," and the use of the moving image to document spiritualist séances was quite rare, too.[5] Notwithstanding the apocryphal anecdotes regarding early cinematic audiences panicking before the image of an oncoming train,[6] film apparently did not invite the same kind of faith as spirit photography.

A more careful look into the history of spirit photography and multiple-exposure techniques, however, reveals that issues of fiction and belief intermingled in virtually every use of superimposition, from spirit photography to the trick movie. As I will argue, in fact, the way in which spiritualists interpreted and used spirit photographs reveals a deep interconnection between consumerism and religious beliefs: prints of spirit photographs were commercialized and consumed within the movement and were regarded by spiritualists not only as evidences of the existence of spirits but also as commodities and visual curiosities. The history of spirit photography was also shaped by questions of fictionality and the market, and the use of superimposition effects in cinema to conjure apparitions such as ghosts, fairies, devils, and other fantastic creatures finds a significant precedent in the late-nineteenth-century debunking of this spiritualist technique. Following the visual technique of superimposition in the worlds of photographic and projected images, from Robertson's phantasmagoria to Mumler's spirit photographs, from photographic amusements to stage magic and the trick film, I will look at superimposition as a kind of visual medium in its own right. Despite its being continuously reinvented and reconstructed, its history reveals the trajectory of a visual culture that was haunted by ghosts, dreams, visions, and the contradictory status of the photographic image. The chapter will show that the representation of spirits as superimposed images was used within spiritualism as well as in openly spectacular contexts, such as stereoscopic photography and early cinema. Moreover, the fact that spirit photographs and visual representations of spirits were regarded as visual curiosities and marketed as commodities within the boundaries of spiritualism suggests that rigid distinctions between entertainment and belief are problematic not only for spiritualist séances and demonstrations but also for spiritualism's visual culture. The examination of spirit photography and related visual effects, therefore, further corroborates my overall argument that the history of spiritualism merged with the history of spectacular attractions and entertainments in the nineteenth century.

PHOTOGRAPHING SPIRITS

In 1862, the spiritualist world was startled by the news that an engraver from Boston, William Mumler, was able to produce the photograph of a spirit. This discovery soon spread through the channels of spiritualist print media and was heralded by the spiritualist journal *Banner of Light* as the beginning of "a new spiritual phase."[7] Mumler had reportedly discovered the phenomenon by chance, while working with some new chemicals. When he developed the plate, the figure of a young woman, in whom he recognized the likeness of his deceased cousin, appeared mysteriously. He soon established a photographic studio in Boston and later one in New York, where he offered his sitters the extraordinary possibility of being photographed with a spirit. Similar to regular portrait photographers, he charged a price for a successful sitting. Using ordinary photographic means, he claimed to have no control over the phenomenon, by which a faint image of the departed appeared beside the persons photographed in his studio (figs. 21–22).

Spirit photography became widely known beyond the spiritualist world in 1869, when Mumler was brought to trial for fraud in New York and the news spread in the American press. Although nine possible technical ways to produce images similar to his spirit photographs were presented and the judge declared himself to be morally convinced of the presence of fraud, Mumler was discharged. The prosecutors had been unable to explain with certainty which procedure Mumler actually used to perform the trick. However, as Louis Kaplan has thoroughly documented, the trial succeeded in making spirit photography an issue of public debate.[8] It became a hot topic in the New York daily press, as well as in widely circulating national magazines, including *Harper's Weekly* and *Frank Leslie's Illustrated Journal*.[9] Such extensive coverage probably played a role in the proliferation of spirit photography in the following years, which resulted in the 1870s in what James Coates, the author of an early twentieth-century history of supernatural photography, called "a little boom": from this decade alone, he listed—"beside a few others of lesser note"—Mumler in the United States, Édouard Buguet in France, and as many as nine active spirit photographers in Britain.[10] Although repeatedly debunked as a photographic trick, spirit photography remained influential in the spiritualist field for decades, starting to decline in popularity only in the middle decades of the twentieth century.

After its virtual disappearance from the historical discourse on photography for decades, scholars have recently dedicated growing attention to spirit photography.[11] However, much work has yet to be done in order to fully comprehend why believers in spirit communication were so fascinated by photographic technologies. Most literature on spirit photography has pointed to the claims of mechanical objectivity and to the indexicality of the photographic medium as the main reasons for spiritualism's use of this technology. In contrast to this perspective, I argue in this section that the evidentiary use of spirit photography has been overestimated and that other aspects of photography's early history are equally useful for understanding its appeal to spiritualists. In particular, I will point to the formation of an industry-shaped market of images and to the rise of trick photography

FIG. 21 One of William Mumler's spirit photographs featured Mary Todd Lincoln with the spirit of her deceased husband, former American president Abraham Lincoln. Lincoln Financial Foundation Collection, item OC-0275. Courtesy of the Allen County Public Library and Indiana State Museum.

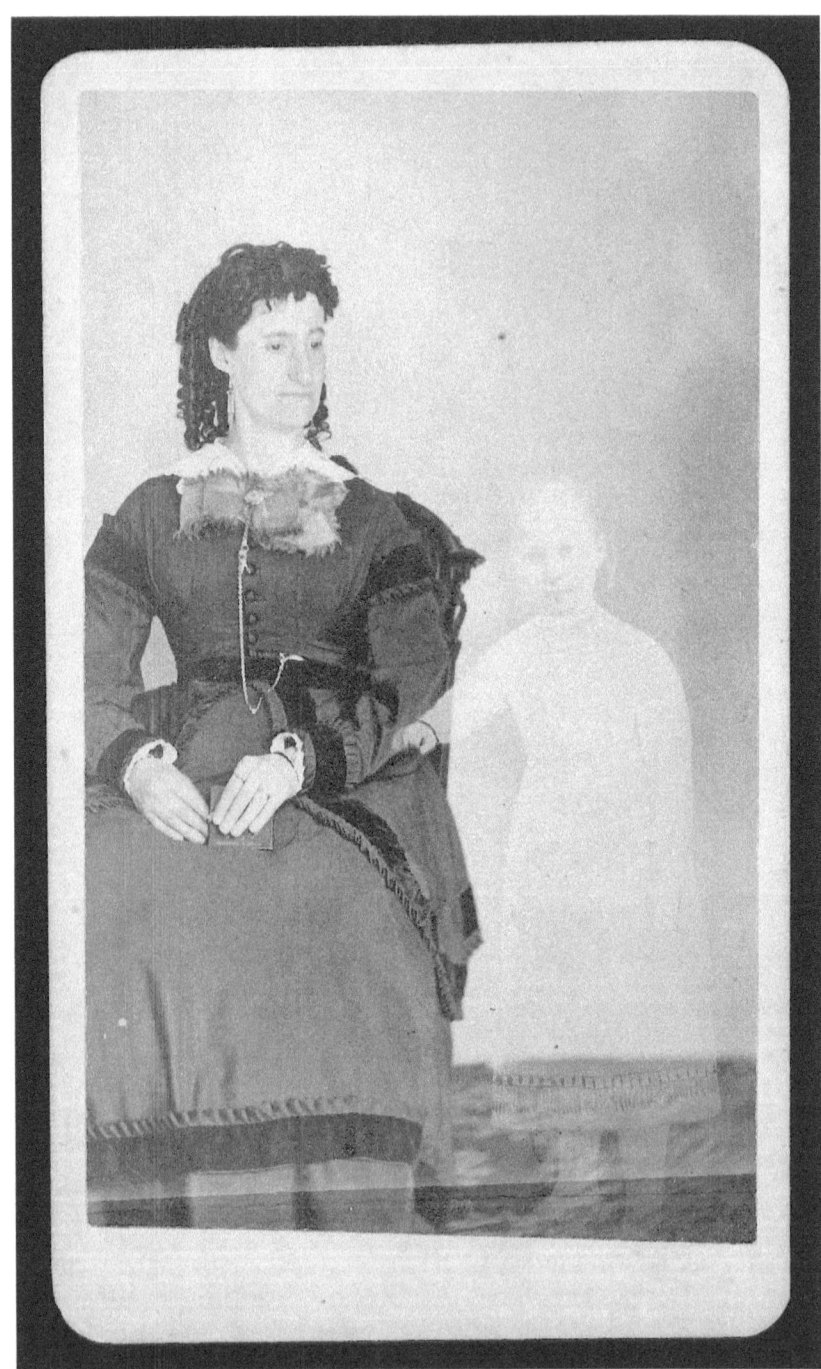

FIG. 22 This spirit photograph by William Mumler depicts a woman, Mrs. Tinkman, with the spirit of her deceased daughter. This spiritualist practice was often employed to create a link between the spirits of the deceased and their relatives or friends. Albumen silver, 9.5 × 5.7 cm. Digital image courtesy of the Getty's Open Content Program, item 84.XD.760.1.7d.

as a means of expression. These transformations, which were under way in the 1860s, can help account for the ways in which this technology was incorporated into the spiritualist field.

AN IMPERFECT MEDIUM: EVIDENCE AND MANIPULATION IN SPIRIT PHOTOGRAPHY

Throughout the history of spiritualism, the phenomenon of spirit photography was greeted again and again as definitive and indisputable evidence supporting spirit communication. However, a thorough look at spiritualist sources demonstrates that the possibility of trickery was also recognized in this context and that many spiritualists regarded the medium of photography with suspicion. To play on the title of the well-known exhibition "The Perfect Medium: Photography and the Occult,"[12] photography came to be regarded among spiritualists as an *imperfect* medium, in whose authority it was rather hazardous to trust. In most cases, in fact, photography was accepted as evidence only in conjunction with testimonies of professional photographers or of those who had recognized the spirit on the plate as bearing the likeness of a deceased relative or friend.

In recent literature in art history, the debate on spirit photography has wavered between two apparently contrasting interpretations. On the one hand, this practice has been seen by many as further evidence of the diffusion during the nineteenth century of an unshaken belief in photography's adherence to truth. For instance, John Harvey dedicated a large part of his book *Photography and Spirit* to the relations between spirit photography and science, arguing that spiritualists exploited the new photographic technology to bridge the gulf between their religious beliefs and rationalism and thus contributed to a "scientification" of spiritualism.[13] On the other hand, some scholars have claimed that spirit photography contributed to the questioning of photography's authority. Jennifer Mnookin and Jennifer Tucker documented how the rise of spirit photography in the 1860s resulted in a debate that questioned the value of photography as juridical evidence[14] and as a scientific instrument.[15] Tucker in particular argued that this controversy "made the issues of trust in photographic production visible to a wider Victorian public and focused attention as never before on the necessary qualifications to make authentic photographs."[16] Working from a similar perspective, Michael Leja linked the debate on spirit photography to a number of deceptive practices that were in use in turn-of-the-century America, focusing in particular on trompe l'oeil painting.[17]

Such contradictory interpretations can be partially explained by examining the different perspectives through which spirit photography was regarded. While committed spiritualists often relied on the scientific status of photography to provide confirmation for their claims, nonspiritualists often underlined the possibility of manipulation. In the photographic field, for instance, news about the discovery of spirit photography was frequently ridiculed. In 1869, the British magazine *Photographic News* observed that "a trick so easy to enact should not have excited more wonder than the sleight-of-hand effect of the commonest street juggler."[18] Some years later, when the French spirit photographer Édouard Buguet visited London, the prestigious *British Journal of Photography* ironically noted that his business was open to everyone who possessed faith *and* money.[19]

It is interesting to note, however, that the evidentiary status of photography was far from going unchallenged within the spiritualist field, too. Although many kept believing in spirit photography and upheld its mechanical exactitude, the fact that photographs could be manipulated, and thus that "any photographer can easily produce 'ghosts' *ad libitum*,"[20] was common knowledge within the spiritualist movement from at least the early 1870s. Mumler's trial and Buguet's subsequent condemnation for fraud in France convinced many spiritualists that spirit photography was unreliable. In his popular book *Lights and Shadows of Spiritualism*, for instance, the medium Daniel Dunglas Home openly exposed spirit photography as a trick, explaining the photographic techniques that could be employed to produce it.[21] Others maintained an ambivalent attitude toward the subject. The highly regarded Bostonian spiritualist Epes Sargent expressed doubts about the genuineness of Mumler's spirit photographs in his book *Planchette*,[22] only to withdraw this claim some time later, when he declared that "renewed investigation has satisfied me that many genuine spirit-photographs have been produced."[23] Even those who argued for the legitimacy of this process admitted that there had been many documented cases of fraud: the prominent English spiritualist William Stainton Moses, for instance, recognized that "it is abundantly certain that Spirit Photography can be, and has been, fraudulently produced," although he firmly denied that this happened in all cases.[24] Photography's technological nature could be a source of distrust, too, if it was true that, as one spiritualist noted, "every phase of modern Spiritualism, except Spirit Photography, we find in the Bible."[25]

The instability of photography's status within the spiritualist field is evident in the multiple ways in which spiritualists tried to collect evidence

FIG. 23
Reproduction of a spirit photograph by Jay J. Hartman. The careful design of the test conditions under which this photograph was taken suggests that the testimonies of people were at least as important as the photographic image itself in establishing the spiritual and scientific value of spirit photographs. Hartman's picture was, in fact, taken "under the most rigid test conditions, in a gallery he had never visited before, with camera, glass, and chemicals of a skeptical photographer, all of the manipulations of the plate being done by a skeptical photographer." From Samuel Watson, *The Religion of Spiritualism: Its Phenomena and Philosophy* (Boston: Colby and Rich, 1880), 98.

supporting its trustworthiness. John Harvey has argued that, while proof of spiritualism usually relied on "the corroborating testimony of honest and reliable witnesses," in the case of spirit photography the evidence was provided by the mechanical passivity of the camera.[26] This, however, is true only within certain limits. The presumed honesty of photography was usually also corroborated through the testimonies of witnesses who attested to the reliability of the photographic procedures. The *Medium and Daybreak* reported the testimony of Julius Plaetz, a professional photographer from Kansas City who, although not professing to be a spiritualist, certified that the spirit photographer Lizzie Carter had been taking photographs at his gallery and that he had not found any evidence of fraud.[27] Spirit photographers such as the American Jay J. Hartman went so far as to organize free public investigations, "addressed to the public generally, and to photographers especially," to show that no manipulation or fraud was involved in the process (fig. 23).[28] In other cases, the authenticity of spirit photographs was confirmed directly by the spirits, through séance communications or direct writing.[29]

Rather than the indexicality of the photographic image, the central issue for believers in spirit photography seems to have been the identity of the spirits appearing on the photographic plate. As Robert S. Cox put it, spiritualists were most concerned with "the emotional connection between the living and the dead as a key for interpreting authenticity."[30] Particular importance was given to the fact that individuals could sometimes recognize the photographed spirits as resembling a departed relative or friend. Mumler's *Personal Experiences* is an especially good work for understanding the weight of this identification in establishing the authenticity of spirit photography; a large part of this memoir, in fact, is based on reports of the testimonies of those who solemnly swore to have recognized the spirit images.[31]

The recognition of a spirit's likeness could withstand any argument that posited the trickery of the photographer. In 1872, for instance, a spiritualist named M. Jones was astonished when he recognized in the faint image of a spirit the features of his wife, who had died about fourteen months before. His identification was confirmed by friends and family, causing him to resist suggestions of the possible manipulation of the image: "Whatever explanation might be given to the above facts by scientists or the advocates of unconscious cerebration, delusion, psychic force, &c., the result is to me a glory and a happiness which I would not exchange for all the science in the world, and which no one can take away."[32] Similarly, when a French tribunal charged spirit photographer Édouard Buguet with fraud, some of his past customers refused to acknowledge that his spirit images were fake: they were so sure that they recognized their loved ones that their belief remained unshaken even when precise demonstrations of the trick were given.[33]

GHOSTS AND THE MARKETPLACE

If belief in photography's mechanical objectivity was shaking within the spiritualist field, how can we explain the fact that photography was so appealing to spiritualists? An initial answer to this question can be found by looking at the ways in which photography was inserted into the marketplace in the first decades after its invention. When spirit photography was introduced in the spiritualist field, photography was being established as an industrial commodity and a commercial medium. Some of the technological advances that stimulated the creation of a mass market for the printed word also made the production of photographic prints profitable.[34] Moreover, the development of more efficient techniques of reproduction and the success of stereoscopic photography, as well as the decrease in costs of portrait photography, facilitated this change. As I will argue, this process also contributed to shaping the circulation of spirit photographs within the spiritualist movement.

The stereoscope, originally a philosophical toy designed to illustrate a theory on vision, was transformed into a successful popular amusement in the 1850s, when it was applied to photography to create a three-dimensional effect. With a production process that allowed the stereographic industry to publish, from the mid-nineteenth century to the 1930s, between three and six million different images,[35] stereoscopic photographs can be considered the first mass visual medium. This turn toward industrialization and commerce was acknowledged by several testimonies of the time. In 1863, one year after Mumler produced his first spirit photograph, Oliver Wendell Holmes published in the *Atlantic Monthly* the third and last of his articles on the subject of photography, entitled "Doings of the Sunbeam." Noting that "few of those who seek a photographer's establishment to have their portraits taken know at all into what a vast branch of commerce this business of sun-picturing has grown,"[36] Holmes related his visit to a New York firm, the E. and H. T. Anthony Company, which was producing stereoscopic prints with manufacturing methods.[37] His description of its organization of production and subdivision of labor—so that "a young person who mounts photographs on cards all day long confessed to having never, or almost never, seen a negative developed"[38]—is still regarded as one of the most compelling documents on the industrialization of photography in the nineteenth century.[39]

Additionally, portrait photography underwent a process of progressive standardization in this period. The carte de visite, a photographic format commercialized by the French entrepreneur André Adolphe Eugène Disdéri in the 1850s and introduced in America in the 1860s, permitted portrait photographers to charge a lower price and contributed to the drastic growth of their business. This new format allowed individuals of lower classes access to portrait photography and helped create a vast international market for celebrity pictures. Quite interestingly, spirit photographs were often associated with cartes de visite. An article from a British photographic journal, for instance, referred to Mumler's photographs as "spirit cartes de visite."[40] The use of this format did not go unacknowledged in the spiritualist world, as demonstrated by an early description of Mumler's photographs in the *Spiritualist Magazine* as "ordinary *cartes de visite*, but with a faint additional figure."[41] As pertaining to portraiture, moreover, spirit photographs were also similar to cartes de visite in terms of content. They often depicted famous mediums in trance with a "spirit extra"—as the faint images of the spirits were called. Mumler, for instance, produced images of Bronson Murray and Fanny Conant, two famed American mediums of the time. Like the cartes de visite of famous actors, actresses, and entertainers, these portraits of mediums with spirits circulated widely within the spiritualist movement, contributing to mediums' celebrity status.[42]

Robert S. Cox has been perhaps the most observant in recognizing the connection between spirit photography and money, noting that while spiritualist séances could be performed privately for free, there were virtually no noncommercial instances of spirit photography.[43] Following this perspective, Mumler was probably the fastest to understand that photography could be sold as a profitable commercial good within the spiritualist movement. His photographic activity fell into the category of portrait photography, the most popular application of photography in mid-nineteenth-century America.[44] As would an ordinary professional studio photographer, Mumler charged ten dollars—a fairly high price at the time—for a successful sitting.

The exorbitant cost of Mumler's spirit pictures was among the main arguments brought against him at the New York trial and one of the factors to which critics generally pointed in order to demonstrate the spuriousness of his enterprise.[45] In the photographic field, references to the commercial character of Mumler's work were extremely common, too. The *Photographic News*, for instance, reproduced in 1869 a jeu d'esprit that had appeared in the American magazine *Brooklyn Eagle*: the author, Corry O'Lanus, recalled that when a photographer asked him whether he wanted to do a photo "with or without the spirit," he had chosen to decline the spirit, since it cost twice the price.[46]

Although mediums in the spiritualist field were often professional and relied on patronage or charged admission to their séances, spirit photographers could be especially expensive. For instance, the commission appointed by the University of Pennsylvania to investigate spiritualism at the request of Henry Seybert, who had left a sum of money to the university in his will, reported that a spirit photographer, Mr. W. M. Keeler, had charged the exorbitant amount of three hundred dollars for a sitting.[47] Spirit photographers justified the high cost of their services by citing the costliness of photographic equipment and claiming that spirit photography was "one of the most exhausting manifestations."[48] Furthermore, spirit photographs were, unlike the phenomena delivered in normal séances, objects that lasted; they could be preserved and collected. In the nineteenth century, professional photographers took postmortem photographs of the departed as souvenirs for their relatives.⁴⁹ As a commercial activity based on the production of posthumous portraits, spirit photography can be compared to postmortem photography and other practices that produced memorabilia for the benefit of the bereaved.

In most cases, spirit photographers were associated with ordinary mediums, thus bringing their photographic skills together with the "gift" of professional mediums. This was the case for Mumler, who worked with his wife, a medium, and for later spirit photographers such as Samuel Guppy, who called for the assistance of a professional photographer, Frederick A. Hudson.⁵⁰ Hudson also partnered with the medium Georgiana Houghton, who published a popular book on spirit photography.⁵¹ In a pamphlet written by a medium that aimed at exposing the trickery in the spiritualist business, the author carefully explained how mediums gained more profit from spirit photographs: a medium made an agreement with spirit photographers, brought her "customers" to them, and shared the results of the transactions.⁵²

Spirit photographs were widely advertised and reproduced. Prints of spirit photographs were commercialized by spiritualist circles and journals and, to a certain extent, outside the spiritualist world: P. T. Barnum stated that he had acquired some for his American Museum some years before Mumler's trial.⁵³ Images such as Mumler's photograph of Mary Todd Lincoln with the spirit of her departed husband, Abraham Lincoln, sold well in the 1870s (see fig. 21),⁵⁴ and the advertisements of professional spirit photographers appeared quite often in spiritualist journals. The American spirit photographer Jay J. Hartman, for instance, advertised in the *American Spiritual Magazine*, offering a fairly standardized service to his Philadelphia customers: they had to send a picture of the departed to him and then fix a date and an hour for the sitting, "at which time the party desiring the picture must be as quiet and passive as possible."⁵⁵ His price was five dollars, but the money would be refunded if no spirit appeared in the picture.

The *Medium and Daybreak* also profited from the craze for spirit photography. In 1882, London's spiritualist journal started a campaign on behalf of the spirit photographer Frederick A. Hudson. Endorsing this spiritualist practice with the assertion that "the more we saw of spirit photography the greater was our confidence in it,"⁵⁶ the journal emphasized the poverty of Hudson "and other benefactors in the same line"⁵⁷ and called readers to make a donation to him. For several editions of the magazine, the editors advertised his "recognized spirit-photographs":

FIG. 24
Spirit photographs circulated widely within the boundaries of the spiritualist movement. This illustration was published as the frontispiece to Samuel Watson, *The Religion of Spiritualism: Its Phenomena and Philosophy* (Boston: Colby and Rich, 1880).

Quite a new generation of Spiritualists have come into the field since Mr. Hudson commenced to take his spirit-photographs nine years ago. At the time large numbers of these interesting pictures were put into circulation; but there are many recent adherents who never saw one of these spiritual results. To gratify such friends, we have pleasure in stating that Mr. Hudson has printed from the original negatives some copies of Recognised Spirit-Photographs, and they may be obtained [for the] price [of] 1s. each, on applying to him at 20, Maxted Road, Peckham Rye, London, S.E. Six copies may be had for 5s. The circulation of these will be a help to Mr. Hudson. They are also sold at this office.[58]

By commodifying reproductions of spirit photographs, journals such as the *Medium and Daybreak* turned them into material goods that could be purchased and collected. The proliferation of spirit photographs within the spiritualist field thus recalls the growing industry whose wonders were narrated by Oliver Wendell Holmes (fig. 24).

In another of Holmes essays, entitled "The Stereoscope and the Stereograph," Holmes went so far as to compare photography to "a universal currency of these banknotes, or promises to pay in solid substance, which the sun has engraved for the great Bank of Nature."[59] According to his argument, a photograph stands in relation to its referent in the same way that a banknote stands in relation to the value inscribed on it. While there have been several interpretations of the meaning of such a comparison,[60] the analogy between photography and the banknote was probably also related to the fact that they are both easily exchanged and moved. The primary aim of money, in fact, is to circulate within the market. Likewise, photographs circulated as commodities within the new market of visual reproductions.[61]

TRICK PHOTOGRAPHY

A further context that helps explain photography's integration into spiritualism is the history of trick photography. The introduction of spirit photography, in fact, must be framed within a period of intense development of darkroom manipulations, as a means of visual expression in art and commercial photography. Jennifer Tucker documented how, in the 1860s, an increasing number of persons "recognized the contingency of claims about photographic truth and were proud of their skills of detecting flaws and errors in photography."[62] The knowledge that photography could be easily manipulated, and that the indexical nature of the image did not guarantee trustworthiness, spread outside the community of amateur and professional photographers. During this time, the establishment of trick photography gave rise to new uses of the photographic medium, opening the way for a new understanding of its fictional and transformative potentials.

As Tom Gunning pointed out, "Perhaps the most extraordinary historical fact about Spirit Photographs lies in the fact that such images existed for years before any Spiritualist seemed to have claimed them."[63] It was, in fact, Sir David Brewster, sometimes erroneously credited with the invention of stereoscopic photography,[64] who declared as early as 1856 that "for the purpose of amusement, the photographer might carry us even into the regions of the supernatural."[65] The process suggested by the

Scottish physicist involved the use of a staged set, in which a female figure was introduced only when the exposure time was nearly finished. "If this operation has been well performed," Brewster explained, "all the objects immediately behind the female figure, having been, previous to her introduction, impressed upon the negative surface, will be seen through her, and she will have the appearance of an aerial personage, unlike the other figures in the picture."[66] The description of this trick inaugurated a tradition of photographic spirits intended for entertainment, rather than for the confirmation of spiritualist beliefs. Using Brewster's method based on exposure time, or a multiple-exposure technique, stereoscopic photographs bearing images of "aerial" ghosts were published in the following years by the London Stereoscopic Company, which commercialized a series called *Ghost in the Stereoscope*.[67]

As publications of the time suggest, there was significant circulation of similar "ghostly" stereoscopic photographs in the marketplace,[68] so Mumler, a jewel engraver and amateur photographer in his spare time, might possibly have been aware of them when he started producing spirit photography in 1862. This hypothesis is corroborated by the fact that in January 1863, two months after the news of Mumler's discovery reached the spiritualist press, the *Spiritual Magazine* mentioned the existence of the *Ghost in the Stereoscope* series, explaining the trick that was employed and giving credit to Brewster for its invention.[69] But even if Mumler had been unaware of the iconic potential of ghost photography, he was certainly familiar with the art of photographic retouching, which was customary in photography at the time and, as a contemporary photography handbook shows, was also employed in metal engraving.[70]

The behavior of persons involved in spirit photography seems to confirm the connection of this practice with the art of trick photography and photographic retouching. Spirit photographers, in fact, regularly preferred to work with technologies that allowed them a high degree of intervention. Thus, Georgiana Houghton explained that "the highly sensitized plates that may now be purchased ready prepared, might be suitable, but that is very doubtful, for, as I have stated, Mr. Hudson always found that the old collodion that had been for a long time in his studio and in his atmosphere was much more receptive to manifestations, while upon the new he could perhaps only obtain the faintest shadows."[71] It is for this reason, too, that the development of photographic materials and techniques is central to understanding developments and shifts in the history of spirit photography. As Jennifer Tucker insightfully noted, for instance, the introduction of the dry-plate process in 1871, which permitted more opportunities for

FIG. 25 American photographer Eadweard Muybridge produced this image for Kate and Robert Johnson in San Francisco. Muybridge ironically played upon the tradition of spirit photography, depicting Robert as a "spirit" haunting their house. *Photograph of Kate Johnson with the "Spirit" of Her Husband, Robert, Adjacent*. Kate and Robert Johnson Photograph Album, 1880, William L. Clements Library. Courtesy of the William L. Clements Library at the University of Michigan.

manipulation, gave new instruments to spirit photographers—"a factor that contributed to the richness of the visual culture of spirit photography from the 1870s on."[72]

Professional photographers also created trick pictures that willingly recalled spirit photography as a means of expression in the late nineteenth century. This is the case with a beautiful, fake spirit photograph by Eadweard Muybridge, which can be found in a residential photo album commissioned by Kate and Robert Johnson in San Francisco (fig. 25). Among the photographs that he executed in their mansion, which were intended as domestic souvenirs, the English photographer made a picture of Kate with the "spirit" of her husband. Interior photographs were common among upper-class American families of the time[73] and could be, as in this case, commissioned from professional photographers. Muybridge's

image, however, reveals the intention to go beyond the aesthetic representation of an interior, culminating in the creation of a picture that recalls the transformative power of photography and, at the same time, the gothic theme of the haunted house. As Corey Keller observes, Muybridge, a pioneer of chronophotography and animated pictures, was particularly sensitive to the opportunity to combine the authority of the photographic image with the "effects" that appealed to viewers and spectators of his photographs, stereographs, panoramas, and illustrated lectures: "He turned not only the photograph's subject but also its making—and perhaps more important, its maker—into a spectacle, and thereby created a market for his work."[74] The sophisticated use of setting in Muybridge's image, moreover, is revealing of how tricks were employed in photographs where elements of fashion and taste played a significant role. Muybridge introduced the element of the ghost into the presentation of a well-appointed, elegant house. In a similar way, spirit photographs (see, for instance, fig. 26) also depicted spirits in elaborate settings that would appeal to the taste of contemporary viewers. Elements of spiritualism's iconography hinted quite openly at consumer culture, as images of spirits were presented within an environment that evoked the prosperity of the middle and upper classes.

Another photographic trick that was widely known within the photographic field during Mumler's time was combination printing.[75] In the late 1850s, photographers such as Oscar Gustave Rejlander and Henry Peach Robinson employed this technique, which involved the careful use of multiple exposure to create a complex photographic canvas. Rejlander, who studied painting in Italy and turned to photography in the 1850s, composed allegorical canvases such as *The Two Ways of Life*, first exhibited in 1857, which consisted of about thirty different negatives. Robinson also used combination printing, but he preferred to focus on more realistic subjects that did not involve neoclassical pictorial themes, as was the case with Rejlander. Robinson's most famous picture, *Fading Away*, a composition of five negatives, depicted a bourgeois family in which a young girl was dying of tuberculosis. As Daniel A. Novak argued, the use of multiple exposure in combination printing can be interpreted as enhancing the relationship

FIG. 26   Some spirit photographs featured more sophisticated tableaux. This photograph taken by William Mumler, for instance, depicts three spirits hovering near a photograph of a living person, which had been sent to Mumler. The image seems to hint ironically at the unsettling play between absence and presence in photographic portrayals of people (and spirits). William H. Mumler's *Three Spirits with a Photograph on a Table Propped Against a Vase with Flowers* (1862–75). Albumen silver. The J. Paul Getty Museum, Los Angeles, item 84.XD.760.1.16.

between photography and narrative, producing what Novak tentatively termed "photographic fiction."[76]

A similar narrative power seems to be at play, to a certain extent, in spirit photography. This is especially true of stereoscopic prints and other ghost photographs made for the purpose of amusement, such as a spirit tintype produced by an obscure photographer in the 1890s that depicted people in a small Michigan community being frightened by apparitions.[77] But, to some degree, spirit photography produced in a spiritualist context also manifested a fictional and, at the same time, realistic link between our world and the beyond. Some of Mumler's photographs illustrate a complex and engaging relationship between the sitter and the spirit, linking them, for instance, through the ambiguous and self-reflexive insertion in the tableau of a framed photographic picture (fig. 26).

FROM MUMLER TO MÉLIÈS: A SHORT HISTORY OF SUPERIMPOSITION

The trajectory from spirit photography to the motion picture found symbolic expression at the very beginning of the film era. As Matthew Solomon has noted,[78] one of the first books ever published on the moving image, *History of the Kinetograph, Kinetoscope, and Kineto-phonograph*, authored by W. K. L. Dickson and his wife, Antonia, in 1895, included a curious illustration entitled *Photography Extraordinary*. It was, in the tradition of often-mocked spirit photographs, a photographic portrait of Dickson with a spectral double behind him (fig. 27). Dickson had contributed to the invention of the first commercial moving-picture technology, the kinetoscope, and was a photography specialist in Edison's laboratory. It was probably to acknowledge cinema's debts to photography, which had served as "the birthplace and nursery of the kinetoscope,"[79] that he inserted this image in his book. It is intriguing, however, to read it as a tribute to the visual technique of superimposition. Dickson's spirit was just one of the ghosts that multiple exposure would eventually conjure through its new dimension—the moving image.

The fact that the practice of spirit photography within spiritualism was also shaped by issues of the market and by fiction helps us find more stable ground for the link between spirit photography and other superimposition effects that were produced for spectacular and commercial reasons. Following from this argument, this section examines the history of superimposition throughout the nineteenth century, when superimposition effects were popularized in spirit photography, as well as in magic-lantern desired realism of effect. It was then that a series of experiments was entered upon at the Orange Laboratory, extending over a period of six years.

The synchronous attachment of photography with the phonograph was early contemplated in order to record and give back the impressions to the eye as well as to the ear. The comprehensive term for this invention is the kineto-phonograph. The dual taking machine is the phono-kinetograph, and the reproducing machine is the phono-kinetoscope, in contradistinction to the kinetograph and kinetoscope, which apply respectively to the taking and reproduction of movable but *soundless* objects.

The initial experiments took the form of microscopic pinpoint photographs, placed on a cylindrical shell, corresponding in size to the ordinary phonograph cylinder. These two cylinders were then placed side by side on a shaft, and the sound record was taken as near as possible synchronously with the photographic image, impressed on the sensitive surface of the shell. The photographic portion of the undertaking was seriously hampered by the materials at hand, which, however excellent in themselves, offered no substance sufficiently sensitive. How to secure clear-cut outlines, or indeed any outlines at all, together with phenomenal speed, was the problem which puzzled the experimenters. The Daguerre, albumen and kindred processes met the first requirements, but failed when subjected to the latter test. These methods were therefore regretfully abandoned, a certain precipitate of knowledge being retained, and a bold leap was made to the Maddox gelatine bromide of silver emulsion, with which the cylinders were coated. This process gave rise to a new and serious difficulty. The bromide of silver haloids, held in suspension with the emulsion, showed themselves in an exaggerated

PHOTOGRAPHY EXTRAORDINARY.

FIG. 27
A fake spirit photograph illustrates W. K. L. Dickson and Antonia Dickson's *History of the Kinetograph, Kinetoscope, and Kineto-phonograph* (1895), one of the first books ever published on the moving picture. From William Kennedy Laurie Dickson and Antonia Dickson, *History of the Kinetograph, Kinetoscope, and Kinetophonograph* (New York: Museum of Modern Art, 2000), 8.

projections, antispiritualist exposés, and trick films. Since the 1850s, when Brewster described a trick for creating photographs of specters and the London Stereoscopic Company began to produce the *Ghost in the Stereoscope* series, superimposition had spread into a number of technologies and cultural environments, including spiritualism, trick photography, the magic lantern, stage magic, and early cinema. Comparable images, produced through similar means, were presented in these various contexts as an audacious trick, as a demonstration of the existence of spirits, or as a way to visualize dreaming. It was this movement into different technological and cultural worlds that ultimately fixed superimposition at the intersection of spiritualism and magic, photography and cinema, realism and fantasy.

By addressing visual effects of superimposition as an integrated field comprising different media and practices, the following sections aim to frame spiritualism's visual culture in the broader context of Victorian spectacular entertainments. In this regard, the examination of superimposition techniques contributes to the overall approach to the study of the supernatural that I propose in this book: to refuse rigid distinctions between the world of religion and the world of entertainment and engage instead with the porosity and flexibility of such boundaries.

PROJECTING GHOSTS

The history of superimposition is connected not only with the photographic medium but also with the projected image. During the nineteenth century, magic-lantern projection developed as a spectacular, recreational, and didactic technology. In this process, a number of techniques were introduced to create visual effects that could stimulate the wonder and the attention of the spectator. One of these, involving the use of two magic lanterns to superpose a figure on a background, has been compared to the use of superimposition in early cinema.[80] This, however, was not the only means by which superimposition intertwined with the projection of images. Magic lanterns were used to project photographic images that featured the trick of multiple exposure, and in at least one case, as I will show, they were used to project spirit photographs, too.

The technique of superimposing one image over another had been common in magic-lantern shows at least since the spectacles of phantasmagoria popularized by Étienne-Gaspard Robertson in the 1790s. Playing on the uncanny relationship between projected images and apparitions of ghosts, Robertson staged his performances in the lugubrious rooms of an abandoned chapel in the Couvent des Capucines in Paris. Although he presented his shows as spectacle and introduced them with a warning against superstition and impostors, Robertson's phantasmagoria played with popular fascination with the worlds of the supernatural and the occult. The concealment of the projector from the spectators contributed to the mysterious atmosphere of these spectacles. Robertson used multiple visual effects, such as dissolves and the illusion of movement, which he achieved through the means of mechanical slides and by moving the lantern.[81] The figures were sometimes projected onto smoke, creating the illusion that apparitions were floating over the audience.

Superimposition in Robertson's phantasmagoria was accomplished with two projectors. The first lantern usually provided the background, while the other was mobile; moving it forward and backward could produce the illusion that the apparition, often a ghost or a skeleton, was moving toward the audience. This trick was often used by lanternists in the nineteenth century, building a long tradition of superimposition with the magic lantern.[82] A similar technique was involved in the illusion known as "Pepper's Ghost," which was first presented at the London Royal Polytechnic in 1863 and combined real actors and projected images.[83]

The employment of a dark background in the superimposition trick was common to magic-lantern projections and spirit photography. In early cinema, filmmakers such as Georges Méliès would eventually adopt the same practice: in *Le mélomane* (The melomaniac; 1903), for instance, the dark background allows Méliès to make his heads appear on the musical staff at the top part of the screen. The common use of superimposition in magic-lantern shows may have played a role in the establishment of superimposition in early film. Indeed, as Deac Rossell, among others, has documented, many pioneers and early practitioners of the moving image had a background in the art of lantern projection.[84]

The magic lantern was also used to project spirit photographs. In April 1882, the *Medium and Daybreak* published a report of an evening ceremony organized in London to celebrate the thirty-fourth anniversary of modern spiritualism. This "general meeting of British spiritualists" drew together representatives from many spiritualist communities outside the capital. Neumeyer Hall, which had been chosen to host the celebration, was soon filled to capacity; chairs had to be placed in every available space to accommodate the number of attendees. For those who had not reserved a place, ordinary tickets were sold at the entrance, where the pressure of the crowd became quite intense. But neither the wait nor the discomfort of the line could ruin the atmosphere of the gathering; as the reporter put it, "On the contrary the principle of love seemed to dominate so completely that it was a pleasure to press the one against the other."[85]

A solo pianist inaugurated the evening's entertainment. This was followed by introductory addresses from the celebration's committee, the performance of a vocalist, "through whose voice the spirit world seems to breathe its harmonies,"[86] and two trance lectures performed by spiritualist mediums. Then it was time for the principal attraction, spirit photography. A lantern-slide operator, Mr. Middleton,[87] set up the projection, while a piano player furnished musical accompaniment. Lights were turned off in order to ensure a suitable condition for the projection. James Burns, the editor of the *Medium and Daybreak*, acted as presenter, introducing every slide with his "descriptive remarks." The projection included illustrations and photographs that represented salient moments in spiritualism over the past decades, as well as a few samples of manifestations, such as slate writing and direct drawing. But the attention soon turned toward spirit photographs. The first series of images of this kind was titled "The Substance of Which Spirit-Photographs Are Made"[88] and included photographs of mediums with a halo of light over their hands or body—a phenomenon that, according to Burns, modern science had been unable to explain. The next sequence, which, with thirty-seven images, accounted for the majority of the slides, exhibited the spirit photographs of Frederick A. Hudson, whose reproductions had been repeatedly offered at a sale price to the readers of the *Medium and Daybreak*. A few examples of spirit images made by other photographers—among them some by William Mumler—completed the forty-minute-long projection, which was followed by a speech from the medium Georgiana Houghton and by a few words of thanks from Hudson.

While in the case of phantasmagoria and other spectacular magic-lantern tricks, the illusion—or, from the believer's perspective, the spirit manifestation—took place right before the spectators' eyes, the projection of spirit photography is, in a certain regard, a different case. The manipulation preceded the show at Neumeyer Hall, having been produced by the camera when the photograph was taken and not directly before the audience. The magic lantern was employed to project onto the stage images that had been previously made: it was not used to conjure the superimposition effect, nor was it involved in the reputedly supernatural phenomenon. The audience, however, did not seem to be completely aware of this distinction. Reportedly, this magic-lantern spiritualist show was seen by many as a mystical event. As the reporter for the *Medium and Daybreak* stated, "the darkness which prevailed during the exhibition was very favourable for the exercise of the clairvoyance,"[89] and several audience members claimed to have seen visions of spirits or to have felt their presence. The magazine account mentioned one spectator who saw the apparition of a horseman, over whose head six different spirits of different nationalities were hovering. Apparently, it was believed, a trace of the supernatural presence that—according to the spiritualists' claims—had produced the images was also carried in the slides projected before the audience. This might suggest that spiritualist meaning was found not only in the photograph as a concrete object but also in its visual representation, regardless of the medium used to show it.

The account of this event, apart from providing proof of the richness of spiritualist visual culture, demonstrates that on at least one occasion—although the number of magic-lantern glass slides featuring spirit photographs used in the London celebration indicates that there could have been more events of this kind—spirit photography intertwined with the technology of the projected image. Although the author of the report insisted that "the sole purpose" of the evening was "the work of the angel-world amongst humanity,"[90] the gathering of the British spiritualist community was presented as a highly spectacular event, with the public taking part in a performance that resembled not only magic-lantern shows of the time but also the spectacle of early film shows. In fact, some of the conditions of display that were highlighted by the author of this report, such as the darkness of the room, the musical accompaniment, the paying public, and the presence of a presenter who gave commentary and explanations, came to be customary some decades later during the projection of silent films.

DEBUNKING SPIRIT PHOTOGRAPHY

The advent of spiritualism in the nineteenth century resulted not only in a craze for spirit séances but also in an unprecedented effort on the part of skeptics to expose claims about spirit activity as superstition and fraud. This gave rise to an impressive body of publications.[91] Spirit photography was demystified as a photographic trick, and fake spirit photographs were described as the result of multiple exposure and other techniques, as skeptics attempted to prove the dishonesty of mediums.

Illusions produced through trick photography, such as Brewster's "ghosts," came to be widely known as "photographic amusements" during the second half of the nineteenth century. An article published in the *British Journal of Photography* included in this category "an extended class of effects, produced by the aid of the camera, which, in their complete state, serve to excite the curiosity or the amusement of the public, and in some measure to justify the occasionally-lengthy correspondence which we have seen in our scientific journals to explain and account for them."[92] In the 1860s, the introduction of spirit photography brought about a significant change in the use and production of these images. Photographs in the style of the *Ghost in the Stereoscope* series were now explicitly linked to spiritualism, and the purpose of amusement came together with the moral duty of exposing superstition and gullibility.

During the late nineteenth century, photographic tricks were often described in popular scientific publications, such as the *Scientific American* and the French journal *La Nature*, which published a series of articles later collected in Albert A. Hopkins's *Magic: Stage Illusions and Scientific Diversions, Including Trick Photography*.[93] Offering explanations for a number of illusory techniques used in stage magic and prestidigitation, this

FIG. 4.—FACSIMILE OF A COMPOSITE PHOTOGRAPH.

FIG. 28 This image, featuring a photographic trick based on multiple exposure, appears in Albert A. Hopkins's book *Magic*, which explained a number of illusory techniques taken from stage magic and prestidigitation. The book reproduced photographic effects similar to those employed in early cinema. This trick was skillfully designed to create a macabre yet comical effect. From Albert A. Hopkins, *Magic: Stage Illusions and Scientific Diversions, Including Trick Photography* (New York: Munn, 1897).

book went through several editions at the turn of the century. It included chapters on chronophotography and the projection of moving pictures and an entire section dedicated to popular "photographic diversions." A detailed explanation of how to create the photographs of so-called spirits was given, in the hope that "they will be made merely for amusement, and, if possible, to expose persons who practice on the gullibility of inexperienced persons."[94] Engravings illustrated how multiple exposure could be used to produce spirit photographs as well as other photographic illusions (fig. 28).

The main context for imitations of spirit photography was stage magic. After the rise of the spiritualist movement in the mid-nineteenth century, magicians engaged in polemical attempts to demonstrate that behind the craze for spirit séances was the trickery of fraudulent mediums. Pointing out that their knowledge of illusionism and optics allowed them to recognize and explain spirit séances, stage magicians exploited the fascination with the supernatural, often performing a kind of antispiritualist show that aimed to reproduce technically the "phenomena" of spiritualism. Although spirit photography could not be conveniently exhibited onstage, exposés of this spiritualist practice can be found in several printed sources that were published in connection with magicians' debunking of spiritualism. Indeed, spirit photography broke with stage magicians' tradition of live performance. Instead of being produced in real time through mirrors or hidden projections, the ghostly illusions were conjured with the photographic medium. The effect, however, was no less spectacular.

A particularly interesting example of antispiritualist spirit photography is the frontispiece engraving for *The Supernatural?*, an 1891 book that featured a chapter on modern spiritualism written by the prominent English magician John Nevil Maskelyne. In this ironic and symbolic picture, the "spirit" of John Nevil Maskelyne appears beside the editor of the book, Lionel A. Weatherly, as if intending to clasp his hand (fig. 29). In his chapter, Maskelyne explained how these images could be produced, pointing to two possible tricks: "double-printing," which involved the superimposition of two negatives on the same print, and "double-exposure," a technique that followed the method illustrated by Brewster. In both cases, the second exposure or print was too brief for the image to be fully fixed. The result, Maskelyne stated, was that "whilst all else is sharp and well-defined, the 'spirit' is represented by a hazy outline, through which all that is behind it shows. There is nothing very 'spiritual' about this, is there?"[95]

Among other fake spirit photographs made by magicians were the two images published in a German book, Carl Willman's *Moderne Wunder* (Modern wonders), in 1886. Willman, a German watchmaker and amateur magician, wrote several books on stage magic and was engaged in exposing spiritualist trickery; in *Moderne Wunder*, he made it clear that "spirit" photographs were produced through fully explainable, artificial means.[96] The book's first engraving, entitled *Jacoby in the Realm of His Ghosts: So-Called Spirit Photography*, was a relatively conventional image in which the magician Jacoby appeared frightened before a spectral apparition (fig. 30). Another one, entitled *The Liberation of the Prestidigitator Jacoby*, involved a more complicated multiple exposure, incorporating apparitions of a ghost, a skull, and a levitating hand (fig. 31). This illustration seems to play ironically with the tradition of escape art, which had been practiced in spiritualism by the Davenport brothers and in stage magic by a number of showmen, including the American Harry Houdini, who would eventually make it his most successful feat at the beginning of the twentieth century.

Magicians and other opponents of spiritualism continued to debunk spirit photography as the product of multiple exposure well beyond the end of the nineteenth century. This tradition probably contributed to the questioning of photography's claims of objectivity, while continuing to foreground mediums' ability to create fictional worlds and, in cases where

A SPIRIT PHOTOGRAPH.

The Wraith of Mr. Maskelyne *appearing to* Dr. Weatherly.

FIG. 29   *A Spirit Photograph: The Wraith of Mr. Maskelyne Appearing to Dr. Weatherly.* Frontispiece to Lionel A. Weatherly, *The Supernatural?* (Bristol: Arrowsmith, 1891).

Jacoby im Reiche seiner Geister.
(Sogenannte Geister-Photographien.)

FIG. 30 *Jacoby in the Realm of His Ghosts: So-Called Spirit Photography* (*Jacoby im Reiche seiner Geister: Sogenannte Geister-Photographier*). From Carl Willmann, *Moderne Wunder: Natürliche Erklärung der älteren wie neueren Geheimnisse der Spiritisten und Antispiritisten, Geisterritierer, Hellseher, Gedankenleser, Heilmedien, Mnemotechniker und Rechenkünstler* (Leipzig: Otto Spamer, 1886), 212.

Die Entfesselung des Prestidigitateurs Jacoby.

FIG. 31 *The Liberation of the Prestidigitator Jacoby (Die Entfesselung der Prestidigitateurs Jacoby)*. From Carl Willmann, *Moderne Wunder: Natürliche Erklärung der älteren wie neueren Geheimnisse der Spiritisten und Antispiritisten, Geisterritierer, Hellseher, Gedankenleser, Heilmedien, Mnemotechniker und Rechenkünstler* (Leipzig: Otto Spamer, 1886), 66.

there was the intent to deceive, to lie. As a debunker of spiritualism pointed out some years later, "So unreliable I consider any photograph to which is attached the slightest taint of spiritualism, that when in this connection I have been asked, 'Can a photograph lie?,' I have frequently replied, 'A spirit photograph is absolutely unable to speak the truth.'"[97]

TOWARD THE TRICK MOVIE

In early cinema, the technique of multiple exposure was successfully introduced in a genre that rose to great popularity during the first years of the moving image: the trick film. The involvement of filmmakers who drew on the tradition of stage magic especially contributed to popularizing this technique in film production. Through their creativity, photographic tricks were applied to the new moving images, and new tricks, such as stop-motion and substitution splicing, were successfully employed. Multiple exposure was used to produce several different effects, including dissolves, the replication of characters or objects, superimposition, and transparency.

André Bazin's essay on superimposition opened with a consideration of the coexistence of realism and fantasy on the cinematic screen. "The fantastic in the cinema," he argued, "is possible only because of the irresistible realism of the photographic image. It is the image that can bring us face to face with the unreal, that can introduce the unreal into the world of the visible." As an example, Bazin mentioned a film from 1933, James Whale's *The Invisible Man*, arguing that as an animated film it would have immediately lost all interest, since what appealed to the audience was "the contradiction between the irrefutable objectivity of the photographic image and the unbelievable nature of the events that it depicts."[98] The observation that realism is needed to bring the viewer into the world of fantasy could be applied to the history of superimposition before cinema. The most astounding paradox of this technique is that it was regarded simultaneously as a spirit manifestation by spiritualists and as a mere trick by magicians, expert photographers, and skeptics in general. In this sense, superimposition brought to cinema what Dan North called "the synthesis between photographic similitude and its fantastic, transformative effect."[99] The fact that multiple exposure was used in two contexts, spiritualism and magic, exploiting, respectively, its realist and its fantastic power, may explain the fascination of early filmmakers with this technique and its extensive employment in the trick film.

The relationship between stage magic and early cinema has been increasingly acknowledged in film history. As Erik Barnouw, the author of a pioneering work on this topic, put it, given the extent to which professional magicians relied on technical means and magic-lantern projection to perform their tricks, it is not surprising that the debut of the Lumière brothers' cinematograph "set off a gold rush" in the magic arena.[100] Practicing theatrical conjurers, such as Gaston Velle, Walter Booth, J. Stuart Blackton, Albert E. Smith, and Georges Méliès, were among the first motion-picture exhibitionists and filmmakers. Magic theaters, such as the Egyptian Hall in London and the Théâtre Robert-Houdin and Théâtre Isola in Paris, were among the locations where early cinematic projection took place. And Tom Gunning, Lucy Fischer, Simon During, and Karen Beckman, among others, have posited that many spectators of the time experienced cinema as a kind of magic show.[101]

Notwithstanding Matthew Solomon's convincing demonstration that magic dialogued with cinema well beyond the novelty period,[102] the most significant contribution of stage magic to film production was certainly the trick film. Trick films were composed of a series of apparitions, transformations, and magical attractions that aimed at astonishing the spectator with the wonder of complex visual tricks. Especially in the earliest years, they did not rely on a convincing narrative plot, but rather on a string of magical effects that were created through photographic tricks such as substitution splicing and multiple exposure. Filmmakers such as Georges Méliès, a professional stage magician who owned the Théâtre Robert-Houdin in Paris, and George Albert Smith, who produced a number of trick films in Britain, were among the leaders of this genre. Devils, fairies, skeletons, and ghosts were—alongside the stage magician, who was often the protagonist of these short movies—the figures that populated this imaginary world.

Images such as those created by Maskelyne and Willman demonstrate that photographic tricks were in use in the world of magic and illusionism well before the invention of cinema. The exposure of spirit photography can thus be seen as evidence of the precinematic involvement of stage magicians in the art of chemicals, darkrooms, and photographic manipulation—an art that was at the root of the success in early cinema of magicians such as Méliès and Smith. It is probably not a coincidence that multiple exposure and other darkroom tricks were first popularized in motion pictures by those filmmakers who came to film production from the profession of stage magic, and who were particularly aware of the artifices used by spiritualist mediums.

In 1898, the British pioneer of trick film, George Albert Smith, produced a film called *Photographing a Ghost*. Although no copies of the original film have been preserved, Smith's catalogue description offers insight into its simple plot, which involved the comical and unfortunate attempt of a photographer to take a picture of a spirit.[103] The text mentioned that the ghost was perfectly transparent, so that the background was visible through him, and that he kept disappearing and reappearing. Before becoming involved in film production, Smith had been a magic lanternist, a portrait photographer, and a stage hypnotist, and took part in the Society for Psychical Research's experiments on hypnotism and thought reading.[104] With such a career trajectory, he would have been well aware of the ramifications of spiritualism's visual culture. The catalogue description suggests that he used multiple exposure to insert the transparent image of the specter into the scene, performing through the moving picture something similar to what Mumler and other spirit photographers had been doing with the still image. In other films created during the same period, Smith skillfully exploited superimposition, and he even obtained a patent for double exposure,[105] which he used for depicting a ghost and a vision in his film *The Corsican Brothers*. According to Frank Gray, he was the first British filmmaker to render ghost illusions and vision scenes through multiple exposure.[106]

Georges Méliès was also involved in the tradition of debunking spiritualism. One of his most successful magic plays, entitled *Le decapité recalcitrant* (The recalcitrant decapitated man), which was popular enough to be performed 1,200 times at the Théâtre Robert-Houdin, featured the decapitation of a spiritualist medium who annoyed the public by assuring them of the trustworthiness of spirit séances. Méliès also shot a movie, *L'armoire des frères Davenport* (The cabinet trick of the Davenport brothers; 1902), mocking the performances of the two famous American stage mediums. And, like Smith, Méliès composed a film on spirit photography, called *Le portrait spirite* (A spiritualist photographer; 1903).

Méliès's familiarity with spirit photography may date back to 1884, when he sojourned in London and learned about modern stage-magic techniques. During this period, he became a devotee of the most famous London magic theater, the Egyptian Hall, and a friend of John Nevil Maskelyne. In the years 1883–84, Maskelyne gave two hundred antispiritualist performances at the Egyptian Hall, during which, as he put it, "I explained every trick, together with several improvements of my own."[107] At the beginning of the 1880s, several spirit photographers were active in London,[108] and it is possible that Maskelyne was already involved in the production of fake spirit photographs like the one he later published in Weatherly's book (see fig. 29).[109] In 1884, Méliès was also in contact with David Devant, another Egyptian Hall magician, who, after 1896, introduced film projections into his shows.[110] Devant was known at the time for making a life-sized portrait of a woman come to life, an illusion that some decades later would be replicated in Méliès's *Le portrait spirite*.

Multiple exposure and superimposition effects were widely used in film production in the following decades, even after the trick film had virtually disappeared as a genre.[111] In 1922, for instance, the American magician Harry Houdini produced and acted in *The Man from Beyond*, a film featuring ghostly apparitions created through multiple exposure. Although Houdini had already been the protagonist of several nonfiction and fiction films,[112] this was the first of his films to rely on the supernatural and, in particular, on themes taken from belief in spiritualism and reincarnation. Using superimposition to visually express spirit apparitions, Houdini exhibited awareness of the iconographic tradition epitomized by spirit photography. Throughout his entire career, he had been involved in the exposure of spiritualist trickery, claiming to consider this a moral duty and comparing mediums to gamblers who "resort to deception and take advantage of the sitters at all angles."[113] His images of specters in *The Man from Beyond* can be considered a kind of homage to the iconography of spirit photography, whose history and practice he had so thoroughly traced and researched.

PARADOXICAL IMAGES

In "A Theory of Play and Fantasy," Gregory Bateson argued that a crucial stage in the evolution of communication occurs when "the organism gradually ceases to respond quite 'automatically' to the mood-signs of another and becomes able to recognize the sign as a signal, that is, to recognize that the other individual's and its own signals are only signals, that can be trusted, distrusted, falsified, denied, amplified, corrected, and so forth."[114] Consequently, the definition of an event as serious or unserious will vary, depending on the meaning that an individual gives to this event. In some cases, however, we may be uncertain about whether the right interpretation of a situation is reality or play. Bateson's argument, recalled by Erving Goffman in his discussion of frame analysis,[115] can be helpful in understanding how the ghostly image created through superimposition wavered between fictional and religious contexts, lacking a precise definition and allowing for its simultaneous annexation to the worlds of belief and entertainment. Flowing through technological and cultural contexts as distinct as spiritualism, the magic-lantern lecture circuit, stage magic, photographic amusements, and early cinema, superimposition effects produced ambivalent images that could carry the viewer into fictional realms or passionate belief, into the marvels of illusion or the spirit world. Depending on the perspective from which they were regarded, they opened the door to realms that were only apparently contradictory. This is probably the reason why superimposition, as a visual practice, was so widely employed in the early years of the motion picture. As Michael Chanan has argued, cinema was, from its very start, "an art of both realism and illusion, veracity and deception, transparency and trickery—in short, a highly paradoxical medium."[116]

Being the subject of different and sometimes divergent interpretations (as the revelation of spirit agency, a mere trick, or a photographic accident), spirit photography seems to have shared with film this paradoxical character. Moreover, before multiple exposure and other superimposition techniques were applied by early filmmakers to the spectacle of the moving image, photographic incarnations of ghosts—regarded as amusements, attractions, and curiosities—were already haunting Western visual culture. Rather than being just a demonstration of photography's evidentiary status, spirit photography was an open field in which realistic and fictional interpretations of images coexisted and interacted with each other. The fact that visual representations of spirits were regarded as visual curiosities and as commodities not only among skeptics but also within the boundaries of spiritualism, as well as their relationship with spectacular entertainments featuring superimposition techniques, shows that the boundary between entertainment and belief was blurred in spiritualism's visual culture—as it was in private and public séance performances.

AFTERWORD

French historian Marc Bloch left us one of the most thoughtful reflections about the relationship between the study of history and our knowledge of the present. In *The Historian's Craft*, he observes that the profession of historian requires a relationship of constant exchange between the past and the present. As he put it, "Misunderstanding of the present is the inevitable consequence of ignorance of the past. But a man may wear himself out just as fruitlessly in seeking to understand the past, if he is totally ignorant of the present."[1]

Bloch's teaching is a useful hint to cultural historians and historians of media, who need to observe the present in order to comprehend the past. While this study is dedicated to beliefs in spirits and séance practices in the Victorian age, the observation of contemporary cases in which show business and entertainment media interact with beliefs in the supernatural influenced its conception and development. In this afterword, therefore, I would like to discuss the claims developed in this book in respect to the role of the supernatural as a cultural and religious discourse in contemporary societies.

One of the recurring questions raised by the study of Victorian spiritualism is why it was such a popular craze in the nineteenth century, while it became much less significant throughout the twentieth century and in our present age. The right answer is probably that this is not true, at least not entirely. If spiritualism markedly declined in the United States, in Britain, and in continental Europe after the 1920s, the spiritist church is today a powerful religious confession in countries such as Brazil, with millions of devotees.[2] Moreover, even if we focus only on the American and British contexts, beliefs in spirits and in the occult are still widespread, as confirmed by several polls.[3] As some have argued, after all, the contemporary interest in Victorian culture might tell us something about our present-day cultural configuration: we are intrigued by Victorian society because we feel that it contains something of our own identity and culture.[4]

The chief argument of this book is that belief in spiritualism did not contrast but was instead allied with entertainment practices, spectacular features, and show business. Set at the beginning of a new era for commercial entertainment, from the mid-nineteenth to the early twentieth centuries, the rise of the spiritualist movement was intimately connected to the development of modern popular culture and the media entertainment industry. This link did not vanish at the dawn of the twentieth century. Ghosts haunt contemporary popular culture as much as they haunted Victorian mansions in the nineteenth century: they are omnipresent in literature, film, television series, video games, and even popular music.[5] Moreover, psychics and mediums continue to play upon the distinctions between mystical beliefs and popular entertainment.[6] From the New Age movement to psychic shops, from esoteric books to professional seers, the realm of the supernatural is still deeply bound with contemporary media culture.

In nineteenth-century spiritualism, mediums usually welcomed nonbelievers and skeptics to their séances. This was due in part to the fact that the key issue was not faith in itself, but rather the participation in a common experience that stimulated a sense of curiosity, excitement, and wonder.[7] Thus, public and private séances allowed sitters and spectators to maintain a flexible interpretation of their involvement, mixing religious piety with entertainment and spectacle. Contemporary products of popular culture that focus on the theme of the supernatural often employ similar strategies. Take, for instance, paranormal television series that broadcast investigations into the supernatural, a genre that has been taken up by networks specializing in nonfiction, such as the Discovery Channel. The documentary form within which these series are framed reinforces the impression of authenticity of the supernatural claims.[8] Viewers are not required to actually believe in them, though: the shows allow spectators to choose different interpretations of the events and are designed to excite the curiosity of skeptics as much as those who are willing to believe in paranormal events. The success of these series suggests that the representation of ghosts and other occult phenomena in contemporary popular culture relies on a mechanism similar to that of nineteenth-century spiritualism: the question of authenticity is secondary to the dimension of the spectatorial experience, so that belief and entertainment are not alternatives, but may coexist in a cultural form that stimulates curiosity and wonder in believers and nonbelievers alike.

Literature addressing the history of representations of ghosts has been mainly divided into two separate traditions, which address, respectively, fictional and "real" (at least, considered to be so) ghosts. While attempts have been made to question how beliefs in spirits have influenced the work of writers, filmmakers, and television producers,[9] less attention has been given to the possibility of comparing the experiences of those who believe in spirits with those who consume a product of fiction on ghosts. Frequently, the fact that someone believes in what she sees, hears, touches, and feels—as might be the case in a spiritualist séance—seems to define her experience as structurally different from the experience of the readers of gothic literature or the spectators of a horror film. In contrast with this perspective, the dynamics examined in this book show that a peculiar appeal of the supernatural lies behind the role played by the occult not only in popular literature and entertainment media, but also in religious beliefs and practices. Both fictional representations of ghosts or other supernatural phenomena and beliefs in spirits excite the fascination with the occult, the supernatural, the unknown. In nineteenth-century spiritualism, this fascination functioned as a trigger for the diffusion of beliefs in spirits, driving several generations of American and British Victorians to the séance table. The same fascination contributes to making spirits a powerful theme in contemporary popular culture, too. The popularity of paranormal television series, as well as horror films and fictional television series such as *Medium* (2005–11) and *Supernatural* (2005–present), is built upon the allure of the occult, upon the emotions that come with the conception of ghosts—whether we believe in them or not. There is an intimate connection between fictional representations of the supernatural and beliefs in extraordinary phenomena.[10]

The complex role that belief and disbelief played in spiritualist séances is particularly meaningful if one considers not its difference, but rather its resemblance, to spectatorial situations that bear an explicitly fictional character, such as attending a theatrical piece or watching a film. Take, for instance, some of the most successful American films from the horror and supernatural genre in the last few decades, such as *The Exorcist* (1973), the *Blair Witch Project* (1999), and more recently *The Conjuring* (2013). As noted by Diana Walsh-Pasulka, all of these movies present supernatural events as something that may be true. They create a strong impression of reality by referring to real characters and events, such as the practice of exorcism, reports of ghostly apparitions, or parapsychological research. This heightens the interest of the public and is employed as a marketing strategy by the studios that produce and distribute the films.[11] In this regard, research presented in this book demonstrates the deep affinity between the spectatorial position invited by such films and the spiritualist séance, or other performances and practices connected to supernatural beliefs. While film, literature, and other forms of fiction are often studied under the assumption that spectators and readers willingly suspend their disbelief, inviting belief is, on the contrary, an important and widespread strategy in the media entertainment industry. As a consequence, we should acknowledge the presence of a deep continuity and analogy between forms of involvement that explicitly encourage beliefs, such as spiritualism, and those that, on the surface, seem to deny it, such as fiction.

By arguing for the interconnection of beliefs in spirits and the rise of industrial entertainment and popular culture in the nineteenth century, *Supernatural Entertainments* addresses forms of participation and spectatorship that do not pertain either to the realm of religion or to that of popular culture, but instead to a combination of the two of them. One of the implications of this work, then, is that there is not always a clear distinction between religious belief and spectacular entertainment. While our understanding of religion is often informed by the idea that faith is in a relationship of conflict to "earthly" matters such as market and spectacle, scholars have recently underlined the necessity of going beyond established dichotomies of spirit and matter.[12] As some point out, "there is no such thing as an immaterial religion": we need to comprehend religious beliefs as something pertaining to both the spiritual and the material realms.[13] This book also shows that there is no such thing as an unspiritual entertainment industry. Since the nineteenth century, the rise of new spectacular and entertainment practices has stimulated the amusement, the fascination, and the wonder of believers and skeptics, of curious and ecstatic spectators. They have all been equally welcome to join the spectacle of spirits.

NOTES

INTRODUCTION

1. See, for instance, Doyle, *History of Spiritualism*.
2. For accounts of the Fox sisters' exhibition at the Corinthian Hall, see Harding Britten, *Modern American Spiritualism*, 42–54; Doyle, *History of Spiritualism*, 1:78–79.
3. Throughout this book, I employ the term "popular" to indicate something regarded with favor, approval, or affection, especially by the general public. Although most literature on popular culture focuses on the twentieth century, numerous scholars have noted that popular culture originated in the nineteenth-century revolution of communication media, as cheap newspapers, increasingly rapid and inexpensive transportation, and electrical media such as the telegraph facilitated the formation of a mass audience for popular literature and the press. See, among many others, Anderson, *Printed Image*; Gitelman, *Scripts, Grooves, and Writing Machines*; Czitrom, *Media and the American Mind*. For approaches to popular culture focusing on early modernity and the Victorian age, see Burke, *Popular Culture*; Bailey, *Popular Culture and Performance*.
4. Estimates given at the time probably exaggerated the dimension of the movement, but they are nonetheless revealing of spiritualism's pervasiveness in Victorian societies. The British psychologist L. S. Forbes Winslow calculated that in the United States alone there were 30,0000 mediums and more than a million persons who firmly believed in spiritualism. Others gave even higher estimates, such as the claim that the number of Americans at least peripherally engaged with the movement numbered 3 million by the 1850s and more than 11 million by the 1870s. The insider Emma Hardinge claimed in 1870 that spiritualism had 100 million followers worldwide. Public personalities who sat at séance tables included Mary Todd Lincoln, widow of the former president of the United States, and scientists such as the eminent British chemist William Crookes, who famously converted to spiritualism in the 1870s. Winslow, *Spiritualistic Madness*, 8; Hardinge Britten, *Modern American Spiritualism*. See also Moore, "Spiritualism and Science," 481. For a most precise estimation of spiritualist activities and adherents in nineteenth-century America, see Nartonis, "Rise of 19th-Century American Spiritualism."
5. Berry, *Experiences in Spiritualism*, 39.
6. Cook, *Arts of Deception*.
7. Huhtamo, *Illusions in Motion*, 364.
8. See Nadis, *Wonder Shows*; Qureshi, *Peoples on Parade*; Cook, *Arts of Deception*.
9. Lorraine Daston and Katharine Park have defined wonders as phenomena pertaining to nature or technology that arouse reactions of astonishment in viewers. A similar approach was used by Barbara Benedict in her history of curiosity in the early modern

period. In employing the notions of wonder and curiosity, I refer to Fred Nadis's book on the display of wonders from magic, science, and religion in nineteenth-century America. Nadis convincingly demonstrates that reactions of curiosity and wonder were kindled by a wide range of attractions that erased the boundaries between technology and the supernatural, science and religion, nature and magic. Daston and Park, *Wonders*; Benedict, *Curiosity*; Nadis, *Wonder Shows*.

10. Bennett, *Birth of the Museum*, 59.
11. On freak shows, see Tromp, *Victorian Freaks*; Garland Thomson, *Freakery*; Durbach, *Spectacle of Deformity*; Bogdan, *Freak Show*.
12. Willis, "On Wonder"; Nadis, *Wonder Shows*; Scott, "Popular Lecture." As Willis points out, novelty was a key element in nineteenth-century spectacular attractions, including spiritualism.
13. Brooker, "Polytechnic Ghost." See also Lightman, *Victorian Popularizers of Science*; Morus, "Worlds of Wonder"; Tresch, "The Prophet and the Pendulum"; Willis, *Mesmerists, Monsters, and Machines*; Kember, Plunkett, and Sullivan, *Popular Exhibitions*.
14. See, among others, Oppenheim, *Other World*; Lachapelle, *Investigating the Supernatural*; Monroe, *Laboratories of Faith*; Moore, *In Search of White Crows*.
15. As Alison Winter brilliantly demonstrates, definitions of science were malleable in early Victorian society, when spiritualism was first developing. What counted as a proper science remained quite open to dispute. Winter, *Mesmerized*, 5–9.
16. See, among others, Sprenger, *Medien des Immediaten*; Stolow, "Salvation by Electricity"; Sconce, *Haunted Media*; Peters, *Speaking into the Air*.
17. Nadis, *Wonder Shows*; Kassung, *Das Pendel*; Morus, *Frankenstein's Children*; Darnton, *Mesmerism*.
18. See Bennett, *Transatlantic Spiritualism*.
19. Booth, *Theatre in the Victorian Age*, 20.
20. Morse, *Leaves from My Life*, 34.
21. The beginning of the twentieth century also signaled an important turning point in the history of spiritualism, as mediumship started to be interpreted more and more as a phenomenon based on the medium's psychic powers rather than on spirit agency. See Owen, *Place of Enchantment*.
22. Friedberg, *Window Shopping*; Nead, *Haunted Gallery*; Gunning, "Cinema of Attraction."
23. Nartonis, "Rise of 19th-Century American Spiritualism."
24. Bakker, "Entertainment Industrialized."
25. Marrus, *Emergence of Leisure*.
26. Brazeal, "Precursor to Modern Media Hype."
27. See Cook, *Arts of Deception*; Harris, *Humbug*.
28. McKendrick, Brewer, and Plumb, *Birth of a Consumer Society*.
29. Fyfe and Lightman, *Science in the Marketplace*, 9.
30. Booth, *Theatre in the Victorian Age*, 3; Altick, *Shows of London*, 423; Richards, *Commodity Culture*.
31. The most comprehensive review of the history of British exhibition culture in the nineteenth century is still Altick, *Shows of London*.
32. See, among others, Moore, *In Search of White Crows*; Oppenheim, *Other World*; Braude, *Radical Spirits*; Owen, *Darkened Room*; Cox, *Body and Soul*; McGarry, *Ghosts of Futures Past*; Monroe, *Laboratories of Faith*; Lachapelle, *Investigating the Supernatural*.
33. Herman, "Whose Knocking?," 418.
34. Thurschwell, *Literature, Technology, and Magical Thinking*; Sword,

Ghostwriting Modernism; Bown, Burdett, and Thurschwell, *Victorian Supernatural*.
35. Lehman, *Victorian Women and the Theatre of Trance*.
36. Solomon, *Disappearing Tricks*; Andriopoulos, *Possessed*.
37. During, *Modern Enchantments*; Lamont, "Magician as Conjuror"; North, *Performing Illusions*.
38. Cox, *Body and Soul*; Herman, "Whose Knocking?" See also Owen, *Darkened Room*; Winter, *Mesmerized*; Monroe, *Laboratories of Faith*; Willis, "On Wonder."
39. Sconce, *Haunted Media*; Peters, *Speaking into the Air*; Noakes, "Telegraphy Is an Occult Art."
40. Many spiritualist writings, despite recognizing the Fox sisters as the first mediums, trace a long history of spirit communication, encompassing the ancient Egyptians, the Roman Empire, and even Jesus Christ, who was supposedly a powerful medium. See, for instance, Howitt, *History of the Supernatural*; Peebles, *Seers of the Ages*; Crowell, *Identity*.
41. See Sutherland, "Populism and Spectacle."
42. See, for instance, Hare, *Experimental Investigation*.
43. Hansen, *Babel and Babylon*; Leahy, "Walking for Pleasure?"; Tromp, *Victorian Freaks*.
44. Coppa, Hass, and Peck, *Performing Magic*.
45. Lightman, *Victorian Popularizers of Science*; Fyfe and Lightman, *Science in the Marketplace*.
46. See, among others, North, *Performing Illusions*; Mangan, *Performing Dark Arts*; During, *Modern Enchantments*.
47. Lamont, *Extraordinary Beliefs*.
48. Schwartz, *Spectacular Realities*, 92.
49. As David Walker points out, spiritualist séances "were acts performed amidst a variety of interpretive frames, both provided and assumed, and . . . they were acts that were offered up to the audience's critical and operational consideration." Walker, "Humbug in American Religion," 37.
50. Manon, "Seeing Through"; Staiti, "Con Artists"; Cook, *Arts of Deception*; Levi, "P. T. Barnum and the Feejee Mermaid."
51. Indeed, spiritualists sometimes suggested that stage magicians were nothing but powerful mediums who did not admit to having mediumistic powers. See Berg, *Spirits a Fraud*.
52. Hartman, *Facts and Mysteries of Spiritism*, 21.
53. Bartlett, "Mirth as Medium."
54. McDannell, *Material Christianity*, 4. A similar perspective has been employed in the anthropology of religion. See, for instance, the works of Michael Taussig, especially *Magic of the State*.
55. See, for instance, Cottom, "On the Dignity of Tables"; Cox, *Body and Soul*; Walker, "Humbug in American Religion."
56. Robertson, *Religion as Entertainment*.
57. Albanese, *Republic of Mind and Spirit*. For a cultural history of trance performances in the Victorian age, see Lehman, *Victorian Women and the Theatre of Trance*.
58. Schechner, *Future of Ritual*; Turner, *Anthropology of Performance*.
59. Moore, "Religion, Secularization," 228–33. Like spiritualist séances, these events were often advertised in the same venues employed by entrepreneurs of the show trade. As proposed by Jackson Lears, American evangelistic revivals should thus be included in the cultural history of commercial advertisement. Lears, *Fables of Abundance*, 56–67.
60. Such conditions are particularly well documented in the report of an evening ceremony organized in

London to celebrate the thirty-fourth anniversary of modern spiritualism, which is discussed at length in chapter 5. "Thirty-Fourth Anniversary of Modern Spiritualism," 257.

61. Adorno, *Stars Down to Earth*, 50.
62. See, for instance, Morselli, *Psicologia e spiritismo*, 2:10. On the relationship of spiritualism with the trivial and the everyday, see Walker, *Out of the Ordinary*; Cottom, *Abyss of Reason*; Cox, *Body and Soul*.
63. See Trachtenberg, "Mirror in the Marketplace"; West, "Fantasy, Photography, and the Marketplace"; Gurevitch, "Stereoscopic Attraction"; Plunkett, "Selling Stereoscopy."
64. Early reports, for instance, stated that the Fox sisters earned as much as one hundred dollars a day during their triumphant New York séances tour. Williams, *Horace Greeley*, 122.
65. Isaacs, "Fox Sisters," 100.
66. Money was also used in tricks on the magician's stage. James Peck suggests that this monetary wizardry and its symbolism were linked to wider concerns about money and attained a particular emphasis in times of economic instability. Peck, "Conjuring Capital."
67. Fritz, *Where Are the Dead?*, 52.
68. Indeed, the most up-to-date marketing strategies are used by members and institutions of many religious faiths. See Kaufman, *Consuming Visions*.

CHAPTER 1

1. Wetherbee, *Shadows*, 231.
2. Ibid., 282.
3. Oppenheim, *Other World*, 7; Owen, *Darkened Room*, 54–55; Lehman, *Victorian Women and the Theatre of Trance*, 115–26.
4. Owen, *Darkened Room*; Lehman, *Victorian Women and the Theatre of Trance*. See also Violi, *Il teatro dei nervi*.
5. Lamont, "Magician as Conjuror."
6. Goffman, *Frame Analysis*, 10.
7. Davis and Postlewait, *Theatricality*; Litvak, *Caught in the Act*.
8. Featherstone, "Spiritualism as Popular Performance"; Bennett, "Sacred Theatres."
9. Davis and Postlewait, *Theatricality*, 8.
10. For an insider account of the Fox sisters, see Capron, *Modern Spiritualism*.
11. Braude, *Radical Spirits*, 15–16. Despite its name, Barnum's Hotel had nothing to do with the American showman P. T. Barnum.
12. During, *Modern Enchantments*, 153.
13. Berry, *Experiences in Spiritualism*, 136. Emphasis in original.
14. Braude, *Radical Spirits*.
15. A well-documented case study is provided in John Patrick Deveney's book about the career of Paschal Beverly Randolph, an African American spiritualist, medium, healer, and writer who performed healing and spiritual practices in different locations throughout the United States in the nineteenth century. Deveney, *Paschal Beverly Randolph*.
16. Bennett, *Birth of the Museum*. On the role of itinerant performers and showmen in nineteenth-century media culture, see Huhtamo, *Illusions in Motion*; Assael, *Circus and Victorian Society*.
17. Morse, *Leaves from My Life*, 23–24.
18. "Thirty-Fourth Anniversary of Modern Spiritualism."
19. Nelson, *Spiritualism and Society*, 14–15.
20. Moore, *In Search of White Crows*, 16.
21. Hardinge Britten, *Modern American Spiritualism*, 57.
22. Berry, *Experiences in Spiritualism*, 162.
23. Zon, *Music and Performance Culture*.

24. Laing, "Voice Without a Face." Examples of sheet music inspired by spiritualism include *Planchette: Song and Chorus*, produced by Lee and Walker in Philadelphia; *Planchette Polka*, produced by C. Y. Fonda in Cincinnati; and *Spirit Rappings*, produced by Oliver Ditson in Boston.
25. Burns, "Facts and Phenomena of Spiritualism."
26. Moore, "To Hold Communion."
27. Morse, *Leaves from My Life*, 51–52.
28. "Her Force Only Magnetic?"
29. Home, *Lights and Shadows of Spiritualism*, 369.
30. Berry, *Experiences in Spiritualism*, 164.
31. "Thirty-Fourth Anniversary of Modern Spiritualism," 263.
32. "Casual Observer."
33. Berry, *Experiences in Spiritualism*, 165.
34. Craft, *Epidemic Delusions*, 294–95.
35. "List of Societies."
36. Mendeleev, *Sullo spiritismo*, 39.
37. Harry Houdini famously declared that his friend Arthur Conan Doyle, a devoted spiritualist, thought the magician to be a powerful medium: "Sir Arthur thinks I have great mediumistic powers and that some of my feats are done with the aid of spirits. Everything I do is accomplished by material means, humanly possible, no matter how baffling it is to the layman." Houdini, *Magician Among the Spirits*, 165.
38. Wetherbee, *Shadows*, 208.
39. Lamont, "Magician as Conjuror," 27.
40. Herr Dobler, *Exposé of the Davenport Brothers*.
41. Nichols, *Biography of the Brothers Davenport*, 12.
42. Lamont, "Magician as Conjuror," 23.
43. Cook, *Arts of Deception*.
44. Herr Dobler, *Exposé of the Davenport Brothers*; Maskelyne, *Modern Spiritualism*.
45. The role of skepticism and antispiritualism as a vehicle of publicity for the spiritualist movement is discussed at length in chapter 3.
46. Doyle, *History of Spiritualism*, 1:99–100.
47. Cooper, *Spiritual Experiences*, 130.
48. Doyle, *History of Spiritualism*, 1:96.
49. Sexton, *Spirit Mediums and Conjurers*, 6.
50. Morse, *Leaves from My Life*, 54.
51. Hardinge Britten, *Modern American Spiritualism*, 245–46.
52. Darnton, *Mesmerism*; Crabtree, *From Mesmer to Freud*; Winter, *Mesmerized*. On mesmerism, see also Natale, "Quella sensibilità esagerata della lastra."
53. Hardinge Britten, *Modern American Spiritualism*, 22.
54. Parssinen, "Mesmeric Performers." See also Winter, *Mesmerized*; Lehman, *Victorian Women and the Theatre of Trance*; Violi, *Il teatro dei nervi*.
55. Wetherbee, *Shadows*, 207.
56. Oppenheim, *Other World*, 7; Owen, *Darkened Room*, 54–55.
57. Redman, *Mystic Hours*.
58. Fritz, *Where Are the Dead?*, 42.
59. Richet, *Traité de métapsychique*, 580–81. Emphasis in original.
60. Coates, "Professional Mediumship."
61. With regard to the class dimension of spiritualism, see (for the British context) Owen, *Darkened Room*, and (for the American context) Braude, *Radical Spirits*. It is worth mentioning that actors, acrobats, and theatrical performers most commonly came, like mediums, from the lower class. On the class dimension in Victorian theater, a most useful reference is Booth, *Theatre in the Victorian Age*.
62. Redman, *Mystic Hours*, 107. Emphasis in original.
63. Fritz, *Where Are the Dead?*, 52.
64. Moore, *In Search of White Crows*, 16.
65. Braude, *Radical Spirits*, 175.
66. Berry, *Experiences in Spiritualism*, 97.

67. Houdini, *Magician Among the Spirits*, 119–20.
68. Lamont, *First Psychic*, xiii.
69. Home, *Incidents in My Life*, 36.
70. Lamont, *First Psychic*, 34.
71. Doyle, *History of Spiritualism*, 1:90.
72. Monroe, *Laboratories of Faith*, 86.
73. Doyle, *History of Spiritualism*, 1:87.
74. There is a significant body of scholarship that has approached trance as a matter of performance. See, in particular, Goldingay, "To Perform Possession"; Bennett, "Sacred Theatres"; King, "Shadow of a Mesmeriser"; Taylor, "Exploiting the Medium."
75. Redman, *Mystic Hours*, 107.
76. Daston and Galison, *Objectivity*.
77. See Noakes, "Telegraphy Is an Occult Art."
78. Hardinge Britten, *Modern American Spiritualism*, 38.
79. "Mediumship of Children."
80. Hartman, *Facts and Mysteries of Spiritism*.
81. Wetherbee, *Shadows*, 97–98.
82. Ibid., 121.
83. Ibid., 129.
84. Lynch, "Spectral Politics."
85. Harper, *Stead, the Man*, 61.
86. Phelps and Forbes-Robertson, *Life and Life-Work*, 259–60; Ireland, *Records of the New York Stage*, 2:640.
87. Shorter, "Emma Hardinge," 385.
88. See, for instance, her autobiographical sketch in the introduction to Hardinge Britten, *Six Lectures on Theology and Nature*.
89. Hardinge Britten, *Mrs. Emma Hardinge on Spirit Mediums*.
90. Sussman, "Performing the Intelligent Machine."
91. Gitelman, *Scripts, Grooves, and Writing Machines*, 190.
92. Schaffer, "Babbage's Dancer and the Impresarios of Mechanism."
93. Morus, *Frankenstein's Children*.
94. Hardinge Britten, *Modern American Spiritualism*, 110.
95. Beecher, *Review of the "Spiritual Manifestations,"* 12.
96. Peebles, *Seers of the Ages*, 208.
97. Oyston, "Biographical Sketch of Mrs. M. A. Hall," 307.
98. "Sleep," 33. Emphasis in original.
99. Ibid., 35.
100. See James, *Dream, Creativity, and Madness*.
101. See, for instance, Dendy, *On the Phenomena of Dreams*. In the nineteenth century, public demonstrations of trance and mediumistic phenomena were held in the same theaters in which anatomical and medical demonstrations were performed. Winter, *Mesmerized*, 73.
102. Fried, *Absorption and Theatricality*. The categories of absorption and theatricality have been employed as an interpretive frame in different fields, including film studies. See Rushton, "Early, Classical, and Modern Cinema"; Rushton, "Absorption and Theatricality in the Cinema"; Wright, "Dropping the Mask."

CHAPTER 2

1. Underhill, *Missing Link*, 34.
2. Ibid., 35. Emphasis in original.
3. Watson, *Religion of Spiritualism*, 351.
4. Braude, *Radical Spirits*, 24.
5. Cox, *Body and Soul*; Herman, "Whose Knocking?"; McGarry, *Ghosts of Futures Past*; Monroe, *Laboratories of Faith*.
6. Lewis, "Domestic Theater," 49–53.
7. See, for instance, Crookes, *Researches*, 99.
8. Doyle, *History of Spiritualism*, 1:65.
9. Berry, *Experiences in Spiritualism*, 39–166.
10. Ibid., 39.
11. *Confessions of a Medium*, 20.
12. Ibid., 22.
13. London Dialectical Society, *Report on Spiritualism*, 43.

14. Wetherbee, *Shadows*, 231.
15. Newton, "Why I Am a Spiritualist," 660.
16. Jewett, *Spiritualism and Charlatanism*, 43–46.
17. Mattison, *Spirit Rapping Unveiled!*; Jewett, *Spiritualism and Charlatanism*; Home, *Lights and Shadows of Spiritualism*; *Confessions of a Medium*.
18. Roubaud, *La danse des tables*, 47.
19. Ibid., 66.
20. Berry, *Experiences in Spiritualism*, 39.
21. As a British spiritualist noted, "Every seance should be entered into with pure, loving motives; seeking instruction, help and comfort; so that every such communion may refresh our own spirits and strengthen us to once more gird up our loins for the duties, trials and disappointments incident to our earth life." Witness, "Private Sitting," 705.
22. "Rules and Conditions for the Spirit-Circle."
23. Monroe, *Laboratories of Faith*, 21.
24. Tromp, *Altered States*; Braude, *Radical Spirits*.
25. Hall, *Spiritualists*.
26. De Morgan, *From Matter to Spirit*, xli.
27. Snow, *Spirit-Intercourse*, 34. Emphasis in original.
28. Fritz, *Where Are the Dead?*, 56.
29. Barrett, *Looking Beyond*, 18.
30. Barkas, *Outlines of Ten Years' Investigations*, 13–14.
31. "Pleasant Physical Seance."
32. Hanich, *Cinematic Emotion*.
33. Vorderer and Knobloch, "Conflict and Suspense in Drama"; Carroll, *Theorizing the Moving Image*, 94–117.
34. Cox, *Body and Soul*.
35. Hardinge Britten, *Modern American Spiritualism*, 41.
36. Hanich, *Cinematic Emotion*.
37. Investigating the reasons for the discrepancy between the benevolent spirits of nineteenth-century spiritualism and the fearful ghosts who are ubiquitous in fictional representations may help us better understand the way in which the consumption of fiction and the participation in séances provided different kinds of emotional rewards. Edgar Allan Poe, who mastered the literary genre of the ghost story in the nineteenth century, observes in *The Philosophy of Composition* that a literary work, at best, should be brief enough that it can be read in a single sitting. In fact, if two sittings are required, the intervention of other events and feelings in the reader's life will jeopardize the unity of effect—that is, the excitement of a particular emotion in the reader, which, according to Poe, is the ultimate aim of literary works and particularly of poetry. Poe's argument recalls to mind that the consumption of fiction is an experience that is structurally limited in time and that this has important repercussions for the nature of the experience and the emotional response it entails. In the case of ghost stories and horror movies, reactions of fear are perceived as pleasurable and are actively sought by readers and spectators, who would find them unpleasant and distressing in the course of ordinary life. Spiritualist séances invited a different degree of involvement. Sitters were challenged to deeply question their set of beliefs about the world and their own lives. Spiritualist séances refused to be confined, like fiction, to the boundaries of an experience limited in time. Poe, *The Raven*; with *The Philosophy of Composition*.
38. See, among others, Stolow, "Salvation by Electricity"; Sconce, *Haunted Media*; Peters, *Speaking into the Air*; Noakes, "Telegraphy Is an Occult Art."
39. An element from the Christian imagination, the idea of evangelical

broadcasting also contributed, as James Carey has shown, to shaping the conceptualization of communication in the United States beginning in the nineteenth century. Carey, *Communication as Culture*.

40. Capron, *Modern Spiritualism*.
41. Burns, "Seed Corn."
42. Tuttle, *Arcana of Spiritualism*, 431. For other examples of the broadcast metaphor in spiritualist sources, see Cox, *Spiritualism Answered by Science*, vii; Cleveland, *Religion of Modern Spiritualism*, 17.
43. Hare, *Experimental Investigation*.
44. Keene, "Domestic Science."
45. Lehman, *Victorian Women and the Theatre of Trance*, 39. See also Kaplan, "Mesmeric Mania"; Winter, *Mesmerized*.
46. McGarry, *Ghosts of Futures Past*, 29.
47. Cottom, *Abyss of Reason*, 22.
48. Roubaud, *La danse des tables*.
49. See, for instance, Gasparin, *Science vs. Modern Spiritualism*; Hayden, *On the Phenomena of Modern Spiritualism*.
50. See Noakes, "Telegraphy Is an Occult Art."
51. Cox, *Body and Soul*, 84.
52. Hartman, *Facts and Mysteries of Spiritism*, 20.
53. On the way in which spiritualist circles were equated with a circuit of magnetic and electric relations, see Sconce, *Haunted Media*, 28–35.
54. Cottom, *Abyss of Reason*, 28.
55. Gasparin, *Science vs. Modern Spiritualism*, x.
56. Watson, *Religion of Spiritualism*, 59.
57. Hare, *Experimental Investigation*, 21.
58. Hofer, *Games We Played*.
59. Van Rensselaer, *Devil's Picture-Books*, 41–42.
60. Huizinga, *Homo Ludens*.
61. Fritz, *Where Are the Dead?*, 62.
62. Henck, *Spirit Voices*.
63. Connor, "Machine in the Ghost," 208. Emphasis in original.
64. *Confessions of a Medium*, 34.
65. Houghton, *Evenings at Home in Spiritual Séance*, 13.
66. Ibid., 13–14. Emphasis in original.
67. Hardinge Britten, *Modern American Spiritualism*, 110.
68. Berry, *Experiences in Spiritualism*, 45–98.
69. Ibid., 97.
70. Hardinge Britten, *Modern American Spiritualism*, 110–12.
71. Duguid, *Hafed Prince of Persia*.
72. Houghton, *Chronicles of the Photographs*.
73. Bartlett, "Mirth as Medium."
74. Hartman, *Facts and Mysteries of Spiritism*, 21.
75. Owen, *Debatable Land*, 367. Robert Dale Owen was the son of the famous social reformer Robert Owen and a socialist reformist himself.
76. Mattison, *Spirit Rapping Unveiled!*, 148–49.
77. Lamont, "Magician as Conjuror."
78. Houghton, *Evenings at Home in Spiritual Séance*, 3.
79. Moore, *In Search of White Crows*, 17.
80. Lewis, *Modern Magic*.
81. The concept of sensation has been employed in scholarship on Victorian spectacles to underline the constant appeal to the senses that characterized spectacular attractions as well as lectures and exhibitions of scientific and technological novelties. As Iwan Rhys Morus observes, "The language of sensation is a constant throughout nineteenth-century descriptions of scientific phenomena. By and large, the vocabulary used is one that engages with the senses quite directly." Morus, "Worlds of Wonder," 808. See also Diamond, *Victorian Sensation*.
82. Lewis, "Domestic Theater," 58.
83. Dumont, *Lady's Oracle*, 7.
84. Gutierrez, *Plato's Ghost*, 56.
85. Hare, *Experimental Investigation*, iii.

86. See Hazen, *Village Enlightenment in America*, 83–105; Lightman, *Victorian Popularizers of Science*; Fyfe and Lightman, *Science in the Marketplace*.
87. Hare, *Experimental Investigation*.
88. Noakes, "Cromwell Varley"; Noakes, "Telegraphy Is an Occult Art."
89. Ellis, *Lucifer Ascending*, 180.
90. Field, *Planchette's Diary*; Cottrell, *Revelations*; Sargent, *Planchette*. The history of the planchette and its commercialization is discussed more thoroughly in chapter 5.
91. American collector and researcher Brandon Hodge has compiled a list of patents filed in the United States for spiritualism-related instruments and toys. See his website *Mysterious Planchette*, at http://www.mysterious-planchette.com/Patents/patents.html (accessed July 2015).
92. These were mentioned, for instance, in advertisements for the psychograph, an inexpensive instrument produced by the spiritualist entrepreneur Hudson Tuttle in the United States in the early 1880s. Its price was one dollar, and it was sent postpaid from Tuttle's address in Ohio. See "The Psychograph."
93. The Ouija board is still marketed today as a game board. Another interesting contemporary toy inspired by beliefs in the supernatural is the Magic 8 Ball, a very simple game introduced in the 1950s and marketed today by Mattel. The ball mimics the tradition of clairvoyance and spiritualist séances, providing answers to yes-or-no questions. Similar toys presently on the market are sold under the names Mystic Eye and Aye-See.
94. "Toy or Game," U.S. Patent 446,054, filed 28 May 1890, granted 10 February 1891.
95. "Danziger's Ouija"; "Ouija, or Wonderful Talking Board."
96. Cornelius, *Aleister Crowley and the Ouija Board*, 18–22; McRobbie, "Strange and Mysterious History."
97. Myrick, "Belief and Custom," 11–19.
98. See Mick LaSalle's (very negative) review of the film, published in the *San Francisco Chronicle*; it is available online as "'Ouija' Review: Is This a Bad Movie? Y.E.S.," *SFGate*, 23 October 2014, http://www.sfgate.com/movies/article/Ouija-a-horror-movie-take-on-an-old-board-5842666.php (accessed 12 January 2015).
99. Brewster, *Stereoscope*, 204. Quite interestingly, skeptics pointed to the illusory techniques explained by Brewster in order to explain spiritualist phenomena and expose them as fraudulent. Page, *Psychomancy*, 43.
100. Willis, "On Wonder"; Fyfe and Lightman, *Science in the Marketplace*.
101. Brewster, *Letters on Natural Magic*.
102. During, *Modern Enchantments*.
103. Newton, "Why I Am a Spiritualist," 654.
104. Herman, "Whose Knocking?," 432.
105. Dulac and Gaudreault, "Circularity and Repetition."
106. Fritz, *Where Are the Dead?*, 43.
107. Ibid., 42–43.
108. Horton, "Were They Having Fun Yet?," 12.
109. Meyrowitz, *No Sense of Place*.
110. For some instances, see Mannoni, *Le grand art*; Pesenti Compagnoni, *Quando il cinema non c'era*; Ceram, *Archaeology of the Cinema*.
111. On media archaeology, see Huhtamo and Parikka, *Media Archaeology*.

CHAPTER 3

1. Podmore, *Modern Spiritualism*, 61.
2. Berg, *Spirits a Fraud*, 23.
3. Doyle, *History of Spiritualism*, 1:83.
4. Capron, *Modern Spiritualism*, 318–19. Arthur Conan Doyle noted, too, that after the publication of this report,

"much testimony in support of the Fox sisters was quickly forthcoming, and the only effect of the professors' 'exposure' was to redouble the public interest in the manifestations." Doyle, *History of Spiritualism*, 1:83.
5. Capron, *Modern Spiritualism*, 319.
6. Cook, *Arts of Deception*.
7. Lewis, *From Traveling Show to Vaudeville*; Altick, *Shows of London*.
8. Lears, *Fables of Abundance*; Diamond, *Victorian Sensation*. Lears argues that the culture of advertisement in America had to do not only with the rising social status that consumer goods carried, but also with the appeal of magical practices for Americans. The fact that magic elixirs were one of the earliest and most successful advertised products suggests that a sense of the wonderful also drove the public's appetite for sensationalism.
9. This was the case, for instance, with "gaffed freaks" such as the Siamese twins, who were in reality two separate persons, and the bearded woman, whose beard was fake. Bogdan, *Freak Show*, 8–10. On freak show performances in the British context, see Tromp, *Victorian Freaks*.
10. Garland Thomson, *Freakery*, 5.
11. Lamont, *First Psychic*; Nichols, *Biography of the Brothers Davenport*.
12. Baldasty, *Commercialization of News*.
13. Fretz, "P. T. Barnum's Theatrical Selfhood," 101.
14. See, for instance, Toll, *On with the Show!*; Springhall, *Genesis of Mass Culture*.
15. See Adams, *E Pluribus Barnum*, 1–5; Harris, *Humbug*, 21–27; Cook, *Arts of Deception*, 1–29; Reiss, "P. T. Barnum, Joice Heth."
16. Brazeal, "Precursor to Modern Media Hype."
17. Cook, *Arts of Deception*, 3. See also Sussman, "Performing the Intelligent Machine"; Leja, *Looking Askance*; During, *Modern Enchantments*.
18. Barnum, *Life of P. T. Barnum*, 157.
19. Ibid.
20. Barnum, *Humbugs of the World*, 61.
21. Adams, *E Pluribus Barnum*, 81; Harris, *Humbug*, 74–79.
22. Barnum, *Humbugs of the World*, 117. On spirit photography, see chapter 5.
23. Fretz, "P. T. Barnum's Theatrical Selfhood," 97. Barnum's interest in spiritualism became the subject of public reports and speculation in 1869. That year, Mumler was brought to trial under accusations of having fraudulently produced his photographs of ghosts; Barnum was called to testify before the court, participating in a lively public debate on spiritualism and fraud. The showman reported on his correspondence with Mumler, who sent him two spirit photographs that were later exhibited on the museum wall. As Michael Leja insightfully noted, when Mumler's defense attorney asked Barnum whether he had, as a public entertainer, presented to his audiences anything that was untrue, "he was only asking why Mumler should be prosecuted for doing the same. Why would a society reward one entertaining charlatan and send another to prison?" Leja, *Looking Askance*, 54.
24. Rice also courted and publicized his problems with the law. He claimed, in fact, to actually enjoy being arrested by the police, which was "the cheapest and most effective advertising my shows could get." Toll, *On with the Show!*, 61.
25. Bogdan, *Freak Show*, 226.
26. Nadis, *Wonder Shows*, 11. On the role of imitation and challenges in American vaudeville, see Glenn, "Give an Imitation of Me."
27. Booth, *Theatre in the Victorian Age*, 20.
28. Diamond, *Victorian Sensation*.

29. See Rubery, *Novelty of Newspapers*; Anderson, *Printed Image*.
30. Anderson, *Printed Image*, 84–118.
31. See Qureshi, *Peoples on Parade*, 101–25; Booth, *Theatre in the Victorian Age*, 27–35; Durbach, *Spectacle of Deformity*.
32. Diamond, *Victorian Sensation*, 248.
33. Altick, *Shows of London*, 423.
34. Fyfe and Lightman, *Science in the Marketplace*; Lightman, *Victorian Popularizers of Science*; Morus, "Worlds of Wonder."
35. Lightman, *Victorian Popularizers of Science*, 168. See also Brooker, "Polytechnic Ghost"; Gunning, "To Scan a Ghost."
36. Kassung, "Selbstschreiber und elektrische Gespenster." Electrical demonstrations were paramount in the nineteenth century, featuring effects that aimed at astonishing the public. Morus, *Frankenstein's Children*.
37. Winter, *Mesmerized*, 112–17; Parssinen, "Mesmeric Performers."
38. This was the case, for instance, with the polemics surrounding Mollie Francher, the "fasting girl" who was believed to have eaten almost nothing for more than ten years, from 1866 to 1878, and claimed to be able to communicate with spirits in the otherworld. After the story of her fast and mediumship hit the pages of the *New York Sun* in November 1878 with the sensational headline "Dead and yet Alive!," American newspapers competed in giving different evaluations of the case. See Stacey, *Fasting Girl*.
39. Natale, "Spiritualism Exposed."
40. On the role of controversies in the history of spiritualism and mediumistic practices, see ibid.; Schüttpelz, "Mediumismus und moderne Medien"; Walker, "Humbug in American Religion." A similar role of controversies has been noted by David J. Hess in reference to parapsychology and the New Age movement. Hess, *Science in the New Age*.
41. Doyle, *History of Spiritualism*, 1:78–79. In a funambulist move, Doyle, a committed believer in spirit communication, commented, "It is amazing to think that people, blinded by prejudice, should be so credulous as to imagine that [the Fox sisters' mediumship] was all the result of deception" (1:84).
42. Capron, *Modern Spiritualism*, 96.
43. *History of Monroe County*, 87.
44. Underhill, *Missing Link*, 196.
45. Turner, Bonner, and Marshall, "Producing Celebrity."
46. See Capron, *Modern Spiritualism*.
47. Capron and Barron, *Singular Revelations*, iii.
48. Doyle, *History of Spiritualism*, 1:83.
49. Isaacs, "Fox Sisters," 85.
50. Underhill, *Missing Link*, 128.
51. Ibid., 128–29.
52. Williams, *Horace Greeley*, 122.
53. Isaacs, "Fox Sisters," 90–91.
54. Capron, *Modern Spiritualism*, 175.
55. The *New York Tribune* participated in the surge of the penny papers, while at the same time publishing writings by many leading intellectuals of its age. Tuchinsky, *Horace Greeley's New-York Tribune*.
56. "Horace Greeley was our first caller. He advised us to charge five dollars admission fee. I told him that would be altogether too much; but he feared greatly for our safety, and thought this exorbitant sum would keep the rabble away." Underhill, *Missing Link*, 128. See Chapin, *Exploring Other Worlds*, 83.
57. Cornell, *Life and Public Career*, 214–16. In the following fall, Kate Fox returned to the house to live for some months with the family. Braude, *Radical Spirits*, 16–17.
58. Williams, *Horace Greeley*, 118–23.

59. Mattison, *Spirit Rapping Unveiled!*, 150. On the connections between spiritualism and the history of transoceanic telegraphy, see Noakes, "Telegraphy Is an Occult Art."
60. Greeley, *Autobiography*, 241.
61. See, for instance, Underhill, *Missing Link*, 446; Hardinge Britten, *Modern American Spiritualism*, 71–72. It was thanks to Greeley that P. T. Barnum and the Fox sisters indirectly crossed paths during this period. Greeley invited the Swedish singer Jenny Lind, who was touring the United States under P. T. Barnum's auspices as the "Swedish Nightingale," to attend one of the séances held at Greeley's farm. During the séance, Lind accused the journalist of tipping the table with his own hands, an accusation he indignantly denied. Van Deusen, *Horace Greeley*, 153; Zabriskie, *Horace Greeley*, 174.
62. Greeley, "Philosophy of Advertising," 582.
63. Ibid. This line is cited, for instance, in Lears, *Fables of Abundance*, 89.
64. Hartman, *Facts and Mysteries of Spiritism*, 66.
65. On the role of historical tradition and legacy in shaping the experience of spiritualists, see Bender, *New Metaphysicals*.
66. Podmore, *Modern Spiritualism*, 4. Maria Hayden's "staff" also included a Mr. Stone, who was an expert in "electrobiology"—the art of inducing hypnotism by gazing at metallic discs. Stone's lectures introduced the medium's public exhibitions.
67. Doyle, *History of Spiritualism*, 1:144. For a careful account of the coverage of Hayden's case in the British press, see Podmore, *Modern Spiritualism*, 4–8.
68. Faraday, "Table-Turning."
69. Crookes, *Researches*. Crookes had discovered the element thallium in 1861. His first work on spiritualism was published in the *Quarterly Journal of Science* in July 1870. See also Hall, *Spiritualists*.
70. Luckhurst, *Invention of Telepathy*, 117–46.
71. See Lee, *Origins of the Popular Press*; Campbell, "W. E. Gladstone, W. T. Stead, Matthew Arnold."
72. Eckley, "Borderland."
73. Sword, *Ghostwriting Modernism*, 20.
74. Schüttpelz, "Mediumismus und moderne Medien."
75. As early as 1853, for instance, a booklet was published that informed its readers about the deceptive character of spirit rappings: "Nothing is more easy than to deceive completely, by calling the attention of persons present to sounds from a certain position or direction, while in reality the sounds are made elsewhere and in a remote quarter." Page, *Psychomancy*, 43.
76. Walker, "Humbug in American Religion."
77. Ibid.
78. Chapin, *Exploring Other Worlds*, 92–94.
79. Walker, "Humbug in American Religion," 37.
80. Barnouw, *The Magician and the Cinema*; Solomon, *Disappearing Tricks*; Natale, "Cinema of Exposure."
81. Weatherly, *Supernatural?*, 190.
82. Maskelyne, *Modern Spiritualism*, 66.
83. Cook, *Arts of Deception*, 199.
84. During, *Modern Enchantments*, 71.
85. Houdini, *Magician Among the Spirits*, 12. Houdini, one of the most celebrated antispiritualist crusaders, occasionally relied on the ambiguous character of spectacular spiritualist demonstrations: at the outset of his career, he conducted phony spiritualist séances in the American Midwest. These performances involved phenomena such as table

movements, self-playing accordions, and the appearance of spirit faces. Nadis, *Wonder Shows*, 122.
86. Salamanca, *Fortress of Freedom*, 325.
87. McLean, *American Vaudeville*, 157.
88. Maskelyne, *Modern Spiritualism*, 66.
89. During, *Modern Enchantments*, 71.
90. See, for instance, North, *Performing Illusions*; Mangan, *Performing Dark Arts*.
91. Nadis, *Wonder Shows*, 120.
92. Burns, "Seed Corn," 2.
93. See Lamont, "Magician as Conjuror."
94. This case is discussed at length in Walker, "Humbug in American Religion," 41–45. For a transcription of a trance lecture performed by Bly, see Bly, *Errors Corrected*.
95. "Dr. Martin Van Buren Bly and the Times."
96. Harris, *Humbug*, 68–89.
97. Ibid., 75. This public taste for exposure of frauds and humbugs in nineteenth-century America is also evident in literature. P. T. Barnum's autobiography, as well as his book *The Humbugs of the World*, a collection of reports about frauds and hoaxes, were hugely popular in the nineteenth century. Along similar lines, Edgar Allan Poe devoted an essay to revealing the fraud behind Maelzel's chess player. Poe's literary works often depicted the act of exposing a deceit: this is the case, for instance, in "The Purloined Letter" and "The Murders in the Rue Morgue." See Tresch, "Potent Magic of Verisimilitude"; Harris, *Humbug*, 87.
98. Harris, *Humbug*.
99. Walker, "Humbug in American Religion," 55.
100. See, for instance, Newton, "Why I Am a Spiritualist," 663. For some examples of professions of firm skepticism, see Wolfe, *Startling Facts in Modern Spiritualism*, 77; Wetherbee, *Shadows*, 69.
101. See, among others, Moore, *In Search of White Crows*; Braude, *Radical Spirits*; Stolow, "Salvation by Electricity."
102. Taussig, "Viscerality, Faith, and Skepticism," 222. See also Walker, "Humbug in American Religion."

CHAPTER 4

1. Manganelli, *Le interviste impossibili*. I would like to thank Domenico Scarpa for directing my attention to this text.
2. The most famous mediums sometimes published autobiographies. See, among others, Home, *Incidents in My Life*; Morse, *Leaves from My Life*; Alvarado, "Eusapia Palladino."
3. Take, for instance, Doyle, *History of Spiritualism*.
4. Nolan, *Film, Lacan, and the Subject of Religion*. On religion and celebrity culture, see also Rojek, "Celebrity and Religion"; Howells, "Heroes, Saints, and Celebrities"; Ward, *Gods Behaving Badly*; Chidester, *Authentic Fakes*.
5. Morgan, "Historicising Celebrity," 367. See also Berlanstein, "Historicizing and Gendering Celebrity Culture"; Inglis, *Short History of Celebrity*; Mole, *Romanticism and Celebrity Culture*; Morgan, "Celebrity."
6. Richards, *Commodity Culture*, 255.
7. For some recent attempts to apply celebrity theory to the study of historical figures prior to the rise of classical cinema, see McDayter, *Byromania*; Inglis, *Short History of Celebrity*; Blake, *Walt Whitman*; Berenson and Giloi, *Constructing Charisma*; Carnevali, *Romantisme et reconnaissance*.
8. Braudy, *Frenzy of Renown*, 5. Emphasis mine.
9. Inglis, *Short History of Celebrity*.
10. The definition of celebrity as a "representational technology" comes from Blake, *Walt Whitman*, 57. See also Morgan, "Celebrity."

11. For a useful survey of literature on celebrity and consumer culture, see Marshall, *Celebrity Culture Reader*.
12. Braudy, "Secular Anointings."
13. Berenson and Giloi, *Constructing Charisma*, 2.
14. See Dinius, *The Camera and the Press*; Siegel, "Daguerreotypie auf Papier." As Leo Braudy underlines, graphic caricatures not only anticipated but also accompanied photography in the visual representation of celebrities throughout the nineteenth century. Braudy, "Secular Anointings," 178.
15. Blake, *Walt Whitman*, 36.
16. Lightman, *Victorian Popularizers of Science*. See also Browne, "Charles Darwin as a Celebrity."
17. Blake, *Walt Whitman*, 29–31; Booth, *Theatre in the Victorian Age*, 20.
18. Diamond, *Victorian Sensation*, 248–85.
19. Luckhurst and Moody, *Theatre and Celebrity in Britain*; Browne, "Charles Darwin as a Celebrity"; Easley, *Literary Celebrity*; Morgan, "Material Culture."
20. McDayter, *Byromania*.
21. Blake, *Walt Whitman*.
22. Cook, *Arts of Deception*.
23. Barnum's autobiography, for instance, was reprinted numberless times and was one of the greatest editorial successes of Victorian America, functioning as the perfect vehicle to make his name known throughout the country. Barnum's capacity to capitalize on the notoriety of others is probably best exemplified by the character of General Tom Thumb. Born Charles Sherwood Stratton, Thumb was a dwarf whom the showman hired to perform a series of feats, such as dancing and impersonating famous characters, and brought to international fame as a performer. In order to give him more appeal as an attraction, Barnum embellished several details about Thumb, including his name, title, age, appearance, and personal story, and he designed strategies to meet the expectations of specific audiences. During the 1856 tour in Britain, for instance, he successfully heralded the contrast between Thumb's appearance and his high countenance and good manners, which would be particularly appreciated, Barnum felt, in Britain. The fabrication of Thumb's celebrity also included publicity of his marriage to Lavinia Warren, also a dwarf. The grandiosity of their wedding reception in New York and the couple's subsequent visit with President Lincoln at the White House made headlines in many newspapers and popular magazines. See *Sketch of the Life*. See also Henderson, "From Barnum to 'Bling Bling.'"
24. Morse, *Leaves from My Life*, 39–59.
25. See, for instance, the discussion of Eusapia Palladino's tour in the United States below. Her arrival there in 1909 was greeted as a major event in the community of spiritualists, while many skeptics took up the challenge of debunking her mediumship and arranged to take part in one of her séances.
26. Carlson, *Haunted Stage*; Roach, *Cities of the Dead*; McPherson, "Siddons Rediviva."
27. Carlson, *Haunted Stage*, 59.
28. Braudy, *Frenzy of Renown*, 6.
29. For instance, Benjamin Franklin was one of the most frequently conjured spirits in early spiritualist séances in America. In 1852, the spirit of Franklin reportedly sent a message to a spiritualist circle in which he suggested that spirit communication was performed through a device that he invented in the spirit world. Sconce, *Haunted Media*, 38. An interesting example of a cinematic

star who spiritually resurfaced after his death is Rudolph Valentino; he appeared in the séances of medium Carla McKinstry in the late 1920s. See Alovisio and Carluccio, *Intorno a Rodolfo Valentino*, 192–93.
30. Edmunds, *Spiritualism*, 47.
31. Crookes, *Researches*, 110.
32. Marryat, *There Is No Death*, 112–13.
33. Carlson, *Haunted Stage*.
34. Tromp, *Altered States*, 32.
35. Rojek, *Celebrity*, 13–17.
36. Lowenthal, "Triumph of Mass Idols." Biographies of mediums are discussed more broadly, as a sort of literary genre, in chapter 5.
37. Di Bello, "Elizabeth Thompson."
38. Morgan, "Material Culture."
39. Dyer, *Stars*, 35.
40. Private life is central to the construction of the emotional link between a celebrity and her fans, and it interacts in complex ways with the fictional character she portrays. An actor famous for his irregular way of life, for instance, could be particularly suited to play the role of a man who redeems his previous errors by committing a heroic act of generosity.
41. As Chris Rojek put it, "Celebrity status implies a split between a private self and a public self." Rojek, *Celebrity*, 11.
42. Isaacs, "Fox Sisters."
43. On the most famous admission of trickery by the Fox sisters, see Davenport, *Death Blow to Spiritualism*. On Margaret Fox's troubled sentimental affair with the Arctic explorer Elisha Kent Kane, see Chapin, *Exploring Other Worlds*.
44. Doyle, *History of Spiritualism*, 1:92.
45. "Departure of Mrs. Fox Jencken to America."
46. Nunn and Biressi, "'Trust Betrayed.'"
47. Diamond, *Victorian Sensation*, 269.
48. Celeste, "Screen Idols," 32.
49. Tromp, *Altered States*, 97–110.
50. Owen, *Darkened Room*, 57–59.
51. Armstrong, "Mrs. Mellon and the Newcastle Society."
52. Tromp, *Altered States*, 109–13; Hall, *Spiritualists*.
53. Roberts, "Rethinking Female Celebrities."
54. Rojek, *Celebrity*, 10. See also Turner, Bonner, and Marshall, "Producing Celebrity."
55. Lamont, "Magician as Conjuror," 23.
56. It might be worth noting, in this regard, that questions of authenticity are raised not only by supernatural phenomena such as spiritualist mediumship, but also by celebrity status. A celebrity's public image is staged by managers and represented through the media in such a way as to stimulate, almost inevitably, questions about the genuineness of this image. See Rojek, *Celebrity*, 17.
57. Alvarado, "Bottazzi and Palladino," 159.
58. Historian of Italian spiritualism Massimo Biondi estimates that, out of all the mediums in the history of the movement, Eusapia Palladino may have been the subject of the largest mass of reports and articles. Biondi, *Tavoli e medium*, 133.
59. Dingwall, "Eusapia Palladino," 178.
60. De Rochas, *L'extériorisation de la motricité*, 16. As noted above, John King was presumed to be the father of Katie King, the female spirit evoked by the medium Florence Cook, who in the 1870s famously convinced William Crookes, one of Britain's leading chemists, of the authenticity of spiritualist claims.
61. Dingwall, "Eusapia Palladino," 180.
62. Biondi, "L'occulto portato in evidenza," 96–97.
63. Brisson, "Une soirée avec Eusapia Paladino," 2.
64. Alvarado, "Eusapia Palladino," 80.

65. Carrington, *Eusapia Palladino and Her Phenomena*, 19. The rumors about Palladino's involvement with stage magic are also discussed in Blondel, "Eusapia Palladino."
66. Morselli, *Psicologia e spiritismo*, 2:11. Morselli also observed that her need to defeat doubts and suspicions made her manifestations stronger and spectacular at first, but they became monotonous after some time, once she knew that she had convinced her sitters. Similar to an accomplished performer, then, Palladino constantly needed new audiences to stimulate her. See also Brancaccio, "Enrico Morselli's Psychology and 'Spiritism.'"
67. Gustave Le Bon, who sat at Palladino's séance table in 1898, reported, "Eusapia is undoubtedly a marvellous subject. It struck me as something wonderful that, while I was holding her hand, she was playing on an imaginary tambourine to which the sounds of the tambourine that was behind the curtain accurately corresponded." Flammarion, *Mysterious Psychic Forces*, 101.
68. Carrington, *Eusapia Palladino and Her Phenomena*, 3.
69. Blondel, "Eusapia Palladino."
70. Carrington, *Eusapia Palladino and Her Phenomena*, 21.
71. See, for instance, Barzini, *Nel mondo dei misteri con Eusapia Palladino*. Lombroso described Palladino as a "vulgar person." Lombroso, "Sui fenomeni spiritici e la loro interpretazione," 984.
72. Arullani, *Sulla medianità di Eusapia Palladino*, 39.
73. Biondi, *Tavoli e medium*, 154.
74. Morselli, *Psicologia e spiritismo*, 2:15.
75. Arullani, *Sulla medianità di Eusapia Palladino*, 13.
76. Alvarado, "Eusapia Palladino," 81; Sommer, "Psychical Research," 26.
77. Carrington, "Eusapia Palladino."
78. Her manager was reportedly "trying to arrange an American premier for the Italian woman where seats will be 200 $ each." "Paladino Tells about Her Stunts." For sources stating that Palladino was paid, see, among others, "Remarks About Eusapia Palladino"; Myers, *Beyond the Borderline of Life*.
79. Doyle, *History of Spiritualism*, 2:192.
80. In 1888, Chiaia attended the Congrès International Spirite in Barcelona, where he publicly read a letter issuing a challenge to Lombroso. The following year, he took part in the most important reunion of spiritualists at the end of the century, the Congrès Spirite et Spiritualiste International in Paris, giving a lecture on Palladino's mediumship that was published in the conference's proceedings. Chiaia, "Expériences médianimiques"; Chiaia, "Un défi à la science."
81. After Chiaia's death in 1905, Palladino's privileged relationship with the popular press continued. In a particularly famous example, two series of sittings that she conducted in Milan in 1906 were related by the prominent journalist Luigi Barzini in *Il Corriere della Sera*. In his articles, later collected in a book, Barzini explained that he was convinced to take part in these séances by the endorsement of Lombroso and by the "international reputation" of the medium. The numerous letters sent to *Il Corriere* upon the publication of his reports demonstrate both the enthusiasm and the discomfort generated among readers by such unusual pieces of journalism. Barzini, *Nel mondo dei misteri con Eusapia Palladino*.
82. Scholars have questioned the reasons that motivated Lombroso's conversion. As his friend and biographer

Hans Kurella suggested, during his scientific career, Lombroso suffered from the contempt of other scholars before his theories started to be taken seriously by the academic establishment. For this reason, he may have had fewer reservations than others about radically new theories and facts. Kurella, *Cesare Lombroso*, 167–76. Kurella's argument is supported by the media archaeologist Siegfried Zielinski, who noted that Lombroso was frequently the butt of ridicule by colleagues and institutions. Zielinski observed that "this ridicule gave him a heightened sensibility, which made him avoid discriminating against forms of knowledge other than those that he practiced professionally." Zielinski, *Deep Time of the Media*, 226. On Lombroso, see also Knepper and Ystehede, *Cesare Lombroso Handbook*.
83. As Arthur Conan Doyle reported, for instance, the Russian Alexandr Aksakov enthusiastically congratulated Chiaia in a personal letter: "Glory to M. Lombroso for his noble words! Glory to you for your devotion!" Doyle, *History of Spiritualism*, 2:193.
84. Alvarado, "Eusapia Palladino," 82.
85. Chiaia, "Una sfida per la scienza." As French parapsychologist Albert de Rochas noted, the letter was beautifully written "to excite the curiosity of the reader." de Rochas, *L'extériorisation de la motricité*, 8.
86. Blondel, "Eusapia Palladino," 144. As Carrington argues, "No other medium, producing 'physical phenomena,' has been studied with so much care, for so long a period, and by so many scientific men, as she." Carrington, *Eusapia Palladino and Her Phenomena*, 1.
87. The French astronomer Camille Flammarion, for instance, distinctly recalled the name of "Professor Chiaia, of Naples, to whom I owe it that I was able to receive Eusapia at my house and obtain the experiments reported above." Flammarion, *Mysterious Psychic Forces*, 135.
88. The Curies, however, refused to endorse Palladino after the experimental séances held at the Institut Général Psychologique in Paris from 1905 to 1908. Quinn, *Marie Curie*, 208–26.
89. Lombroso, *After Death—What?*; Lombroso, "Sui fenomeni spiritici e la loro interpretazione."
90. Richet, *Traité de métapsychique*, 5. Scientists such as de Rochas and Morselli followed suit. Morselli, *Psicologia e spiritismo*; de Rochas, *L'extériorisation de la motricité*.
91. Arullani, *Sulla medianità di Eusapia Palladino*, 32–33. On the relationship between X-rays and beliefs in the supernatural, see Natale, "Invisible Made Visible," 352–55; Natale, "Cosmology of Invisible Fluids"; Grove, "Röntgen's Ghosts."
92. Richet, *Traité de métapsychique*, 38–39.
93. Ibid., 530.
94. When Ercole Chiaia passed away in 1905, a solemn ceremony was held in his memory in Naples. Psychical researchers came from all regions of Italy to attend. Cesare Lombroso was not among them, but he sent a letter that praised, with inspired words, Chiaia's merits: "You are right to honour highly the memory of Ercole Chiaia. In a country where there is such a horror of what is new, it required great courage and a noble soul, to become the apostle of theories which have met even with ridicule, and to do so with that tenacity, that energy, which always characterised Chiaia. It is to him that many owe—(myself among others)—the privilege of seeing a new world open out to our psychical investigation—and this by

the only way which exists to convince men of culture, that is to say, by direct observation." "Tributes to the Memory of Ercole Chiaia," 261.

95. The funds that paid for Palladino's trip to America were obtained from donors, with the pledge, in many cases, that her mediumship would be properly investigated by scientific men: "Some subscribers made it a condition of their donation that the case be seen only by scientific men. This pledge was not kept and the very first thing done was to take the case before the newspaper reporters and to reveal the fact that magazine articles were at the base of the enterprise." Hyslop, "Eusapia Palladino," 170.

96. The American Society for Psychical Research was founded in 1885, three years after its British counterpart, the Society for Psychical Research. Regarded today as "one of the most prolific popularisers in the history of psychical research," Carrington was the author of many successful books on parapsychology and related topics and a well-known figure in early twentieth-century spiritualism. Alvarado and Nahm, "Psychic Phenomena," 94. Among his publications, besides *Eusapia Palladino and Her Phenomena* (1909), it is worth mentioning Carrington, *Coming Science*; Carrington, *Problems of Psychical Research*.

97. See Alvarado, "Eusapia Palladino," 91–92.

98. "Weird Scenes on Ocean Liner."

99. The *New York Times* explicitly mentioned that Carrington was "managing her interests in this country." "Paladino Tells About Her Stunts."

100. Ibid.

101. "Her Force Only Magnetic?"

102. "Extension of Human Faculty."

103. Palladino, "My Own Story."

104. Alvarado, "Eusapia Palladino," 77.

105. On the racialization of stars of Italian origin in America, see Alovisio and Carluccio, *Intorno a Rodolfo Valentino*; Dalle Vacche, *Diva*.

106. Corbett, "Performing Identities."

107. "Spirits at Sea."

108. "Topics of the Times."

109. "Spirits at Sea."

110. Kerscheval, "Mme. Palladino."

111. "Woman's World."

112. He had come close, however, to arranging for a sitting with medium Leonora Piper in 1899. Sommer, "Psychical Research," 30.

113. Münsterberg, "Psychology and Mysticism," 78.

114. This book has often been republished with the title *The Film: A Psychological Study*. See Münsterberg, *Film*. For a discussion of Münsterberg's contribution to film theory, see Bruno, "Film, Aesthetics, Science"; Carroll, "Film/Mind Analogies"; Wicclair, "Film Theory."

115. Münsterberg, *Film*, viii.

116. Münsterberg, *American Problems*.

117. Ibid., 144. Münsterberg's essay relating his exposure of Eusapia Palladino was originally published in the *Metropolitan Magazine* in 1910, under the title "My Friends the Spiritualists: Some Theories and Conclusions Concerning Eusapia Palladino."

118. In the history of spiritualism, mediums often demonstrated a surprising ability to survive public exposures. A common argument was that they might sometimes trick, but that did not mean that all of their manifestations were false. For instance, the French astronomer and committed spiritualist believer Camille Flammarion candidly admitted in 1907 "that during the last forty years, almost all the celebrated mediums have been present at one time or another in my salon in the avenue of the

Observatoire in Paris, and that I have detected them nearly all in trickery"—only to add that this did not mean "that they always deceive; those who affirm this are wrong." Flammarion, *Mysterious Psychic Forces*, 63–64. This thesis helped many mediums, including Eusapia Palladino, to survive even the most disgraceful of exposés. The Italian medium was able, on many occasions, to revitalize her reputation. As historian Massimo Biondi notes, the alternation of triumphs and shameful exposures was a recurrent pattern throughout her long career. Each time, Palladino found a way to overcome these scandals and punctually reappeared with reinvigorated grandeur. Biondi, *Tavoli e medium*, 100.
119. Sommer, "Psychical Research," 28. As Biondi points out, the decisive character of Münsterberg's debunking might be due to the fact that the medium was lacking an adviser as capable as Ercole Chiaia. Biondi, *Tavoli e medium*, 158.
120. Jastrow, "Unmasking of Palladino"; Davis, "New York Exposure"; Miller, "Palladino's Tricks."
121. Davis, "New York Exposure," 423.
122. Carrington, "Would Bolster Up Palladino's Case." See also Myers, *Beyond the Borderline of Life*, 147.
123. A similar argument had been used by some of Palladino's supporters after a negative report was written about her experimental séances conducted in Cambridge in 1895 before members of the Society for Psychical Research. The renowned psychical researcher Julien Ochorowicz, for one, strenuously defended her, arguing that while there were traces of trickery in her performances—which had also been detected in her longer series of experimental séances in Italy, Poland, and France—most of these should be attributed to "unconscious fraud." Ochorowicz, "La question de la fraude," 97–101. Similar commentaries were frequently issued in connection to Palladino's mediumship: see, for instance, Dariex, "Que doit-on penser." On Ochorowicz's intervention, see also Alvarado, "Ochorowicz on Eusapia Palladino."
124. Alvarado, "Eusapia Palladino," 82.
125. Berenson and Giloi, *Constructing Charisma*, 15.
126. Roberts, "Rethinking Female Celebrities."
127. Braude, *Radical Spirits*; Owen, *Darkened Room*.
128. Braude, *Radical Spirits*, 82.
129. Dalle Vacche, *Diva*, 6.
130. "Palladino Talks to the Reporters."
131. Kaufman, *Consuming Visions*.
132. Noakes, "Instruments," 131–32.
133. On the celebrity culture of Victorian science, see Browne, "Charles Darwin as a Celebrity"; Lightman, *Victorian Popularizers of Science*.

CHAPTER 5

1. Burns, "Seed Corn," 1.
2. Ibid.
3. Brake, *Print in Transition*; Eisenstein, *Printing Revolution*; Stolow, *Orthodox by Design*, 20–21.
4. Geary, "Domestic Novel," 366–67.
5. On the rise of the book as a commodity in Britain, see McKitterick, *Cambridge History of the Book*.
6. Lehuu, *Carnival on the Page*, 17; Rubery, *Novelty of Newspapers*.
7. Boyer and Cohen, *Religion and the Culture of Print*, 5.
8. Bann, "Ghostly Hands," 673.
9. Bennett, "Spirited Away."
10. Gomel, "'Spirits in the Material World,'" 198. Additionally, scholars such as Emily D. Edwards and Sabine Doering-Manteuffel have studied the ways in which spiritualism and

occultism were used and elaborated by popular culture. Edwards, *Metaphysical Media*; Doering-Manteuffel, *Das Okkulte*.
11. Braude, *Radical Spirits*.
12. Davis, *Present Age and Inner Life*.
13. Wetherbee, *Shadows*.
14. Fritz, *Where Are the Dead?*
15. Braude, *Radical Spirits*, 26.
16. Podmore, *Modern Spiritualism*, 165.
17. Burns, "Seed Corn." See also Oppenheim, *Other World*, 45; Lavoie, *Theosophical Society*, 152–53; Owen, *Darkened Room*, 24.
18. Burns, "Seed Corn," 2.
19. Ibid.
20. Hardinge Britten, *Modern American Spiritualism*.
21. "Beautiful Artistic Design."
22. Gaunt, "Henry Bielfeld," 6.
23. "Subscription Price." See Henkin, *Postal Age*.
24. "Subscription Price."
25. Herman, "Whose Knocking?"
26. Lears, *Fables of Abundance*.
27. Horn, *Next World*.
28. Dods, *Philosophy of Mesmerism*, 217.
29. "Recognised Spirit-Photographs."
30. For an excellent online repository of spiritualist and occultist periodicals, see the website of the International Association for the Preservation of Spiritualist and Occult Periodicals at http://www.iapsop.com/archive (accessed July 2015).
31. Ann Braude counted at least 214 spiritualist periodicals published during the nineteenth century in the United States alone. Most of these periodicals, however, had a short life. Braude, "News from the Spirit World," 401.
32. Nord, *Communities of Journalism*; Anderson, *Imagined Communities*.
33. Braude, "News from the Spirit World," 404–7.
34. Lachapelle, *Investigating the Supernatural*.
35. Bennett, *Transatlantic Spiritualism*.
36. Qureshi, *Peoples on Parade*, 79.
37. For an example of a spiritualist exhibition pamphlet, see Sexton, *Spirit Mediums and Conjurers*.
38. Lehuu, *Carnival on the Page*, 36–75.
39. See, among others, Bown, Burdett, and Thurschwell, *Victorian Supernatural*; Wolfreys, *Victorian Hauntings*; Thurschwell, *Literature, Technology, and Magical Thinking*; Kontou, *Spiritualism and Women's Writing*; Kontou, "Sensation Fiction."
40. Leeder, "Early Cinema and the Supernatural"; Fry, *Cinema of the Occult*; Ruffles, *Ghost Images*.
41. Edwards, *Metaphysical Media*; Fry, *Cinema of the Occult*.
42. Hanich, *Cinematic Emotion*.
43. See Schaper, "Fiction and the Suspension of Disbelief"; Jacobsen, "Looking for Literary Space"; Holland, "Willing Suspension."
44. Religious studies scholar Diana Walsh-Pasulka provides an interesting reflection on this issue by examining urban legends and stories surrounding films such as *The Exorcist* (1973) and *The Passion of the Christ* (2004). As she demonstrates, the reception of these films included "the belief that the sacred or supernatural is at work in the lives of those whom produce, star in, and view the movies." She compares the films with religious icons, arguing that both are representations that possess numinous qualities. In this sense, fictional narratives such as films can also be objects of popular devotion credited with miracles and sacred powers, defying the understanding of fiction as something that is rigidly separated from reality—as this is experienced by readers or viewers. Walsh-Pasulka, "Passion Tickets."
45. Whalen, introduction to *The Life of P. T. Barnum*, viii. Biographies published

in the press and in book form were also one of the main supports that allowed for the formation of modern celebrity culture. See chapter 4.
46. Biographies of mediums were frequently featured as the leading piece in a magazine. For some examples, see Colville, "W. J. Colville"; Oxley, "William Oxley"; Armitage, "Autobiographical Sketch"; Wallis, "Story of My Life"; Oyston, "Biographical Sketch of Mrs. M. A. Hall."
47. Nichols, *Biography of the Brothers Davenport*.
48. Smith, "Performativity." See also Corbett, "Performing Identities."
49. Alvarado, "Eusapia Palladino," 77.
50. See, for instance, Armitage, "Autobiographical Sketch."
51. Redman, *Mystic Hours*, 20–21.
52. Wallis, "Story of My Life," 353.
53. Armitage, "Autobiographical Sketch," 229.
54. Redman, *Mystic Hours*, 246.
55. Ibid., 247–48.
56. Ibid., 278–80.
57. See Law and Hughes, *Biographical Passages*; Benton, *Literary Biography*; Epstein, *Recognizing Biography*; Batchelor, *Art of Literary Biography*.
58. Turley, "Usable Life."
59. Kris and Kurz, *Legend, Myth, and Magic*.
60. Ortoleva, "Vite geniali."
61. On the use of automatism and mediumship to validate the authenticity of spiritualist texts, see Bacopoulos-Viau, "Scripting the Mind."
62. Senex, "Diffusion of Spiritualism," 313.
63. Fanciullacci, *Il pellegrinaggio nei cieli*.
64. Sword, *Ghostwriting Modernism*, 13.
65. See Snow, *Spirit-Intercourse*, 111–28.
66. Rhode, "America's 'Medium' Poets," 260.
67. White, *Voices from Spirit-Land*, viii.
68. Ibid.
69. These pseudo-journalistic accounts were ridiculed in popular publications such as Algernon Mortimer's *The Very Latest News*, in which a newspaper from the future is reproduced by the press of a fictional printer, Mr. J. Smith, after he attends a spiritualist séance.
70. A. T .T. P., "Spirit-Messenger," 117.
71. A. T .T. P., "Historical Controls."
72. Colville, "Graphic Record," 577.
73. Ibid.
74. Ibid., 578.
75. Wolf-Braun, "Parapsychologische und psychiatrische Konstruktionen," 161.
76. Gomel, "'Spirits in the Material World,'" 189.
77. Doyle, *History of Spiritualism*, 2:219.
78. Alovisio and Carluccio, *Intorno a Rodolfo Valentino*, 192–93.
79. "Book Written and Illustrated by Spirits."
80. Ibid.
81. Duguid, *Hafed Prince of Persia*, 27.
82. Ibid., 50.
83. See, for some instances, Howitt, *History of the Supernatural*, 173–207; Crowell, *Identity*.
84. Malley, *From Archaeology to Spectacle*.
85. Sword, *Ghostwriting Modernism*, 27.
86. American Library Association, *A.L.A. Cataloging Rules*, 6.
87. Lee, "Copyright of Automatic Writing."
88. Hartman, *Facts and Mysteries of Spiritism*, 19.
89. William James was involved in psychical research, being a member of the Society for Psychical Research in Britain and a founder of its American counterpart. He also studied spiritualist phenomena, such as automatic writing and drawing. In 1904, for instance, an article by James on automatic drawing appeared in *Popular Science*; see James, "Case of Automatic Drawing."

90. Solomons and Stein, "Normal Motor Automatism," 509.
91. Stein, "Cultivated Motor Automatism."
92. "Report of the General Meeting," 342.
93. Duguid, *Hafed Prince of Persia*, 18.
94. Gitelman, *Scripts, Grooves, and Writing Machines*; Kittler, *Gramophone, Film, Typewriter*.
95. Sword, *Ghostwriting Modernism*, 25.
96. Dadmun, *Spiritualism Examined and Refuted*, 337; Kardec, *Book on Mediums*, 292.
97. De Morgan, *From Matter to Spirit*, 52–53. Emphasis in original.
98. Ibid., 53. It was claimed that the two drawings had been made by the spirits themselves through the phenomena of direct drawing, in order to explain graphically how the process of automatic writing was carried on.
99. Kipling, "Wireless," 259.
100. Mattison, *Spirit Rapping Unveiled!*, 74.
101. Ibid., 64–65.
102. Sconce, *Haunted Media*.
103. Watson, *Religion of Spiritualism*, 25.
104. Monroe, *Laboratories of Faith*, 113.
105. In her dissertation on automatic writing in France, Alexandra Bacopoulos-Viau has provided a very useful case study of this process, showing how French spiritism (in particular through its founder and central figure, Allan Kardec) characterized the written word as a source of scientific legitimization. Through the standardization of techniques of automatic writing, in which the spirit dictated to the medium in trance, Kardec professed to have provided empirical proofs, explicitly likening them to scientific evidences by mechanical means. Bacopoulos-Viau, "Scripting the Mind."
106. G. W. Cottrell, however, reported a different story about the birth of this device, claiming that it was invented by a sect of French monks. Cottrell, *Revelations*.
107. Sargent, *Planchette*, 3.
108. Ibid., 1.
109. Cottrell, *Revelations*.
110. Braude, *Radical Spirits*, 25.
111. Shea, *Patience of Pearl*, 26.
112. An Anxious Mamma, "To the Editor."
113. A digital copy of the sheet music of Lee and Walker is available online in the JScholarship collection: https://jscholarship.library.jhu.edu/handle/1774.2/27681 (accessed July 2015).
114. See, for instance, "Ouija, or Wonderful Talking Board." For information on the Two Worlds Publishing Company, see "Two Worlds Publishing," *Mysterious Planchette*, http://www.mysteriousplanchette.com/Manu_Portal/twoworlds.html (accessed July 2015).
115. Dods, *Philosophy of Mesmerism*, 217.

CHAPTER 6

1. Bazin, "Life and Death of Superimposition."
2. Nead, *Haunted Gallery*, 2.
3. Gunning, "Phantom Images and Modern Manifestations."
4. Jost, *Le temps d'un regard*; Solomon, *Disappearing Tricks*; Solomon, "Magic, Spiritualism, and Cinema"; Beckman, *Vanishing Women*; Nead, *Haunted Gallery*. See also Gunning, "To Scan a Ghost."
5. One of the most interesting exceptions was the use of film to document spiritualist materializations of the medium Eva C., by German spiritualist Albert von Schrenck-Notzing. Fischer, "Reciprocal Adaptation."
6. Bottomore, "Panicking Audience?"
7. Child, "Spirit Photographs."
8. Kaplan, *Strange Case of William Mumler*.

9. These articles have been reprinted in ibid.
10. Coates, *Photographing the Invisible*, 57.
11. The literature on spirit photography is extensive. Most notably, the use of photography in spiritualism has been the subject of critical and historical analysis in Chéroux et al., *Perfect Medium*; Kaplan, "Where the Paranoid"; Kaplan, *Strange Case of William Mumler*; Jolly, *Faces of the Living Dead*; Harvey, *Photography and Spirit*; Ferris, *Disembodied Spirit*; Gunning, "Phantom Images and Modern Manifestations"; Gunning, "To Scan a Ghost." See also Fischer and Loers, *Im Reich der Phantome*; Lamarche and Rannou, *La photographie hantée*; Turzio, Renzo, and Violi, *Locus solus*; Durant, "Blur of the Otherworldly"; Schoonover, "Ectoplasms, Evanescence, and Photography"; Matheson, "The Ghost Stamp, the Detective"; Owen, "'Borderland Forms'"; Gettings, *Ghosts in Photographs*; Medeiros, *Fotografia e verdade*. Useful references on the reception of spirit photography in art history are Krauss, "Tracing Nadar"; Batchen, "Ectoplasm." On spirit photography and skepticism, see Mnookin, "Image of Truth"; Tucker, *Nature Exposed*; Leja, *Looking Askance*.
12. Chéroux et al., *Perfect Medium*.
13. See Harvey, *Photography and Spirit*.
14. Mnookin, "Image of Truth."
15. Tucker, *Nature Exposed*.
16. Ibid., 124.
17. Leja, *Looking Askance*.
18. "Spirit Photographs, and Modes of Producing Them."
19. "Present State of Spirit Photography."
20. Fritz, *Where Are the Dead?*, 81. Emphasis in original.
21. Home, *Lights and Shadows of Spiritualism*, 360–66.
22. Sargent, *Planchette*.
23. Ibid., 221.
24. Stainton Moses, "Researches in Spiritualism," 389.
25. Watson, *Religion of Spiritualism*, 48.
26. Harvey, *Photography and Spirit*, 12.
27. Plaetz, "Julius Plaetz, Photographer."
28. Shindler, *Southerner Among the Spirits*, 50–53.
29. Stainton Moses, *Spirit-Identity*, 61.
30. Cox, *Body and Soul*, 120.
31. Mumler, *Personal Experiences*.
32. Fritz, *Where Are the Dead?*, 82.
33. Monroe, *Laboratories of Faith*, 176–78.
34. Anderson, *Printed Image*, 2.
35. Babbitts, "Stereographs," 129.
36. Holmes, "Doings of the Sunbeam," 1.
37. The firm of E. and H. T. Anthony, located on Broadway, ran from 1841 to 1902 and, along with companies such as the London Stereoscopic Company, succeeded in commercializing photography as an industrial commodity.
38. Holmes, "Doings of the Sunbeam," 2.
39. West, "Fantasy, Photography, and the Marketplace."
40. "Spirit Cartes de Visite."
41. "Spirit Photographs" (1863), 269. Emphasis in original.
42. Hacking, "Camille Silvy's Repertory." See chapter 4 on the celebrity culture of spiritualism.
43. Cox, *Body and Soul*, 134.
44. Taft, *Photography and the American Scene*, 22–45.
45. Kaplan, *Strange Case of William Mumler*, 180–210.
46. "Cost of Spirit Photography."
47. Seybert Commission for Investigating Modern Spiritualism, *Preliminary Report*, 91.
48. Burns, "Spirit Photography," 83.
49. Troyer, "Embalmed Vision"; Ruby, *Secure the Shadow*.
50. Coates, *Photographing the Invisible*, 35.
51. Houghton, *Chronicles of the Photographs*.
52. *Revelations of a Spirit Medium*, 113–14.
53. Barnum, *Humbugs of the World*, 117.

54. Cox, *Body and Soul*, 134.
55. Hartman, "Hartman, J. Jay."
56. Burns, "Spirit Photography," 82.
57. Ibid., 83.
58. "Recognised Spirit-Photographs."
59. Holmes, "Stereoscope and Stereograph."
60. See, among others, Trachtenberg, *Reading American Photographs*, 19; West, "Fantasy, Photography, and the Marketplace."
61. For a broader discussion of Holmes's comparison between of photography and banknotes, see Natale, "Photography and Communication Media."
62. Tucker, *Nature Exposed*, 69.
63. Gunning, "To Scan a Ghost," 112.
64. Although Brewster did not invent the fluoroscope, he introduced a convenient and inexpensive lenticular stereoscope in 1850, often called the "American stereoscope," which contributed to the massive diffusion of stereoscopic views in the following period. The inventor of the stereoscope was the English scientist Charles Wheatstone.
65. Brewster, *Stereoscope*, 205.
66. Ibid., 206.
67. Some of these images acknowledged their debt to the text, bearing the inscription "Kindly Suggested by Sir David Brewster."
68. "Minor Topics of the Month."
69. "Spirit Photographs" (1863).
70. Hockin, *Practical Hints on Photography*, 78–79.
71. Houghton, *Chronicles of the Photographs*, 271.
72. Tucker, *Nature Exposed*, 73.
73. Carter, "Picturing Rooms."
74. Keller, "Magnificent Entertainment," 217.
75. For a thorough discussion of Victorian combination printing, see Orvell, *Real Thing*.
76. Novak, *Realism, Photography*; Novak, "Photographic Fictions."
77. The image to which I am referring is a spirit tintype made by Roose, a photographer from Camden, Michigan, around 1890. It is located in the Wm. B. Becker Collection at the American Museum of Photography.
78. Solomon, *Disappearing Tricks*.
79. Dickson and Dickson, *History of the Kinetograph*, 19.
80. Mannoni, "Méliès, magie et cinéma," 50.
81. The literature on Robertson's phantasmagoria is vast. See, among others, Mannoni, *Le grand art*; Milner, *La fantasmagorie*; Gunning, "Fantasmagorie et fabrication de l'illusion."
82. Barber, "Phantasmagorical Wonders."
83. Brooker, "Polytechnic Ghost."
84. Rossell, *Living Pictures*, 153.
85. "Thirty-Fourth Anniversary of Modern Spiritualism," 257.
86. Ibid., 258.
87. This Mr. Middleton could be Thomas John Middleton—who was active in London in those years as a magic-lantern manufacturer—or a member of his family. See the National Portrait Gallery's directory of British artists' suppliers (1650–1950) at http://www.npg.org.uk/research/programmes/directory-of-suppliers/m.php (accessed July 2015).
88. "Thirty-Fourth Anniversary of Modern Spiritualism," 260.
89. Ibid., 263.
90. Ibid., 257.
91. See Natale, "Spiritualism Exposed."
92. Statham, "On Photographic Surprises."
93. Hopkins, *Magic*.
94. Ibid., 435.
95. Maskelyne, "Modern Spiritualism," 203–4.
96. Willmann, *Moderne Wunder*, 211.
97. Fawkes, *Spiritualism Exposed*, 99.
98. Bazin, "Life and Death of Superimposition."

99. North, *Performing Illusions*, 49.
100. Barnouw, *The Magician and the Cinema*, 38.
101. Gunning, "'Primitive' Cinema," 10; Fischer, "Lady Vanishes"; During, *Modern Enchantments*, 135–77; Beckman, *Vanishing Women*.
102. Solomon, *Disappearing Tricks*, 1–10.
103. Chanan, "Treats of Trickery," 117–18.
104. Gray, "Smith the Showman."
105. Brosnan, *Movie Magic*, 11.
106. Gray, "George Albert Smith's Visions and Transformations," 177.
107. Maskelyne, "Modern Spiritualism," 190.
108. Coates, *Photographing the Invisible*, 57–60.
109. Weatherly, *Supernatural?*
110. Additionally, some of the producers of fake spirit photographs, such as Maskelyne, were directly engaged in the making of motion pictures during their novelty period. Maskelyne appeared in an 1896 film by Robert Paul and produced trick movies with his son Nevil in the following years. The Egyptian Hall was used as a movie theater from the beginning of 1896.
111. Maciak, "Spectacular Realism."
112. Solomon, *Disappearing Tricks*, 80–101.
113. Houdini, *Magician Among the Spirits*, 245.
114. Bateson, "Theory of Play and Fantasy," 40.
115. Goffman, *Frame Analysis*, 2–5.
116. Chanan, "Treats of Trickery," 117.

AFTERWORD

1. Bloch, *Historian's Craft*, 43.
2. Hess, *Spirits and Scientists*.
3. Spencer, "To Absent Friends," 343.
4. Heilmann and Llewellyn, *Neo-Victorianism*.
5. Blanco and Peeren, *Popular Ghosts*.
6. Goldingay, "To Perform Possession." On the connections between beliefs in the supernatural and contemporary popular culture, see Hill, *Paranormal Media*; Edwards, *Metaphysical Media*; Carluccio and Ortoleva, *Diversamente vivi*; Clark, *From Angels to Aliens*.
7. Cox, *Body and Soul*.
8. According to film scholar Dirk Eitzen, the essence of the documentary genre does not lie in a particular style of presentation, but instead in the type of reception: contrary to fictional movies, "documentaries are presumed to be truthful." Eitzen, "When Is a Documentary?," 88.
9. See, for instance, Thurschwell, *Literature, Technology, and Magical Thinking*; Castle, *Female Thermometer*; Fry, *Cinema of the Occult*; Edwards, *Metaphysical Media*.
10. Kripal, *Mutants and Mystics*.
11. Walsh-Pasulka, "Passion Tickets."
12. See, among others, McDannell, *Material Christianity*; Arweck and Keenan, *Materializing Religion*; Chidester, *Authentic Fakes*; Robertson, *Religion as Entertainment*.
13. Meyer et al., "Origin and Mission," 210.

BIBLIOGRAPHY

Adams, Bluford. *E Pluribus Barnum: The Great Showman and the Making of U.S. Popular Culture.* Minneapolis: University of Minnesota Press, 1997.

Adorno, Theodor W. *The Stars Down to Earth and Other Essays on the Irrational in Culture.* London: Routledge, 1994.

Albanese, Catherine L. *A Republic of Mind and Spirit: A Cultural History of American Metaphysical Religion.* New Haven: Yale University Press, 2007.

Allen, Richard. *Projecting Illusion: Film Spectatorship and the Impression of Reality.* Cambridge: Cambridge University Press, 1995.

Alovisio, Silvio, and Giulia Carluccio, eds. *Intorno a Rodolfo Valentino: Materiali italiani 1923–1933.* Turin: Kaplan, 2009.

Altick, Richard D. *The Shows of London.* Cambridge: Harvard University Press, 1978.

Alvarado, Carlos S. "Bottazzi and Palladino: The 1907 Seances." *Journal of Scientific Exploration* 26, no. 1 (2012): 159–67.

———. "Eusapia Palladino: An Autobiographical Essay." *Journal of Scientific Exploration* 25, no. 1 (2011): 77–101.

———. "Ochorowicz on Eusapia Palladino, Dissociation, and Mediumistic Fraud." *Journal of the Society for Psychical Research* 74, no. 898 (2010): 57–60.

Alvarado, Carlos S., and Renaud Evrard. "The Psychic Sciences in France: Historial Notes on the *Annales des Sciences Psychiques.*" *Journal of Scientific Exploration* 26, no. 1 (2012): 117–40.

Alvarado, Carlos S., and Michael Nahm. "Psychic Phenomena and the Vital Force: Hereward Carrington on 'Vital Energy and Psychical Phenomena.'" *Journal of the Society for Psychical Research* 75, no. 903 (2011): 91–103.

American Library Association. *A.L.A. Cataloging Rules for Author and Title Entries.* Chicago: American Library Association, 1941.

Anderson, Benedict. *Imagined Communities: Reflections on the Origin and Spread of Nationalism.* London: Verso, 1983.

Anderson, Patricia. *The Printed Image and the Transformation of Popular Culture, 1790–1860.* Oxford: Oxford University Press, 1991.

Andrews, James. *The Psychology of Scepticism and Phenomenalism.* Glasgow: James Maclehose, 1874.

Andriopoulos, Stefan. *Ghostly Apparitions: German Idealism, the Gothic Novel, and Optical Media.* New York: Zone Books, 2013.

———. *Possessed: Hypnotic Crimes, Corporate Fiction, and the Invention of Cinema.* Chicago: University of Chicago Press, 2008.

An Anxious Mamma. "To the Editor of *Once a Week.*" *Once a Week* 4 (1867): 569.

Apke, Bernd, Veit Loers, Pia Witzmann, and Ingrid Ehrhardt. *Okkultismus und Avantgarde: Von Munch bis Mondrian, 1900–1915.* Ostfildern: Edition Tertium, 1995.

Ariès, Philippe. *Western Attitudes Toward Death: From the Middle Ages to the Present.* Baltimore: Johns Hopkins University Press, 1974.

Armitage, Joseph. "An Autobiographical Sketch." *Medium and Daybreak* 16, no. 783 (1885): 226–31.

Armstrong, William. "Mrs. Mellon and the Newcastle Society." *Medium and Daybreak* 447, no. 9 (1878): 678.

Arthur, T. S. *The Angel and the Demon: A Tale of Modern Spiritualism.* Philadelphia: J. W. Bradley, 1859.

Arullani, Pier Francesco. *Sulla medianità di Eusapia Palladino.* Turin: Rosenberg & Sellier, 1907.

Arweck, Elisabeth, and William J. F. Keenan, eds. *Materializing Religion: Expression, Performance, and Ritual.* Aldershot: Ashgate, 2006.

Assael, Brenda. *The Circus and Victorian Society.* Charlottesville: University of Virginia Press, 2005.

A. T .T. P. "Historical Controls." *Medium and Daybreak* 9, no. 436 (1878): 497–99.

———. "The Spirit-Messenger: England's Mission in the Soudan—A Control by Sir Christopher Wren Recorded by A.T.T.P." *Medium and Daybreak* 16, no. 777 (1885): 116–17.

Auerbach, Nina. "Ghosts of Ghosts." *Victorian Literature and Culture* 32, no. 1 (2004): 277–84.

Babbitts, Judith. "Stereographs and the Construction of a Visual Culture in the United States." In *Memory Bytes: History, Technology, and Digital Culture,* edited by Lauren Rabinovitz and Abraham Geil, 126–49. Durham: Duke University Press, 2004.

Bacon, George Allen. *The Attitude of Scientific Men Toward the Spiritual Phenomena: An Address Delivered Before the National Spiritualist Association.* Boston: Banner of Light, 1896.

Bacopoulos-Viau, Alexandra. "Automatism, Surrealism, and the Making of French Psychopathology: The Case of Pierre Janet." *History of Psychiatry* 23, no. 3 (2012): 259–76.

———. "Scripting the Mind: Automatic Writing in France, 1857–1930." Ph.D. diss., University of Cambridge, 2013.

Bailey, Peter. *Popular Culture and Performance in the Victorian City.* Cambridge: Cambridge University Press, 1998.

Bakker, Gerben. "Entertainment Industrialized: The Emergence of the International Film Industry, 1890–1940." *Enterprise and Society* 4, no. 4 (2003): 579–85.

Baldasty, Gerald A. *The Commercialization of News in the Nineteenth Century.* Madison: University of Wisconsin Press, 1993.

Ballou, Adin. *An Exposition of Views Respecting the Principal Facts, Causes, and Peculiarities Involved in Spirit Manifestations.* Boston: Bela Marsh, 1853.

Banks, Joe. "Rorschach Audio: Ghost Voices and Perceptual Creativity." *Leonardo Music Journal* 11 (2001): 77–83.

Bann, Jennifer. "Ghostly Hands and Ghostly Agency: The Changing Figure of the Nineteenth-Century Specter." *Victorian Studies* 51, no. 4 (2009): 663–86.

Barber, X. Theodore. "Phantasmagorical Wonders: The Magic Lantern Ghost Show in Nineteenth-Century America." *Film History* 3, no. 2 (1989): 73–86.

Barkas, Thomas P. *Outlines of Ten Years' Investigations into the Phenomena of Modern Spiritualism, Embracing Letters, Lectures, & C.* London: Frederick Pitman, 1862.

Barnouw, Eric. *The Magician and the Cinema.* Oxford: Oxford University Press, 1981.

Barnum, Phineas T. *The Humbugs of the World: An Account of Humbugs, Delusions, Impositions, Quackeries, Deceits and Deceivers Generally, in All Ages.* New York: Carleton, 1866.

———. *The Life of P. T. Barnum, Written by Himself.* Urbana: University of Illinois Press, 2000.

Barrett, J. O. *Looking Beyond: A Souvenir of Love to the Bereft of Every Home.* Boston: W. White, 1871.

Bartlett, Mackenzie. "Mirth as Medium: Spectacles of Laughter in the Victorian Séance Room." In *The Ashgate Research Companion to Nineteenth-Century Spiritualism and the Occult*, edited by Tatiana Kontou and Sarah Willburn, 267–84. Aldershot: Ashgate, 2012.

Barzini, Luigi. *Nel mondo dei misteri con Eusapia Palladino.* Milan: Baldini, Castoldi, 1907.

Batchelor, John, ed. *The Art of Literary Biography.* Oxford: Clarendon Press, 1995.

Batchen, Geoffrey. "Ectoplasm: Photography in the Digital Age." In *Each Wild Idea: Writing, Photography, History*, 128–44. Cambridge: MIT Press, 2001.

Bateson, Gregory. "A Theory of Play and Fantasy." *Psychiatric Research Reports* 2 (1955): 39–51.

Bazin, André. "The Life and Death of Superimposition (1946)." *Film-Philosophy* 6, no. 1 (2002). http://www.film-philosophy.com/vol6-2002/n1bazin. Accessed July 2015.

Bear, Jordan. "From Magician to Metal Brain: The Embodiment of Illusion in Early European Film Theory." *Studies in European Cinema* 5, no. 1 (2008): 17–29.

Beard, George M. "The Psychology of Spiritism." *North American Review* 129, no. 272 (1879): 65–80.

"A Beautiful Artistic Design." *Medium and Daybreak* 2, no. 66 (1871): 233.

Beckman, Karen. "Impossible Spaces and Philosophical Toys: An Interview with Zoe Beloff." *Grey Room* 22 (2006): 68–85.

———. *Vanishing Women: Magic, Film, and Feminism.* Durham: Duke University Press, 2003.

Bednarowski, Mary Farrell. "Spiritualism in Wisconsin in the Nineteenth Century." *Wisconsin Magazine of History* 59, no. 1 (1975): 2–19.

Beecher, Charles. *A Review of the "Spiritual Manifestations": Read Before the Congregational Association of New York and Brooklyn.* New York: Thomas Bosworth, 1853.

Bender, Courtney. *The New Metaphysicals: Spirituality and the American Religious Imagination.* Chicago: University of Chicago Press, 2010.

Benedict, Barbara M. *Curiosity: A Cultural History of Early Modern Inquiry.* Chicago: University of Chicago Press, 2001.

Bennett, Bridget. "Sacred Theatres: Shakers, Spiritualists, Theatricality, and the Indian in the 1830s and 1840s." *The Drama Review (TDR)* 49, no. 3 (2005): 114–34.

———. "Spirited Away: The Death of Little Eva and the Farewell Performances of 'Katie King.'" *Journal of American Studies* 40, no. 1 (2006): 1–16.

———. *Transatlantic Spiritualism and Nineteenth-Century American Literature.* New York: Palgrave Macmillan, 2007.

Bennett, Tony. *The Birth of the Museum: History, Theory, Politics.* London: Routledge, 1995.

Benton, Michael. *Literary Biography: An Introduction.* Malden, Mass.: Wiley-Blackwell, 2009.

Berenson, Edward, and Eva Giloi, eds. *Constructing Charisma: Celebrity, Fame, and Power in Nineteenth-Century Europe.* New York: Berghahn Books, 2010.

Berg, Joseph F. *Spirit Rappings a Fraud: A Lecture Delivered December 16th, 1852*. Philadelphia: William S. Young, 1853.

Berlanstein, L. R. "Historicizing and Gendering Celebrity Culture: Famous Women in Nineteenth-Century France." *Journal of Women's History* 16, no. 4 (2004): 65–91.

Berry, Catherine. *Experiences in Spiritualism: A Record of Extraordinary Phenomena, Witnessed Through the Most Powerful Mediums*. London: James Burns, 1876.

Berton, Mireille. "Alfred Binet entre illusionnisme, spiritisme et cinéma des origines." In *Recherches & Éducations*, edited by Champy-Remoussenard, 197–201. Nancy: Presses Universitaires de Nancy, 2008.

———. "Georges Méliès, la magie et les fantômes: Le spectateur didéré." In *Les âmes errantes: Fantômes et revenants dans la France du XIXe siècle*, edited by Stéphanie Sauget, 131–42. Paris: Creaphis, 2012.

Biondi, Massimo. "L'occulto portato in evidenza: Teatri, giornali, tribunali." In *Spiriti inquilini: Le case "infestate" tra palcoscenici e tribunali*, edited by Gabriele Mina, 91–103. Nardò: Besa, 2008.

———. *Tavoli e medium: Storia dello spiritismo in Italia*. Rome: Gremese Editore, 1988.

Blake, David Haven. *Walt Whitman and the Culture of American Celebrity*. New Haven: Yale University Press, 2006.

Blanco, María del Pilar, and Esther Peeren, eds. *Popular Ghosts: The Haunted Spaces of Everyday Culture*. London: Continuum, 2010.

Bloch, M. *The Historian's Craft*. New York: Alfred A. Knopf, 1953.

Blondel, Christine. "Eusapia Palladino: La méthode experimentale et la 'diva des savants.'" In *Des savants face à l'occulte, 1870–1940*, edited by Bernardette Bensaude-Vincent and Christine Blondel, 143–71. Paris: La Découverte, 2002.

Bly, Martin Van Buren. *Errors Corrected: An Address by the Spirit of Stephen Treadwell*. New York: S. T. Munson, 1857.

Boddy, Janice. "Spirit Possession Revisited: Beyond Instrumentality." *Annual Review of Anthropology* 23 (1994): 407–34.

Bogdan, Robert. *Freak Show: Presenting Human Oddities for Amusement and Profit*. Chicago: University of Chicago Press, 1988.

"A Book Written and Illustrated by Spirits." *Medium and Daybreak* 9, no. 420 (1878): 251.

Booth, Michael R. *Theatre in the Victorian Age*. Cambridge: Cambridge University Press, 1991.

Bottomore, Stephen. "The Panicking Audience? Early Cinema and the 'Train Effect.'" *Historical Journal of Film, Radio, and Television* 19, no. 2 (1999): 177–216.

Bown, Nicola, Carolyn Burdett, and Pamela Thurschwell, eds. *The Victorian Supernatural*. Cambridge: Cambridge University Press, 2004.

Boyer, Paul S., and Charles L. Cohen. *Religion and the Culture of Print in Modern America*. Madison: University of Wisconsin Press, 2008.

Brake, Laurel. *Print in Transition, 1850–1910: Studies in Media and Book History*. Basingstoke: Palgrave Macmillan, 2001.

Brancaccio, Maria Teresa. "Enrico Morselli's Psychology and 'Spiritism': Psychiatry, Psychology, and Psychical Research in Italy in the Decades Around 1900." *Studies in History and Philosophy of Biological and Biomedical Sciences* 48 (2014): 75–84.

Braude, Ann. "News from the Spirit World: A Checklist of American Spiritualist

Periodicals, 1847–1900." *Proceedings of the American Antiquarian Society* 99, no. 2 (1990): 399–462.

———. *Radical Spirits: Spiritualism and Women's Rights in Nineteenth-Century America*. Boston: Beacon Press, 1989.

Braudy, Leo. *The Frenzy of Renown: Fame and Its History*. New York: Oxford University Press, 1986.

———. "Secular Anointings: Fame, Celebrity, and Charisma in the First Century of Mass Culture." In *Constructing Charisma: Celebrity, Fame, and Power in Nineteenth-Century Europe*, edited by Edward Berenson and Eva Giloi, 165–82. New York: Berghahn Books, 2010.

Brazeal, Donald K. "Precursor to Modern Media Hype: The 1830s Penny Press." *Journal of American Culture* 28, no. 4 (2005): 405–14.

Brewster, David. *Letters on Natural Magic, Addressed to Sir Walter Scott*. London: J. Murray, 1832.

———. *The Stereoscope: Its History, Theory, and Construction, with Its Application to the Fine and Useful Arts and to Education*. London: John Murray, 1856.

Brisson, Adolphe. "Une soirée avec Eusapia Paladino." *Le Temps*, 17 December 1898, 2–3.

Brooker, Jeremy. "The Polytechnic Ghost: Pepper's Ghost, Metempsychosis, and the Magic Lantern at the Royal Polytechnic Institution." *Early Popular Visual Culture* 5, no. 2 (2007): 189–206.

Brosnan, John. *Movie Magic: The Story of Special Effects in the Cinema*. New York: St. Martin's Press, 1974.

Brown, J. H. *Spectropia, or Surprising Spectral Illusions: Showing Ghosts Everywhere, and of Any Color*. New York: James G. Gregory, 1864.

Browne, Janet. "Charles Darwin as a Celebrity." *Science in Context* 16, no. 1–2 (2003): 175–94.

Brownson, Orestes Augustus. *The Spirit-Rapper: An Autobiography*. Boston: Little, Brown, 1854.

Bruno, Giuliana. "Film, Aesthetics, Science: Hugo Münsterberg's Laboratory of Moving Images." *Grey Room* 36 (2009): 88–113.

Burke, Peter. *Popular Culture in Early Modern Europe*. Farnham: Ashgate, 2009.

Burns, James. "The Facts and Phenomena of Spiritualism: A Lecture by J. Burns to Be Given at the Opening of the New Hall, Blackburn." *Medium and Daybreak* 16, no. 779 (1885): 160.

———. "Seed Corn." London, 1872.

———. "Spirit Photography." *Medium and Daybreak* 13, no. 619 (1882): 81–84.

Buse, Peter, and Andrew Stott, eds. *Ghosts: Deconstruction, Psychoanalysis, History*. New York: Palgrave Macmillan, 1999.

Bush, Edward. *Spiritualism Explained and Exposed*. Wakefield: E. Bush, 1920.

Cahagnet, Louis Alphonse. *The Celestial Telegraph; Or, Secrets of the Life to Come, Revealed Through Magnetism*. New York: Partridge and Brittan, 1855.

Campbell, Kate. "W. E. Gladstone, W. T. Stead, Matthew Arnold, and a New Journalism: Cultural Politics in the 1880s." *Victorian Periodicals Review* 36, no. 1 (2003): 20–40.

Capron, Eliab Wilkinson. *Modern Spiritualism: Its Facts and Fanaticisms, Its Consistencies and Contradictions*. Boston: Bela Marsh, 1855.

Capron, Eliab Wilkinson, and Henry D. Barron. *Singular Revelations: Explanation and History of the Mysterious Communion with Spirits, Comprehending the Rise and Progress of the Mysterious Noises in Western*

New-York, Generally Received as Spiritual Communications. Auburn, N.Y.: Capron and Barron, 1850.

Carey, James W. *Communication as Culture: Essays on Media and Society.* Boston: Unwin Hyman, 1988.

Carlson, Marvin A. *The Haunted Stage: The Theatre as Memory Machine.* Ann Arbor: University of Michigan Press, 2001.

Carluccio, Giulia, and Peppino Ortoleva, eds. *Diversamente vivi: Zombi, vampiri, mummie, fantasmi.* Milan: Il Castoro, 2010.

Carnevali, Barbara. *Romantisme et reconnaissance: Figures de la conscience chez Rousseau.* Geneva: Droz, 2012.

Carrington, Hereward. *The Coming Science.* Boston: Maynard, 1908.

———. *Eusapia Palladino and Her Phenomena.* New York: B. W. Dodge, 1909.

———. "Eusapia Palladino: The Despair of Science." *McClure's Magazine* 38 (1909): 660–75.

———. *The Problems of Psychical Research: Experiments and Theories in the Realm of the Supernormal.* New York: W. Rickey, 1914.

———. "Would Bolster Up Palladino's Case." *New York Times,* 13 May 1910, 8.

Carroll, Noël. "Film/Mind Analogies: The Case of Hugo Münsterberg." *Journal of Aesthetics and Art Criticism* 46, no. 4 (1988): 489–99.

———. *Theorizing the Moving Image.* Cambridge: Cambridge University Press, 1996.

Carter, Sarah Anne. "Picturing Rooms: Interior Photography, 1870–1900." *History of Photography* 34, no. 3 (2010): 251–67.

Castle, Terry. *The Female Thermometer: Eighteenth-Century Culture and the Invention of the Uncanny.* New York: Oxford University Press, 1995.

"The Casual Observer Among the Spirits." *Once a Week* 11 (1874): 336–39.

Celeste, Reni. "Screen Idols: The Tragedy of Falling Stars." *Journal of Popular Film and Television* 33, no. 1 (2005): 29–38.

Ceram, C. W. *Archaeology of the Cinema.* New York: Harcourt, Brace, and World, 1965.

Chanan, Michael. "The Treats of Trickery." In *Cinema: The Beginnings and the Future,* edited by Christopher Williams, 117–22. London: University of Westminster Press, 1996.

Chapin, David. *Exploring Other Worlds: Margaret Fox, Elisha Kent Kane, and the Antebellum Culture of Curiosity.* Amherst: University of Massachusetts Press, 2004.

Chéroux, Clément. *Fautographie: Petite histoire de l'erreur photographique.* Crisnée: Yellow Now, 2003.

Chéroux, Clément, Andreas Fischer, Pierre Apraxine, Denis Canguilhem, and Sophie Schmit, eds. *The Perfect Medium: Photography and the Occult.* New Haven: Yale University Press, 2005.

Chiaia, Ercole. "Un défi à la science." In *Congrès International Spirite de Barcelone,* 1888, 123–27. Paris: Librairie des Sciences Psychologiques, 1889.

———. "Expériences médianimiques." In *Compte rendu du Congrès Spirite et Spiritualiste International,* 326–34. Paris: Librairie Spirite, 1890.

———. "Una sfida per la scienza." *Fanfulla della Domenica* 34 (1888): 127–31.

Chidester, David. *Authentic Fakes: Religion and American Popular Culture.* Berkeley: University of California Press, 2005.

Child, A. B. "Spirit Photographs." *Banner of Light,* 1862, 4.

Clark, Lynn Schofield. *From Angels to Aliens: Teenagers, the Media, and the Supernatural.* Oxford: Oxford University Press, 2003.

Clark, Uriah. *Plain Guide to Spiritualism.* Boston: William White, 1863.

Clery, Emma J. *The Rise of Supernatural Fiction, 1762–1800.* Cambridge: Cambridge University Press, 1995.

Cleveland, William. *The Religion of Modern Spiritualism and Its Phenomena, Compared with the Christian Religion and Its Miracles.* Cincinnati: Light of Truth, 1896.

Coates, James. *Photographing the Invisible: Practical Studies in Spirit Photography, Spirit Portraiture, and Other Rare but Allied Phenomena.* Chicago: Advanced Thought, 1911.

———. "Professional Mediumship." *Medium and Daybreak* 9, no. 433 (1878): 459.

Cohen, Patricia Cline. "Sex and Sexuality: The Public, the Private, and the Spirit Worlds." *Journal of the Early Republic* 24, no. 2 (2004): 310–18.

Colville, W. J. "A Graphic Record of Actual Experiences in Spirit-Life: Given by the Guides of W. J. Colville, Through His Mediumship." *Medium and Daybreak* 16, no. 806 (1885): 577–79.

———. "W. J. Colville: His Development and Experiences as a Medium." *Medium and Daybreak* 9, no. 442 (1878): 594–95.

Confessions of a Medium. London: Griffith and Farran, 1882.

Connor, Steven. *Dumbstruck: A Cultural History of Ventriloquism.* Oxford: Oxford University Press, 2000.

———. "The Machine in the Ghost: Spiritualism, Technology, and the 'Direct Voice.'" In *Ghosts: Deconstruction, Psychoanalysis, History,* edited by Peter Buse and Andrew Stott, 203–55. New York: St. Martin's Press, 1999.

Cook, James W. *The Arts of Deception: Playing with Fraud in the Age of Barnum.* Cambridge: Harvard University Press, 2001.

Cooper, Robert. *Spiritual Experiences, Including Seven Months with the Brothers Davenport.* London: Heywood, 1867.

Coppa, Francesca, Lawrence Hass, and James Peck, eds. *Performing Magic on the Western Stage: From the Eighteenth Century to the Present.* New York: Palgrave Macmillan, 2008.

Corbett, Mary Jean. "Performing Identities: Actresses and Autobiography." *Biography* 24, no. 1 (2001): 15–23.

Cornelius, J. Edward. *Aleister Crowley and the Ouija Board.* Port Townsend: Feral House, 2005.

Cornell, William Mason. *The Life and Public Career of Hon. Horace Greeley.* Boston: Lee and Shepard, 1872.

Cosandey, Roland, André Gaudreault, and Tom Gunning, eds. *Une invention du diable? Cinéma des premiers temps et religion.* Sainte-Foy: Presses de l'Université Laval, 1992.

Coste, Albert. *Les phénomènes psychiques occultes: État actuel de la question.* Montpellier: Camille Coulet, 1895.

"Cost of Spirit Photography." *Photographic News* 12, no. 566 (1869): 330.

Cottom, Daniel. *Abyss of Reason: Cultural Movements, Revelations, and Betrayals.* New York: Oxford University Press, 1991.

———. "On the Dignity of Tables." *Critical Inquiry* 14, no. 4 (1988): 765–83.

Cottrell, G. W. *Revelations of the Great Modern Mystery Planchette, and Theories Respecting It.* Boston: G. W. Cottrell, 1868.

Cox, Edward William. *Spiritualism Answered by Science; with Proofs of a Psychic Force.* London: Longman, 1872.

Cox, Robert S. *Body and Soul: A Sympathetic History of American Spiritualism.* Charlottesville: University of Virginia Press, 2003.

Crabtree, Adam. *From Mesmer to Freud: Magnetic Sleep and the Roots of Psy-*

chological Healing. New Haven: Yale University Press, 1993.
Craft, Amos N. *Epidemic Delusions.* Cincinnati: Walden and Stowe, 1881.
Crary, Jonathan. *Techniques of the Observer: On Vision and Modernity in the Nineteenth Century.* Cambridge: MIT Press, 1990.
Crookes, William. *Researches in the Phenomena of Spiritualism.* London: J. Burns, 1874.
———. "Some Possibilities of Electricity." *Fortnightly Review* 51 (1892): 174–76.
Crowell, Eugene. *The Identity of Primitive Christianity and Modern Spiritualism.* New York: G. W. Carleton, 1874.
Cruikshank, George. *A Discovery Concerning Ghosts; with a Rap at the "Spirit-Rappers."* London: F. Arnold, 1863.
Czitrom, Daniel J. *Media and the American Mind: From Morse to McLuhan.* Chapel Hill: University of North Carolina Press, 1982.
Dadmun, John H. *Spiritualism Examined and Refuted.* Philadelphia: Privately printed, 1893.
Dalle Vacche, Angela. *Diva: Defiance and Passion in Early Italian Cinema.* Austin: University of Texas Press, 2008.
Damiani, Giovanni. "A Neapolitan Medium." *Spiritual Magazine* 7 (1872): 287.
"Danziger's Ouija, or, the Wonderful Talking Board." *Pittsburg Dispatch*, 1 February 1891, 12.
Darby, M. E. *An Investigation of Modern Spiritualism: An Exposé.* South Shields: R. Simpson and Sons, 1888.
Dariex, Xavier. "Que doit-on penser des phénoménes médianimiques d'Eusapia Paladino?" *Annales des Sciences Psychiques* 6 (1896): 65–78.
Darnton, Robert. *Mesmerism and the End of the Enlightenment in France.* Cambridge: Harvard University Press, 1968.

Daston, Lorraine, and Peter Galison. *Objectivity.* New York: Zone Books, 2007.
Daston, Lorraine, and Katharine Park. *Wonders and the Order of Nature, 1150–1750.* New York: Zone Books.
Davenport, Reuben Briggs. *The Death Blow to Spiritualism: Being the True Story of the Fox Sisters, as Revealed by Authority of Margaret Fox and Catherine Fox Jencken.* New York: G. W. Dillingham, 1888.
Davis, Andrew Jackson. *The Present Age and Inner Life.* Hartford: Charles Partridge, 1853.
Davis, Colin. "Hauntology, Spectres, and Phantoms." *French Studies* 59, no. 3 (2005): 373–79.
Davis, Tracy C., and Thomas Postlewait. *Theatricality: Theatre and Performance Theory.* Cambridge: Cambridge University Press, 2003.
Davis, W. S. "The New York Exposure of Eusapia Palladino." *Journal of the American Society of Psychical Research* 4, no. 8 (1910): 401–24.
Dawes, Amy. "The Female of the Species: Magiciennes of the Victorian and Edwardian Eras." *Early Popular Visual Culture* 5, no. 2 (2007): 127–50.
Dawes, Edwin A. "The Magic Scene in Britain in 1905: An Illustrated Overview." *Early Popular Visual Culture* 5, no. 2 (2007): 109–26.
Dawson, Gowan. "Stranger than Fiction: Spiritualism, Intertextuality, and William Makepeace Thackeray's Editorship of the *Cornhill Magazine*, 1860–62." *Journal of Victorian Culture* 7, no. 2 (2002): 220–38.
Deacy, Christopher, and Gaye Williams Ortiz. *Theology and Film: Challenging the Sacred/Secular Divide.* Malden, Mass.: Blackwell, 2008.
Debord, Guy. *Society of the Spectacle.* Detroit: Black and Red, 1970.

De Certeau, Michel. *The Possession at Loudun.* Chicago: University of Chicago Press, 2000.

De Fontenay, Guillaume. *À propos d'Eusapia Paladino: Les séances de Monfort-l'Amaury (25–28 juillet 1897).* Paris: Société d'Éditions Scientifiques, 1898.

Delanne, Gabriel. *Le phénomène spirite: Temoignage des savants.* Paris: Chamuel, 1897.

De Morgan, Sophia Elizabeth. *From Matter to Spirit: The Result of Ten Years' Experience in Spirit Manifestations.* London: Longman, Roberts, and Green, 1863.

Dendy, Walter C. *On the Phenomena of Dreams, and Other Transient Illusions.* London: Whittaker, Treacher, 1832.

"Departure of Mrs. Fox Jencken to America." *Medium and Daybreak* 16, no. 794 (1885): 381.

de Rochas, Albert. *L'extériorisation de la motricité: Recueil d'expériences et d'observations.* Paris: Bibliothèque Chacornac, 1906.

Deveney, John Patrick. *Paschal Beverly Randolph: A Nineteenth-Century Black American Spiritualist, Rosicrucian, and Sex Magician.* Albany: SUNY Press, 1997.

Diamond, Michael. *Victorian Sensation; or, The Spectacular, the Shocking, and the Scandalous in Nineteenth-Century Britain.* London: Anthem Press, 2003.

Di Bello, Patrizia. "Elizabeth Thompson and 'Patsy' Cornwallis West as Carte-De-Visite Celebrities." *History of Photography* 35, no. 3 (2011): 240–49.

Dickson, William Kennedy Laurie, and Antonia Dickson. *History of the Kinetograph, Kinetoscope, and Kinetophonograph.* New York: Museum of Modern Art, 2000.

Didi-Huberman, Georges. *Invention of Hysteria: Charcot and the Photographic Iconography of the Salpêtrière.* Cambridge: MIT Press, 2003.

Dingwall, Eric John. "Eusapia Palladino: Queen of the Cabinet." In *Very Peculiar People: Portrait Studies in the Queer, the Abnormal, and the Uncanny,* 178–217. New Hyde Park, N.Y.: University Books, 1962.

Dinius, Marcy J. *The Camera and the Press: American Visual and Print Culture in the Age of the Daguerreotype.* Philadelphia: University of Pennsylvania Press, 2012.

Doane, Mary Ann. *The Emergence of Cinematic Time: Modernity, Contingency, the Archive.* Cambridge: Harvard University Press, 2002.

Dods, John Bovee. *The Philosophy of Mesmerism and Electrical Psychology.* London: James Burns, 1886.

Doering-Manteuffel, Sabine. *Das Okkulte: Eine Erfolgsgeschichte im Schatten der Aufklärung.* Munich: Siedler, 2008.

Don, C. Rawson. "Mendeleev and the Scientific Claims of Spiritualism." *Proceedings of the American Philosophical Society* 122, no. 1 (1978): 1–8.

Doyle, Arthur Conan. *The Case for Spirit Photography.* London: Hutchinson, 1922.

———. *The History of Spiritualism.* 2 vols. London: Cassell, 1926.

"Dr. Martin Van Buren Bly and the Times." *Spiritual Magazine* 2, no. 1 (1861): 29–32.

Duguid, David. *Hafed Prince of Persia: His Experiences in Earth-Life and Spirit-Life, Being Spirit Communications Received Through Mr. David Duguid, the Glasgow Trance-Painting Medium.* London: James Burns, 1876.

Dulac, Nicolas, and André Gaudreault. "Circularity and Repetition at the Heart of the Attraction: Optical Toys and the Emergence of a New Cultural Series." In *The Cinema* of Attractions Reloaded, edited by Wanda Strauven, 227–44. Amsterdam: Amsterdam University Press, 2006.

Dumont, Henrietta. *The Lady's Oracle: An Elegant Pasttime for Social Parties and the Family Circle.* Philadelphia: H. C. Peck and Theo. Bliss, 1851.

Durant, Mark Alice. "The Blur of the Otherworldly." *Art Journal* 62, no. 3 (2003): 7–17.

Durbach, Nadja. *Spectacle of Deformity: Freak Shows and Modern British Culture.* Berkeley: University of California Press, 2010.

During, Simon. *Modern Enchantments: The Cultural Power of Secular Magic.* Cambridge: Harvard University Press, 2002.

Dyer, Richard. *Only Entertainment.* London: Routledge, 1992.

———. *Stars.* London: British Film Institute, 1998.

Easley, Alexis. *Literary Celebrity, Gender, and Victorian Authorship, 1850–1914.* Newark: University of Delaware Press, 2011.

Eckley, Grace. "Borderland: On the Edge of the 'Immense Ocean of Truth.'" *Publishing Research Quarterly* 9, no. 1 (1993): 34–43.

Edmunds, Simeon. *Spiritualism: A Critical Survey.* London: Aquarian, 1966.

Edwards, Emily D. *Metaphysical Media: The Occult Experience in Popular Culture.* Carbondale: Southern Illinois University Press, 2005.

Eisenstein, Elizabeth L. *The Printing Revolution in Early Modern Europe.* Cambridge: Cambridge University Press, 2005.

Eitzen, Dirk. "When Is a Documentary? Documentary as a Mode of Reception." *Cinema Journal* 35, no. 1 (1995): 81–102.

Elcott, Noam M. "Darkened Rooms: A Genealogy of Avant-Garde Filmstrips from Man Ray to the London Film-Makers' Co-op and Back Again." *Grey Room* 30 (2008): 6–37.

Ellis, Bill. *Lucifer Ascending: The Occult in Folklore and Popular Culture.* Lexington: University Press of Kentucky, 2004.

Enns, Anthony. "Psychic Radio: Sound Technologies, Ether Bodies, and Spiritual Vibrations." *Senses and Society* 3, no. 2 (2008): 137–52.

———. "Voices of the Dead: Transmission/Translation/Transgression." *Culture, Theory, and Critique* 46, no. 1 (2005): 11–27.

Epstein, William H. *Recognizing Biography.* Philadelphia: University of Pennsylvania Press, 1987.

Eugeni, Ruggero. *La relazione d'incanto: Studi su cinema e ipnosi.* Milan: Vita e Pensiero, 2002.

"Eusapia Paladino: An Unsolved Mystery." *American Review of Reviews* 41 (1910): 234–36.

"The Extension of Human Faculty in Eusapia Palladino." *Current Literature* 68, no. 1 (1910): 49–53.

Fanciullacci, Gino. *Il pellegrinaggio nei cieli: Poema dettato da uno spirito al medium Gino Fanciullacci.* Florence: Arte della Stampa, 1881.

Faraday, Michael. "Table-Turning." *The Times,* 30 June 1853, 8.

Fawkes, F. Attfield. *Spiritualism Exposed.* Bristol: Arrowsmith, 1920.

Featherstone, Simon. "Spiritualism as Popular Performance in the 1930s: The Dark Theatre of Helen Duncan." *New Theatre Quarterly* 27, no. 2 (2011): 141–52.

Feilding, Everard, W. W. Baggally, and Hereward Carrington. *Report on a Series of Sittings with Eusapia Palladino.* London: Society for Psychical Research, 1909.

Ferris, Alison, ed. *The Disembodied Spirit.* Brunswick: Bowdoin College Museum of Art, 2003.

Field, Kate. *Planchette's Diary.* New York: J. S. Redfield, 1868.

Finkelstein, Norman. "'Making the Ghost Walk About Again and Again': History as Séance in the Work of Susan Howe." *Lit: Literature Interpretation Theory* 20, no. 3 (2009): 215–40.

Fischer, Andreas. "The Reciprocal Adaptation of Optics and Phenomena: The Photographic Recording of Materializations." In *The Perfect Medium: Photography and the Occult,* edited by Clément Chéroux, Andreas Fischer, Pierre Apraxine, Denis Canguilhem, and Sophie Schmit, 171–216. New Haven: Yale University Press, 2005.

Fischer, Andreas, and Veit Loers, eds. *Im Reich der Phantome: Fotografie des Unsichtbaren.* Ostfildern-Ruit: Cantz, 1997.

Fischer, Lucy. "The Lady Vanishes: Women, Magic, and the Movies." *Film Quarterly* 33, no. 1 (1979): 30–40.

Flammarion, Camille. *Mysterious Psychic Forces: An Account of the Author's Investigations in Psychical Research, Together with Those of Other European Savants.* Boston: Small, Maynard, 1907.

Flournoy, Théodore. *Spiritism and Psychology.* New York: Harper and Brothers, 1911.

"The Fox Sisters." *Journal of the Society for Psychical Research* 4 (1889): 15–16.

Fretz, Eric. "P. T. Barnum's Theatrical Selfhood and the Nineteenth-Century Culture of Exhibition." In *Freakery: Cultural Spectacles of the Extraordinary Body,* edited by Rosemarie Garland Thomson, 97–107. New York: New York University Press, 1996.

Fried, Michael. *Absorption and Theatricality: Painting and Beholder in the Age of Diderot.* Berkeley: University of California Press, 1980.

Friedberg, Anne. *Window Shopping: Cinema and the Postmodern.* Berkeley: University of California Press, 1994.

Fritz. *Where Are the Dead? Or, Spiritualism Explained.* Manchester: A. Ireland, 1873.

Fry, Carrol L. *Cinema of the Occult: New Age, Satanism, Wicca, and Spiritualism in Film.* Bethlehem: Lehigh University Press, 2008.

Fyfe, Aileen, and Bernard V. Lightman, eds. *Science in the Marketplace: Nineteenth-Century Sites and Experiences.* Chicago: University of Chicago Press, 2007.

Gagnier, Regenia. "Mediums and the Media: A Response to Judith Walkowitz." *Representations* 22 (1988): 29–36.

Galvan, Jill Nicole. *The Sympathetic Medium: Feminine Channeling, the Occult, and Communication Technologies, 1859–1919.* Ithaca: Cornell University Press, 2010.

Garland Thomson, Rosemarie. *Freakery: Cultural Spectacles of the Extraordinary Body.* New York: New York University Press, 1996.

Gasparin, Agénor. *Science vs. Modern Spiritualism: A Treatise on Turning Tables, the Supernatural in General, and Spirits.* New York: Kiggins and Kellogg, 1857.

Gaudreault, André. "The Diversity of Cinematographic Connections in the Intermedial Context of the Turn of the 20th Century." In *Visual Delights: Essays on the Popular and Projected Image in the 19th Century,* edited by Simon Popple and Vanessa Toulmin, 8–15. Trowbridge, Wiltshire: Flicks Books, 2000.

Gaunt, Paul J. "Henry Bielfeld." *Psypioneer Journal* 6, no. 7 (2010): 2–8.

Geary, Susan. "The Domestic Novel as a Commercial Commodity: Making a Best Seller in the 1850s." *Papers of* the *Bibliographical Society of America* 70, no. 3 (1976): 365–93.

Geimer, Peter. "L'autorité de la photographie: Révélations d'un suaire." *Études Photographiques* 6 (1999). http://etudesphotographiques.revues.org/189. Accessed July 2015.

———, ed. *Ordnungen der Sichtbarkeit: Fotografie in Wissenschaft, Kunst und Technologie*. Frankfurt am Main: Suhrkamp, 2002.

Gettings, Fred. *Ghosts in Photographs: The Extraordinary Story of Spirit Photography*. New York: Harmony Book, 1978.

Ginzburg, Carlo. *Myths, Emblems, Clues*. London: Hutchinson Radius, 1990.

Giovetti, Paola. "Cesare Lombroso e il paranormale." *Luce e Ombra* 109, no. 3 (2009): 193–200.

Gitelman, Lisa. *Scripts, Grooves, and Writing Machines: Representing Technology in the Edison Era*. Stanford: Stanford University Press, 1999.

Glendinning, Andrew. *The Veil Lifted: Modern Developments of Spirit Photography*. London: Whittaker, 1894.

Glenn, Susan A. "Give an Imitation of Me: Vaudeville Mimics and the Play of the Self." *American Quarterly* 50, no. 1 (1998): 47–76.

Goffman, Erving. *Frame Analysis: An Essay on the Organization of Experience*. Cambridge: Harvard University Press, 1974.

Goldingay, Sarah. "To Perform Possession and to Be Possessed in Performance: The Actor, the Medium, and an 'Other.'" In *Spirit Possession and Trance: New Interdisciplinary Perspectives*, edited by Bettina E. Schmidt and Lucy Huskinson, 205–22. London: Continuum, 2010.

Gomel, Elana. "'Spirits in the Material World': Spiritualism and Identity in the *Fin de Siècle*." *Victorian Literature and Culture* 35, no. 1 (2007): 189–213.

Gordon, Rae Beth. "From Charcot to Charlot: Unconscious Imitation and Spectatorship in French Cabaret and Early Cinema." *Critical Inquiry* 27, no. 3 (2001): 515–49.

Gray, Frank. "George Albert Smith's Visions and Transformations." In *Visual Delights: Essays on the Popular and Projected Image in the Nineteenth Century*, edited by Simon Popple and Vanessa Toulmin, 170–80. Trowbridge: Flicks Books, 2000.

———. "Smith the Showman: The Early Years of George Albert Smith." *Film History* 10, no. 1 (1998): 8–20.

Greeley, Horace. *The Autobiography of Horace Greeley: Or, Recollections of a Busy Life*. New York: E. B. Treat, 1872.

———. "The Philosophy of Advertising." *Hunt's Merchants' Magazine and Commercial Review* 23, no. 22 (1850): 580–83.

Grove, Allen W. "Röntgen's Ghosts: Photography, X-rays, and the Victorian Imagination." *Literature and Medicine* 16, no. 2 (1997): 141–73.

Gunning, Tom. "An Aesthetic of Astonishment: Early Film and the (In)Credulous Spectator." *Art and Text* 34 (1989): 31–45.

———. "The Cinema of Attraction: Early Cinema, Its Spectator, and the Avant-Garde." In *Film and Theory: An Anthology*, edited by Robert Stam and Toby Miller, 229–35. Malden, Mass.: Blackwell, 2000.

———. "Fantasmagorie et fabrication de l'illusion: Pour une culture optique du dispositif cinématographique." *Cinémas* 14, no. 1 (2003): 67–89.

———. "Phantom Images and Modern Manifestations: Spirit Photography, Magic Theater, Trick Films, and Photography's Uncanny." In *Fugitive Images: From Photography to Video*, edited by Patrice Petro, 42–71. Bloomington: Indiana University Press, 1995.

———. "'Primitive' Cinema: A Frame-Up? Or the Trick's on Us." *Cinema Journal* 28, no. 2 (1989): 3–12.

———. "To Scan a Ghost: The Ontology of Mediated Vision." *Grey Room* 26 (2007): 94–127.

Guppy, Samuel. *Mary Jane: Or, Spiritualism Chemically Explained, with Spirit Drawings*. London: J. King, 1863.

Gurevitch, Leon. "The Stereoscopic Attraction: Three-Dimensional Imaging and the Spectacular Paradigm 1850–2013." *Convergence: The International Journal of Research into New Media Technologies* 19, no. 4 (2013): 396–405.

Gurney, Edmund, Frederic William Henry Myers, and Frank Podmore. *Phantasms of the Living*. London: Society for Psychical Research, 1886.

Gutierrez, Cathy. *Plato's Ghost: Spiritualism in the American Renaissance*. Oxford: Oxford University Press, 2009.

Hacking, Ian. "Telepathy: Origins of Randomization in Experimental Design." *Isis* 79, no. 3 (1988): 427–51.

Hacking, Juliet. "Camille Silvy's Repertory: The Carte-de-Visite and the London Theatre." *Art History* 33, no. 5 (2010): 856–85.

Hahn, Marcus, and Erhard Schüttpelz, eds. *Trancemedien und neue Medien um 1900: Ein anderer Blick auf die Moderne*. Bielefeld: Transcript, 2009.

Hall, Trevor H. *The Spiritualists: The Story of Florence Cook and William Crookes*. New York: Helix Press, 1963.

Hammond, William A. "The Physics and Physiology of Spiritualism." *North American Review* 110, no. 227 (1870): 233–60.

Hanich, Julian. *Cinematic Emotion in Horror Films and Thrillers: The Aesthetic Paradox of Pleasurable Fear*. New York: Routledge, 2010.

Hansen, G. P. "Magicians on the Paranormal: An Essay with a Review of Three Books." *Journal of the American Society for Psychical Research* 86, no. 2 (1992): 151–85.

Hansen, Miriam. *Babel and Babylon: Spectatorship in American Silent Film*. Cambridge: Harvard University Press, 1991.

Hardinge Britten, Emma. *Modern American Spiritualism: A Twenty Years' Record of the Communion Between Earth and the World of Spirits*. New York: Author, 1870.

———. *Mrs. Emma Hardinge on Spirit Mediums*. Brighton: R. Lewis, 1868.

———. *Six Lectures on Theology and Nature*. Chicago: Scott, 1860.

Hare, Robert. *Experimental Investigation of the Spirit Manifestations, Demonstrating the Existence of Spirits and Their Communion with Mortals*. New York: Partridge and Brittan, 1856.

Harper, Edith Katherine. *Stead, the Man: Personal Reminiscences*. London: Rider, 1914.

Harris, Neil. *Humbug: The Art of P. T. Barnum*. Chicago: University of Chicago Press, 1981.

Hartman, J. Jay. "Hartman, J. Jay: Spirit Artist, 831 Vine St., Philadelphia." *American Spiritual Magazine* 2, no. 10 (1876): 310.

Hartman, Joseph. *Facts and Mysteries of Spiritism: Learned by a Seven Years' Experience and Investigation*. Philadelphia: Thomas W. Hartley, 1885.

Harvey, John. *Photography and Spirit*. London: Reaktion Books, 2007.

Hayden, William B. *On the Phenomena of Modern Spiritualism*. Boston: Otis Clapp, 1855.

Hazen, Craig James. *The Village Enlightenment in America: Popular Religion and Science in the Nineteenth Century*. Urbana: University of Illinois Press, 2000.

Heilmann, Ann, and Mark Llewellyn. *Neo-Victorianism: The Victorians in the Twenty-First Century, 1999–2009*.

New York: Palgrave Macmillan, 2010.

Henck, E. C. *Spirit Voices: Odes, Dictated by Spirits of the Second Sphere, for the Use of Harmonial Circles*. Philadelphia: G. D. Henck, 1855.

Henderson, Amy. "From Barnum to 'Bling Bling': The Changing Face of Celebrity Culture." *Hedgehog Review* 7, no. 1 (2005): 37–46.

Henkin, David M. *The Postal Age: The Emergence of Modern Communications in Nineteenth-Century America*. Chicago: University of Chicago Press, 2006.

Henson, Louise. "'Half Believing, Half Incredulous': Elizabeth Gaskell, Superstition, and the Victorian Mind." *Nineteenth-Century Contexts* 24, no. 3 (2002): 251–69.

"Her Force Only Magnetic? A Seance for Newspaper Men Given by Mme Pallandino." *Kansas City Times* 30, no. 59 (1909): 7.

Herman, Daniel. "Whose Knocking? Spiritualism as Entertainment and Therapy in Nineteenth-Century San Francisco." *American Nineteenth Century History* 7, no. 3 (2006): 417–42.

Herr Dobler [George Smith-Buck]. *Exposé of the Davenport Brothers*. Belfast: D. and J. Allen, 1869.

Hess, David J. *Science in the New Age: The Paranormal, Its Defenders and Debunkers, and American Culture*. Madison: University of Wisconsin Press, 1993.

———. *Spirits and Scientists: Ideology, Spiritism, and Brazilian Culture*. University Park: Pennsylvania State University Press, 1991.

Hill, Annette. *Paranormal Media: Audiences, Spirits, and Magic in Popular Culture*. London: Routledge, 2011.

History of Monroe County, New York. Philadelphia: Everts, Ensigns, and Everts, 1877.

Hockin, John Brent. *Practical Hints on Photography: Its Chemistry and Manipulations*. London: Hockin, 1860.

Hofer, Margaret K. *The Games We Played: The Golden Age of Board and Table Games*. New York: Princeton Architectural Press, 2003.

Holland, Norman N. "The Willing Suspension of Disbelief: A Neuro-Psychoanalytic View." *Literature and Psychoanalysis: Proceedings of the Nineteenth International Conference on Literature and Psychoanalysis*, 2002, 275–280.

Holloway, J. "Enchanted Spaces: The Séance, Affect, and Geographies of Religion." *Annals of the Association of American Geographers* 96, no. 1 (2006): 182–87.

Holmes, Oliver Wendell. "Doings of the Sunbeam." *Atlantic Monthly* 12, no. 69 (1863): 1–16.

———. "The Stereoscope and Stereograph." *Atlantic Monthly* 3, no. 20 (1859): 738–49.

Home, Daniel Dunglas. *Incidents in My Life*. London: F. Pitman, 1864.

———. *Lights and Shadows of Spiritualism*. New York: G. W. Carleton, 1877.

Hopkins, Albert A. *Magic: Stage Illusions and Scientific Diversions, Including Trick Photography*. New York: Munn, 1897.

Horn, Henry J. *Strange Visitors: A Series of Original Papers, Dictated Through a Clairvoyant*. New York: Carleton, 1869.

Horn, Susan G. *The Next World: Fifty-Six Communications from Eminent Historians, Authors, Legislators, Etc., Now in Spirit-Life*. London: J. Burns, 1890.

Horton, Susan R. "Were They Having Fun Yet? Victorian Optical Gadgetry, Modernist Selves." In *Victorian Literature and the Victorian Visual Imagination*, edited by Carol T. Christ and John O. Jordan, 1–23.

Berkeley: University of California Press, 1995.

Houdini, Harry. *A Magician Among the Spirits*. New York: Harper and Brothers, 1924.

Houghton, Georgiana. *Chronicles of the Photographs of Spiritual Beings and Phenomena Invisible to the Material Eye*. London: E. W. Allen, 1882.

——. *Evenings at Home in Spiritual Séance*. London: Trübner, 1881.

Howells, Richard. "Heroes, Saints, and Celebrities: The Photograph as Holy Relic." *Celebrity Studies* 2, no. 2 (2011): 112–30.

Howitt, William. *The History of the Supernatural in All Ages and Nations, and in All Churches, Christian and Pagan: Demonstrating a Universal Faith*. London: Longman, Green, Longman, Roberts, and Green, 1863.

Huhtamo, Erkki. *Illusions in Motion: Media Archaeology of the Moving Panorama and Related Spectacles*. Cambridge: MIT Press, 2013.

Huhtamo, Erkki, and Jussi Parikka, eds. *Media Archaeology: Approaches, Applications, and Implications*. Berkeley: University of California Press, 2011.

Huizinga, Johan. *Homo Ludens: A Study of the Play Element in Culture*. London: Maurice Temple Smith, 1970.

Hyman, R. "The Psychology of Deception." *Annual Review of Psychology* 40, no. 1 (1989): 133–54.

Hyslop, James H. "Eusapia Palladino." *Journal of the American Society for Psychical Research* 4, no. 4 (1910): 169–85.

Imoda, Enrico. *Fotografie di fantasmi*. Turin: Fratelli Bocca, 1912.

"In a Seance with Eusapia Paladino." *New York Times*, 19 April 1908, C3.

Inglis, Fred. *A Short History of Celebrity*. Princeton: Princeton University Press, 2010.

Ireland, Joseph Norton. *Records of the New York Stage, from 1750 to 1860*. 2 vols. New York: T. H. Morrell, 1867.

Isaacs, Ernest. "The Fox Sisters and American Spiritualism." In *The Occult in America: New Historical Perspectives*, edited by Howard Kerr and Charles L. Crow, 79–110. Urbana: University of Illinois Press, 1983.

Jacobsen, Mary. "Looking for Literary Space: The Willing Suspension of Disbelief Re-visited." *Research in the Teaching of English* 1, no. 16 (1982): 21–38.

James, Tony. *Dream, Creativity, and Madness in Nineteenth-Century France*. Oxford: Oxford University Press, 1995.

James, William. "A Case of Automatic Drawing." *Popular Science Monthly*, 1904, 195–201.

Janet, Pierre. "Le spiritisme contemporain." *Revue Philosophique* 33 (1892): 413–42.

Jastrow, Joseph. *Fact and Fable in Psychology*. Boston: Houghton Mifflin, 1900.

——. "Psychological Notes upon Sleight-of-Hand Experts." *Science* 3, no. 71 (1896): 685–89.

——. "The Psychology of Deception." *Popular Science* 34, no. 10 (1888): 145–57.

——. "The Psychology of Spiritualism." *Science* 8, no. 202 (1886): 567–68.

——. "The Unmasking of Palladino: An Actual Observation of the Complete Machinery of the Famous Italian Medium." *Collier's Weekly* 45, no. 8 (1910): 21–22.

Jewett, Pendie L. *Spiritualism and Charlatanism; or, The Tricks of the Media: Embodying an Exposé of the Manifestations of Modern Spiritualism by a Committee of Business Men of New-York*. New York: S. W. Green, 1873.

Johnson, Ray. "Tricks, Traps, and Transformations: Illusion in Victorian

Spectacular Theatre." *Early Popular Visual Culture* 5, no. 2 (2007): 151–65.

Jolly, Martyn. *Faces of the Living Dead: The Belief in Spirit Photography*. West New York, N.J.: Mark Batty, 2006.

Jost, François. "L'écran de fumée." In *I limiti della rappresentazione: Censura, visibile, modi di rappresentazione nel cinema. Atti del 6. Convegno Internazionale di Studi sul Cinema, Udine 17–20 Marzo 1999*, edited by Leonardo Quaresima, Alessandra Raengo, and Laura Vichi, 71–75. Udine: Forum, 2000.

———. "Métaphysique de l'apparition dans le cinéma des premiers temps." In *Une invention du diable? Cinéma des premiers temps et religion*, edited by Roland Cosandey, André Gaudreault, and Tom Gunning, 263–72. Sainte-Foy: Presses de l'Université Laval, 1992.

———. *Le temps d'un regard: Du spectateur aux images*. Quebec: Nuit blanche, 1998.

Kaplan, Fred. "The Mesmeric Mania: The Early Victorians and Animal Magnetism." *Journal of the History of Ideas* 35, no. 4 (1974): 691–702.

Kaplan, Louis. *The Strange Case of William Mumler, Spirit Photographer*. Minneapolis: University of Minnesota Press, 2008.

———. "Where the Paranoid Meets the Paranormal: Speculations on Spirit Photography." *Art Journal* 62, no. 3 (2003): 19–29.

Kardec, Allan. *The Book on Mediums, or Guide for Mediums and Invocators*. York Beach, Maine: Samuel Weiser, 1970.

Kassung, Christian. *Das Pendel: Eine Wissensgeschichte*. Munich: W. Fink, 2007.

———. "Selbstschreiber und elektrische Gespenster. Übertragungen zwischen Physik und Okkultismus." In *Von der Dämonologie zum Unbewußten. Die Transformation der Anthropologie um 1800*, edited by Erhard Schüttpelz and Maren Sziede, 1–20. Berlin: De Gruyter, 2015.

Kaufman, Suzanne K. *Consuming Visions: Mass Culture and the Lourdes Shrine*. Ithaca: Cornell University Press, 2005.

Keene, Melanie. "Domestic Science: Making Chemistry Your Cup of Tea." *Endeavour* 32, no. 1 (2008): 16–19.

Keller, Corey, ed. *Brought to Light: Photography and the Invisible, 1840–1900*. San Francisco: San Francisco Museum of Modern Art, 2008.

———. "Magnificent Entertainment: The Spectacular Eadweard Muybridge." In *Eadweard Muybridge*, edited by Philip Brookman, 217–28. London: Tate, 2010.

Kember, Joe. "The Functions of Showmanship in Freak Show and Early Film." *Early Popular Visual Culture* 5, no. 1 (2007): 1–23.

———. "Productive Intermediality and the Expert Audiences of Magic Theatre and Early Film." *Early Popular Visual Culture* 8, no. 1 (2010): 31–46.

Kember, Joe, John Plunkett, and Jill A. Sullivan, eds. *Popular Exhibitions, Science, and Showmanship, 1840–1910*. London: Pickering and Chatto, 2012.

Kerscheval, John. "Mme. Palladino, Psychic Puzzle." *Duluth News Tribune*, 12 December 1909.

King, W. D. "Shadow of a Mesmeriser: The Female Body on the "Dark" Stage." *Theatre Journal* 49, no. 2 (1997): 189–206.

Kipling, Rudyard. "Wireless." In *The Writings in Prose and Verse of Rudyard Kipling*, vol. 22, *Traffics and Discoveries*, edited by Charles Wolcott Balestier, 237–68. New York: C. Scribner's Sons, 1911.

Kittler, Friedrich A. *Discourse Networks, 1800/1900*. Stanford: Stanford University Press, 1990.

———. *Draculas Vermächtnis: Technische Schriften*. Leipzig: Reclam, 1993.

———. *Gramophone, Film, Typewriter*. Stanford: Stanford University Press, 1999.

Kluitenberg, Eric, ed. *Book of Imaginary Media: Excavating the Dream of the Ultimate Communication Medium*. Rotterdam: NAI, 2006.

Knepper, Paul, and Per Ystehede, eds. *The Cesare Lombroso Handbook*. Abingdon, Oxon: Routledge, 2012.

Kontou, Tatiana. "Sensation Fiction, Spiritualism, and the Supernatural." In *The Cambridge Companion to Sensation Fiction*, edited by Andrew Mangham, 141–53. Cambridge: Cambridge University Press, 2013.

———. *Spiritualism and Women's Writing: From the Fin de Siècle to the Neo-Victorian*. Basingstoke: Palgrave Macmillan, 2009.

Kottler, Malcolm Jay. "Alfred Russel Wallace, the Origin of Man, and Spiritualism." *Isis* 65, no. 2 (1974): 145–92.

Kovacs, Katherine Singer. "Georges Méliès and the Féerie." In *Film Before Griffith*, edited by John L. Fell, 244–57. Berkeley: University of California Press, 1983.

Krauss, Rolf H. *Beyond Light and Shadow: The Role of Photography in Certain Paranormal Phenomena*. Munich: Nazraeli Press, 1995.

Krauss, Rosalind. "Tracing Nadar." *October* 5 (1978): 29–47.

Kripal, Jeffrey J. *Mutants and Mystics: Science Fiction, Superhero Comics, and the Paranormal*. Chicago: University of Chicago Press, 2011.

Kris, Ernst, and Otto Kurz. *Legend, Myth, and Magic in the Image of the Artist: A Historical Experiment*. New Haven: Yale University Press, 1979.

Kurella, Hans. *Cesare Lombroso, a Modern Man of Science*. London: Rebman, 1911.

Lachapelle, Sofie. *Investigating the Supernatural: From Spiritism and Occultism to Psychical Research and Metapsychics in France, 1853–1931*. Baltimore: Johns Hopkins University Press, 2011.

Laing, Dave. "A Voice Without a Face: Popular Music and the Phonograph in the 1890s." *Popular Music* 10, no. 1 (1991): 1–9.

Lamarche, Bernard, and Pierre Rannou. *La photographie hantée par la photographie spirite*. Rimouski: Musée régional de Rimouski, 2009.

Lamont, Peter. *Extraordinary Beliefs: A Historical Approach to a Psychological Problem*. Cambridge: Cambridge University Press, 2013.

———. *The First Psychic: The Peculiar Mystery of a Notorious Victorian Wizard*. London: Little, Brown, 2005.

———. "Magician as Conjuror: A Frame Analysis of Victorian Mediums." *Early Popular Visual Culture* 4, no. 1 (2006): 21–33.

Lavoie, Jeffrey D. *The Theosophical Society: The History of a Spiritualist Movement*. Boca Raton: BrownWalker Press, 2012.

Law, Joe, and Linda K. Hughes, eds. *Biographical Passages: Essays in Victorian and Modernist Biography*. Columbia: University of Missouri Press, 2000.

Leahy, Helen Rees. "Walking for Pleasure? Bodies of Display at the Manchester Art-Treasured Exhibition in 1857." *Art History* 30, no. 4 (2007): 545–65.

Lears, Jackson. *Fables of Abundance: A Cultural History of Advertising in America*. New York: Basic Books, 1994.

Ledger-Lomas, Michael. "Mass Markets: Religion." In *The Cambridge History* of the Book in Britain, vol. 6, 1830–1914, edited by David McKitterick, 324–58. Cambridge: Cambridge University Press, 2009.

Lee, Alan J. *The Origins of the Popular Press in England, 1855–1914*. London: Croom Helm, 1976.

Lee, Blewett. "Copyright of Automatic Writing." *Virginia Law Review* 13, no. 1 (1926): 22–26.

———. "Spiritualism and Crime." *Columbia Law Review* 22, no. 5 (1922): 439–49.

Leeder, Murray. "Early Cinema and the Supernatural." Doctoral thesis, University of Ottawa, 2011.

———. "Ghost-Seeing and Detection in Stir of Echoes." *Clues: A Journal of Detection* 30, no. 2 (2012): 76–88.

———. "M. Robert-Houdin Goes to Algeria: Spectatorship and Panic in Illusion and Early Cinema." *Early Popular Visual Culture* 8, no. 2 (2010): 209–25.

———. "Skeletons Sail an Etheric Ocean: Approaching the Ghost in John Carpenter's *The Fog*." *Journal of Popular Film and Television* 37, no. 2 (2009): 70–79.

Lehman, Amy. *Victorian Women and the Theatre of Trance: Mediums, Spiritualists, and Mesmerists in Performance*. Jefferson, N.C.: McFarland, 2009.

Lehuu, Isabelle. *Carnival on the Page: Popular Print Media in Antebellum America*. Chapel Hill: University of North Carolina Press, 2000.

Leja, Michael. *Looking Askance: Skepticism and American Art from Eakins to Duchamp*. Berkeley: University of California Press, 2004.

Leonardi, Nicoletta. *Il paesaggio americano dell'Ottocento: Pittori, fotografi e pubblico*. Rome: Donzelli, 2003.

Levi, Steven C. "P. T. Barnum and the Feejee Mermaid." *Western Folklore* 36, no. 2 (1977): 149–54.

Lewis, Angelo John. *Modern Magic: A Practical Treatise on the Art of Conjuring, by Professor Hoffmann*. London: G. Routledge and Sons, 1877.

Lewis, Robert M. "Domestic Theater: Parlor Entertainment as Spectacle, 1840–1880." In *Ceremonies and Spectacles: Performing American Culture*, edited by Teresa Ferreira de Almeida Alves, Teresa Cid, Heinz Ickstadt, and Charles Altieri, 48–62. Amsterdam: VU University Press, 2000.

———. *From Traveling Show to Vaudeville: Theatrical Spectacle in America, 1830–1910*. Baltimore: Johns Hopkins University Press, 2003.

Life Beyond the Grave: Described by a Spirit, Through a Writing Medium. London: E. W. Allen, 1876.

Lightman, Bernard V. *Victorian Popularizers of Science: Designing Nature for New Audiences*. Chicago: University of Chicago Press, 2007.

"List of Societies." *Herald of Progress* 1 (1880): 117.

Litvak, Joseph. *Caught in the Act: Theatricality in the Nineteenth-Century English Novel*. Berkeley: University of California Press, 1992.

Lombroso, Cesare. *After Death—What? Spiritistic Phenomena and Their Interpretation*. Boston: Small, Maynard, 1909.

———. "Sui fenomeni spiritici e la loro interpretazione." *La Lettura: Rivista Mensile del Corriere della Sera* 6, no. 11 (1906): 978–87.

Lombroso, Gina. *Cesare Lombroso: Storia della vita e delle opere narrata dalla figlia*. Turin: Bocca, 1915.

London Dialectical Society. *Report on Spiritualism*. London: Longman, Green, Reader, and Dyer, 1871.

Lowenthal, Leo. "The Triumph of Mass Idols." In *The Celebrity Culture Reader*, edited by P. David Marshall,

124–52. New York: Routledge, 2006.
Luckhurst, Mary, and Jane Moody, eds. *Theatre and Celebrity in Britain: 1660–2000*. Basingstoke: Palgrave Macmillan, 2005.
Luckhurst, Roger. *The Invention of Telepathy, 1870–1901*. Oxford: Oxford University Press, 2002.
Lum, Dyer D. *The Spiritual Delusion: The Philosophy and Phenomena Critically Examined*. Philadelphia: J. B. Lippincott, 1873.
Lux, Anna, and Sylvia Paletschek. "Editorial: Okkultismus in Der Moderne: Zwischen Wissenschaft, Religion Und Unterhaltung." *Historische Anthropologie* 21, no. 3 (2013): 315–23.
Lyden, John. *Film as Religion: Myths, Morals, and Rituals*. New York: New York University Press, 2003.
Lynch, Eve M. "Spectral Politics: The Victorian Ghost Story and the Domestic Servant." In *The Victorian Supernatural*, edited by Nicola Bown, Carolyn Burdett, and Pamela Thurschwell, 67–86. Cambridge: Cambridge University Press, 2004.
Maciak, Phillip. "Spectacular Realism: The Ghost of Jesus Christ in D. W. Griffith's Vision of History." *Adaptation* 5, no. 2 (2012): 219–40.
Mahan, Asa. *The Phenomena of Spiritualism Scientifically Explained and Exposed*. London: Hodder and Stoughton, 1875.
Malley, Shawn. *From Archaeology to Spectacle in Victorian Britain: The Case of Assyria, 1845–1854*. Farnham: Ashgate, 2012.
Mangan, Michael. *Performing Dark Arts: A Cultural History of Conjuring*. Bristol: Intellect, 2007.
Manganelli, Giorgio. *Le interviste impossibili*. Milan: Adelphi, 1997.
Mannoni, Laurent. *Le grand art de la lumière et de l'ombre: Archéologie du cinéma*. Paris: Nathan, 1995.

———. "Méliès, magie et cinéma." In *Méliès, magie et cinéma*, edited by Jacques Malthête and Laurent Mannoni, 18–71. Paris: Paris Musées, 2002.
Manon, Hugh S. "Seeing Through Seeing Through: The *Trompe l'Oeil* Effect and Bodily Difference in the Cinema of Tod Browning." *Framework* 47, no. 1 (2006): 60–82.
Marrus, Michael Robert, ed. *The Emergence of Leisure*. New York: Harper and Row, 1974.
Marryat, Florence. *There Is No Death*. New York: Lovell, Coryell, 1891.
Marshall, P. David, ed. *The Celebrity Culture Reader*. London: Routledge, 2006.
Marvin, Frederic R. *The Philosophy of Spiritualism and the Pathology and Treatment of Mediomania: Two Lectures*. New York: Asa K. Butts, 1874.
Marx, Peter W. "Enter Ghost and Hamlet. Zur Vielstimmigkeit des Hamburger Hamlet 1776." *Deutsche Vierteljahrsschrift für Literaturwissenschaft und Geistesgeschichte* 85, no. 4 (2011): 508–23.
Maskelyne, John Nevil. "Modern Spiritualism." In *The Supernatural?*, edited by Lionel A. Weatherly, 153–232. Bristol: Arrowsmith, 1891.
———. *Modern Spiritualism: A Short Account of Its Rise and Progress, with Some Exposures of So-Called Spirit Media*. London: F. Warne, 1876.
Masuzawa, Tomoko. "Troubles with Materiality: The Ghost of Fetishism in the Nineteenth Century." *Comparative Studies in Society and History* 42, no. 2 (2000): 242–67.
Matheson, Neil. "The Ghost Stamp, the Detective, and the Hospital for Boots: *Light* and the Postwar Battle over Spirit Photography." *Early Popular Visual Culture* 4, no. 1 (2006): 35–51.
Mattison, Hiram. *Spirit Rapping Unveiled!* New York: Mason Brothers, 1853.

McDannell, Colleen. *Material Christianity: Religion and Popular Culture in America*. New Haven: Yale University Press, 1995.

McDayter, Ghislaine. *Byromania and the Birth of Celebrity Culture*. Albany: SUNY Press, 2009.

McGarry, Molly. *Ghosts of Futures Past: Spiritualism and the Cultural Politics of Nineteenth-Century America*. Berkeley: University of California Press, 2008.

McKendrick, Neil, John Brewer, and J. H. Plumb. *The Birth of a Consumer Society: The Commercialization of Eighteenth-Century England*. Bloomington: Indiana University Press, 1982.

McKitterick, David, ed. *The Cambridge History of the Book in Britain*. Vol. 6, *1830–1914*. Cambridge: Cambridge University Press, 2009.

McLean, Albert F. *American Vaudeville as Ritual*. Lexington: University of Kentucky Press, 1965.

McMullin, Stanley Edward. *Anatomy of a Seance: A History of Spirit Communication in Central Canada*. Montreal: McGill-Queen's University Press, 2004.

McPherson, Heather. "Siddons Rediviva: Death, Memory, and Theatrical Afterlife." In *Romanticism and Celebrity Culture, 1750–1850*, edited by Tom Mole, 120–40. Cambridge: Cambridge University Press, 2009.

McRobbie, Linda Rodriguez. "The Strange and Mysterious History of the Ouija Board." *Smithsonian Magazine*, 27 October 2013. Available at http://www.smithsonianmag.com/history/the-strange-and-mysterious-history-of-the-ouija-board-5860627/.

Medeiros, Margarida. *Fotografia e verdade*. Lisbon: Assírio & Alvim, 2010.

"The Mediumship of Children." *Medium and Daybreak* 9, no. 423 (1878): 296.

Mendeleev, Dmitrij IvanoviĐ. *Sullo spiritismo*. Turin: Bollati Boringhieri, 1992.

Meyer, Birgit, David Morgan, Crispin Paine, and S. Brent Plate. "The Origin and Mission of Material Religion." *Material Religion* 40, no. 3 (2010): 207–11.

Meyrowitz, Joshua. *No Sense of Place: The Impact of Electronic Media on Social Behavior*. Oxford: Oxford University Press, 1985.

Mihm, Stephen. *A Nation of Counterfeiters: Capitalists, Con Men, and the Making of the United States*. Cambridge: Harvard University Press, 2007.

Miller, Dan E. "The Social Construction of Hypnosis." In *Symbolic Interaction: An Introduction to Social Psychology*, edited by Nancy J. Herman and Larry T. Reynolds, 351–62. New York: Rowman Altamira, 1994.

Miller, Dickinson. "Palladino's Tricks All Laid Bare." *New York Times*, 12 May 1910, 1.

Milner, Max. *La fantasmagorie: Essai sur l'optique fantastique*. Paris: Presses Universitaires de France, 1982.

Milutis, Joe. *Ether: The Nothing that Connects Everything*. Minneapolis: University of Minnesota Press, 2006.

"Minor Topics of the Month." *Art-Journal* 3 (1857): 357–59.

Mnookin, Jennifer L. "Image of Truth: Photographic Evidence and the Power of Analogy." *Yale Journal of Law and the Humanities* 10 (1998): 1–74.

Mole, Tom. *Romanticism and Celebrity Culture, 1750–1850*. Cambridge: Cambridge University Press, 2009.

Monroe, John Warne. *Laboratories of Faith: Mesmerism, Spiritism, and Occultism in Modern France*. Ithaca: Cornell University Press, 2008.

Moore, Paul S. *Now Playing: Early Moviegoing and the Regulation of Fun*. Albany: SUNY Press, 2008.

Moore, Rachel O. *Savage Theory: Cinema as Modern Magic*. Durham: Duke University Press, 2000.

Moore, R. Laurence. *In Search of White Crows: Spiritualism, Parapsychology, and American Culture*. New York: Oxford University Press, 1977.

———. "Religion, Secularization, and the Shaping of the Culture Industry in Antebellum America." *American Quarterly* 41, no. 2 (1989): 216–42.

———. "Spiritualism and Science: Reflections on the First Decade of Spirit Rappings." *American Quarterly* 24, no. 4 (1972): 474–500.

Moore, William D. "To Hold Communion with Nature and the Spirit-World: New England's Spiritualist Camp Meetings, 1865–1910." *Perspectives in Vernacular Architecture* 7 (1997): 230–48.

Morgan, David. *Protestants and Pictures: Religion, Visual Culture, and the Age of American Mass Production*. New York: Oxford University Press, 1999.

Morgan, Simon. "Celebrity: Academic 'Pseudo-Event' or a Useful Concept for Historians?" *Cultural and Social History* 8, no. 1 (2011): 95–114.

———. "Historicising Celebrity." *Celebrity Studies* 1, no. 3 (2010): 366–68.

———. "Material Culture and the Politics of Personality in Early Victorian England." *Journal of Victorian Culture* 17, no. 2 (2012): 127–46.

Morse, Edward S. "Spiritualism as a Survival." *Science* 7, no. 178 (1898): 749–50.

Morse, J. J. *Leaves from My Life: A Narrative of Personal Experiences in the Career of a Servant of the Spirits*. London: James Burns, 1877.

Morselli, Enrico. *Psicologia e spiritismo: Impressioni e note critiche sui fenomeni medianici di Eusapia Paladino*. 2 vols. Turin: Bocca, 1908.

Mortimer, Algernon Reginald Hillearn. *The Very Latest News, Communicated Through the Medium of Mr J. Smith*. Edinburgh: William P. Nimmo, 1871.

Morus, Iwan Rhys. *Frankenstein's Children: Electricity, Exhibition, and Experiment in Early-Nineteenth-Century London*. Princeton: Princeton University Press, 1998.

———. "Worlds of Wonder: Sensation and the Victorian Scientific Performance." *Isis* 101, no. 4 (2010): 806–16.

Mumler, William H. *The Personal Experiences of William H. Mumler in Spirit-Photography*. Boston: Colby and Rich, 1875.

Münsterberg, Hugo. *American Problems from the Point of View of a Psychologist*. New York: Moffat, 1910.

———. *The Film: A Psychological Study*. New York: Dover, 1970.

———. "Psychology and Mysticism." *Atlantic Monthly* 83, no. 595 (1899): 67–85.

Myers, Gustavus. *Beyond the Borderline of Life*. Boston: Ball, 1910.

Myrick, Jean M. "Belief and Custom Surrounding the Ouija Board." M.A. thesis, Memorial University of Newfoundland, 1999.

Nadis, Fred. *Wonder Shows: Performing Science, Magic, and Religion in America*. New Brunswick: Rutgers University Press, 2005.

Nartonis, David K. "The Rise of 19th-Century American Spiritualism, 1854–1873." *Journal for the Scientific Study of Religion* 49, no. 2 (2010): 361–73.

Natale, Simone. "The Cinema of Exposure: Spiritualist Exposés, Technology, and the Dispositif of Early Cinema." *Recherches Sémiotiques / Semiotic Inquiry* 31, no. 1 (2011): 101–17.

———. "A Cosmology of Invisible Fluids: Wireless, X-rays, and Psychical Research Around 1900." *Canadian Journal of Communication* 36, no. 2 (2011): 163–75.

———. "Un dispositivo fantasmatico: Cinema e spiritismo." *Bianco e Nero* 573 (2012): 82–91.

———. "Geisterglauben, Unterhaltung, und Show Business im 19. Jahrhundert." *Historische Anthropologie* 21, no. 3 (2013): 324–42.

———. "The Invisible Made Visible: X-rays as Attraction and Visual Medium at the End of the Nineteenth Century." *Media History* 17, no. 4 (2011): 345–58.

———. "The Medium on the Stage: Trance and Performance in Nineteenth-Century Spiritualism." *Early Popular Visual Culture* 9, no. 3 (2011): 239–55.

———. "Mediums and Stars: Mediumship, Show Business, and Celebrity in Nineteenth-Century Spiritualism." In *The Spiritualist Movement: Speaking with the Dead in America and Around the World*, edited by Christopher Moreman, 237–51. Santa Barbara: Praeger, 2013.

———. "Photography and Communication Media in the Nineteenth Century." *History of Photography* 36, no. 3 (2012): 451–56.

———. "Quella sensibilità esagerata della lastra: Raggi X e revival del mesmerismo nella fotografia di fine Ottocento." *AFT—Rivista di Storia e Fotografia* 48 (2008): 53–61.

———. "A Short History of Superimposition: From Spirit Photography to Early Cinema." *Early Popular Visual Culture* 10, no. 2 (2012): 125–45.

———. "Spettacoli spettrali: Spiritismo, cinema e fantasmi." In *Diversamente vivi: Zombie, vampiri, mummie, fantasmi*, edited by Giulia Carluccio and Peppino Ortoleva, 157–62. Milan: Il Castoro, 2010.

———. "Spiritualism Exposed: Scepticism, Credulity, and Spectatorship in End-of-the-Century America." *European Journal of American Culture* 29, no. 2 (2010): 131–44.

———. "Spiritual Stars: Religion and Celebrity in the Career of Spiritualist Mediums." *Celebrity Studies* 4, no. 1 (2013): 94–96.

Nead, Lynda. *The Haunted Gallery: Painting, Photography, Film Circa 1900*. New Haven: Yale University Press, 2007.

Nelson, Geoffrey K. *Spiritualism and Society*. London: Routledge, 1969.

Newbold, William Romaine. "Possession and Mediumship." *Popular Science* 50 (1896): 220–31.

Newton, A. E. "Why I Am a Spiritualist." *North American Review* 147, no. 385 (1888): 654–68.

Nichols, Thomas Low. *A Biography of the Brothers Davenport*. London: Saunders, Otley, 1864.

Nicholson, H. "Henry Irving and the Staging of Spiritualism." *New Theatre Quarterly* 16, no. 3 (2009): 278–87.

Noakes, Richard J. "Cromwell Varley FRS, Electrical Discharge, and Victorian Spiritualism." *Notes and Records of the Royal Society of London* 61, no. 1 (2007): 5.

———. "Instruments to Lay Hold of Spirits: Technologising the Bodies of Victorian Spiritualism." In *Bodies/Machines*, edited by Iwan Rhys Morus, 125–64. Oxford: Berg, 2002.

———. "Telegraphy Is an Occult Art: Cromwell Fleetwood Varley and the Diffusion of Electricity to the Other World." *British Journal for the History of Science* 32, no. 4 (1999): 421–59.

Nolan, Steve. *Film, Lacan, and the Subject of Religion: A Psychoanalytic Approach to Religious Film Analysis*. London: Continuum, 2009.

Nord, David Paul. *Communities of Journalism: A History of American Newspapers and Their Readers.* Urbana: University of Illinois Press, 2001.

———. *Faith in Reading: Religious Publishing and the Birth of Mass Media in America.* Oxford: Oxford University Press, 2004.

North, Dan. *Performing Illusions: Cinema, Special Effects, and the Virtual Actor.* London: Wallflower Press, 2008.

Novak, Daniel A. "Photographic Fictions: Nineteenth-Century Photography and the Novel Form." *Novel* 43, no. 1 (2010): 23–30.

———. *Realism, Photography, and Nineteenth-Century Fiction.* Cambridge: Cambridge University Press, 2008.

Nunn, Heather, and Anita Biressi. "'A Trust Betrayed': Celebrity and the Work of Emotion." *Celebrity Studies* 1, no. 1 (2010): 49–64.

Oberter, Rachel. "Esoteric Art Confronting the Public Eye: The Abstract Spirit Drawings of Georgiana Houghton." *Victorian Studies* 48, no. 2 (2006): 221–32.

Ochorowicz, Julien. "La question de la fraude dans les expériences avec Eusapia Paladino." *Annales des Sciences Psychiques* 6 (1896): 79–123.

Oppenheim, Janet. *The Other World: Spiritualism and Psychical Research in England, 1850–1914.* Cambridge: Cambridge University Press, 1985.

Ortoleva, Peppino. *Mediastoria.* Milan: Net, 2002.

———. *Il secolo dei media: Riti, abitudini, mitologie.* Milan: Il Saggiatore, 2009.

———. "Vite geniali: Sulle biografie aneddotiche degli inventori." *Intersezioni* 1 (1996): 41–61.

Orvell, Miles. *The Real Thing: Imitation and Authenticity in American Culture, 1880–1940.* Chapel Hill: University of North Carolina Press, 1989.

Ottmann, Solveig. *Symphonie der Zeit: Die kommunizierenden Röhren zwischen Gothic und den Anfängen des Radios.* Saarbrücken: Verlag Dr. Müller, 2008.

"The Ouija, or Wonderful Talking Board." *Two Worlds* 4, no. 199 (1891): 515.

Owen, Alex. "'Borderland Forms': Arthur Conan Doyle, Albion's Daughters, and the Politics of the Cottingley Fairies." *History Workshop* 38 (1994): 48–85.

———. *The Darkened Room: Women, Power, and Spiritualism in Late Victorian England.* Philadelphia: University of Pennsylvania Press, 1990.

———. *The Place of Enchantment: British Occultism and the Culture of the Modern.* Chicago: University of Chicago Press, 2004.

Owen, Robert Dale. *The Debatable Land Between This World and the Next.* New York: G. W. Carleton, 1872.

———. *Footfalls on the Boundary of Another World.* Philadelphia: J. B. Lippincott, 1860.

Oxley, William. "William Oxley: His Life and Times, from a Spiritual Viewpoint, Written by Himself." *Medium and Daybreak* 16, no. 770–71 (1885): 2–4, 25–28.

Oyston, C. G. "Biographical Sketch of Mrs. M. A. Hall, Gateshead." *Medium and Daybreak* 16, no. 789 (1885): 305–7.

Page, Charles Grafton. *Psychomancy: Spirit-Rappings and Table-Tippings Exposed.* New York: D. Appleton, 1853.

Pagliaroli, Jessy C. "Kodak Catholicism: Miraculous Photography and Its Significance at a Post-Conciliar Marian Apparition Site in Canada." *CCHA Historical Studies* 70 (2004): 71–93.

"Paladino Tells About Her Stunts." *New York Times*, 13 November 1909, 3.

Palladino, Eusapia. "My Own Story." *Cosmopolitan Magazine* 48 (1910): 292–300.

"Palladino Talks to the Reporters." *Grand Forks Daily Herald* 29, no. 15 (1909): 3.

Pareti, Germana. *La tentazione dell'occulto: Scienza ed esoterismo nell'età vittoriana*. Turin: Bollati Boringhieri, 1990.

Parssinen, Terry M. "Mesmeric Performers." *Victorian Studies* 21, no. 1 (1977): 87–104.

Peck, James. "Conjuring Capital: Magic and Finance from Eighteenth-Century London to the New Las Vegas." In *Performing Magic on the Western Stage: From the Eighteenth Century to the Present*, edited by Francesca Coppa, Lawrence Hass, and James Peck, 107–30. New York: Palgrave Macmillan, 2008.

Peebles, J. M. *Seers of the Ages: Embracing Spiritualism, Past and Present*. Boston: William White, 1869.

Permutt, Cyril. *Beyond the Spectrum: A Survey of Supernormal Photography*. Cambridge: Stephens, 1983.

Pesenti Compagnoni, Donata. *Quando il cinema non c'era: Storie di mirabili visioni, illusioni ottiche e fotografie animate*. Turin: Utet, 2001.

Peters, John Durham. *Speaking into the Air: A History of the Idea of Communication*. Chicago: University of Chicago Press, 1999.

Pettit, Michael. "Joseph Jastrow, the Psychology of Deception, and the Racial Economy of Observation." *Journal of the History of the Behavioral Sciences* 43, no. 2 (2007): 159–75.

Phelps, Elizabeth Stuart. *The Gates Ajar*. Boston: Fields, Osgood, 1869.

Phelps, W. May, and Johnston Forbes-Robertson. *The Life and Life-Work of Samuel Phelps*. London: Sampson Low, Marston, Searle, and Rivington, 1886.

"Photographing the Spirit Form in Daylight." *Medium and Daybreak* 9, no. 433 (1878): 449–50.

Pierson, Michele. *Special Effects: Still in Search of Wonder*. New York: Columbia University Press, 2002.

Plaetz, Julius. "Julius Plaetz, Photographer, on Spirit Photography." *Medium and Daybreak* 13, no. 628 (1882): 231.

"Planchette." *Scientific American* 52, no. 16 (1885): 247.

"A Pleasant Physical Seance." *Medium and Daybreak* 9, no. 435 (1878): 485.

Plunkett, John. "Selling Stereoscopy, 1890–1915: Penny Arcades, Automatic Machines, and American Salesmen." *Early Popular Visual Culture* 6, no. 3 (2008): 239–55.

Podmore, Frank. *Modern Spiritualism: A History and a Criticism*. London: Methuen, 1902.

Poe, Edgar Allan. *The Raven; with The Philosophy of Composition*. Wakefield, R.I.: Moyer Bell, 1996.

Porter, Jennifer E. "The Spirit(s) of Science: Paradoxical Positivism as Religious Discourse Among Spiritualists." *Science as Culture* 14, no. 1 (2005): 1–21.

"The Present State of Spirit Photography." *British Journal of Photography* 21, no. 740 (1874): 324.

Prono, Franco. "Cinema/fotografia: Il dibattito sulla tecnologia nelle riviste fotografiche italiane del primo Novecento." In *Cinema muto italiano: Tecnica e tecnologia*, vol. 1, *Discorsi, precetti, documenti*, edited by Giulia Carluccio and Federica Villa, 30–46. Rome: Carocci, 2006.

"The Psychograph or Dial Planchette!" *Buchanan's Journal of Man* 2, no. 4 (1889): 129.

"The Psychological Review." *Medium and Daybreak* 9, no. 420 (1878): 247.

"The Psychology of Spiritism." *British Medical Journal* 2, no. 2018 (1899): 611–12.

Quinn, Susan. *Marie Curie: A Life*. New York: Simon and Schuster, 1995.

Qureshi, Sadiah. *Peoples on Parade: Exhibitions, Empire, and Anthropology in Nineteenth-Century Britain.* Chicago: University of Chicago Press, 2011.

Rausky, Franklin. *Mesmer: Ou, la révolution thérapeutique.* Paris: Payot, 1977.

R. C. "Spirit Photography, as Demonstrated Through Mr. Parkes." *Spiritual Magazine* 1 (1875): 287–88.

"Recognised Spirit-Photographs for Sale." *Medium and Daybreak* 13, no. 629 (1882): 248.

Redman, George A. *Mystic Hours; or, Spiritual Experiences.* New York: C. Partridge, 1859.

Reiss, Benjamin. "P. T. Barnum, Joice Heth, and Antebellum Spectacles of Race." *American Quarterly* 51, no. 1 (1999): 78–107.

"Remarks About Eusapia Palladino." *Annals of Psychical Science* 5 (1907): 221–25.

"Report of the General Meeting." *Journal of the Society for Psychical Research* 2, no. 30 (1886): 338–46.

Revelations of a Spirit Medium, or Spiritualistic Mysteries Exposed. St. Paul: Farrington, 1891.

"The Rev. T. L. Harris and American Spiritualism." *Spiritual Magazine* 1, no. 4 (1860): 145–54.

Rhode, Robert D. "America's 'Medium' Poets." *Modern Language Quarterly* 13, no. 3 (1952): 259–63.

Richard, Michel P., and Albert Adato. "The Medium and Her Message: A Study of Spiritualism at Lily Dale, New York." *Review of Religious Research* 22, no. 2 (1980): 186–97.

Richards, Thomas. *The Commodity Culture of Victorian England: Advertising and Spectacle, 1851–1914.* Stanford: Stanford University Press, 1990.

Richet, Charles. *Traité de métapsychique.* Paris: Librairie Félix Alcan, 1922.

Richmond, Cora L. V. *Discourses Through the Mediumship of Mrs. Cora L. V. Tappan: The New Science.* London: J. Burns, 1875.

Roach, Joseph R. *Cities of the Dead: Circum-Atlantic Performance.* New York: Columbia University Press, 1996.

Roberts, Mary Louise. "Rethinking Female Celebrities: The Eccentric Stars of Nineteenth-Century France." In *Constructing Charisma: Celebrity, Fame, and Power in Nineteenth-Century Europe,* edited by Edward Berenson and Eva Giloi, 103–16. New York: Berghahn Books, 2010.

Robertson, C. K., ed. *Religion as Entertainment.* New York: P. Lang, 2002.

Rojek, Chris. *Celebrity.* London: Reaktion Books, 2001.

———. "Celebrity and Religion." In *The Celebrity Culture Reader,* edited by P. David Marshall, 389–417. New York: Routledge, 2006.

Ronell, Avital. *The Telephone Book: Technology—Schizophrenia—Electric Speech.* Lincoln: University of Nebraska Press, 1989.

Rossell, Deac. *Living Pictures: The Origins of the Movies.* Albany: SUNY Press, 1998.

Roubaud, Felix. *La danse des tables: Phénomènes physiologiques démontrés.* Paris: Librairie nouvelle, 1853.

Rubery, Matthew. *The Novelty of Newspapers: Victorian Fiction After the Invention of the News.* Oxford: Oxford University Press, 2009.

Ruby, Jay. *Secure the Shadow: Death and Photography in America.* Cambridge: MIT Press, 1995.

Ruffles, Tom. *Ghost Images: Cinema of the Afterlife.* Jefferson, N.C.: McFarland, 2004.

"Rules and Conditions for the Spirit-Circle." *Medium and Daybreak* 13, no. 645 (1882): 503.

Rushton, Richard. "Absorption and Theatricality in the Cinema: Some Thoughts on Narrative and

Spectacle." *Screen* 48, no. 1 (2007): 109–12.

———. "Early, Classical, and Modern Cinema: Absorption and Theatricality." *Screen* 45, no. 3 (2004): 226–44.

Russell, Charles Taze. *What Say the Scriptures About Spiritualism? Proofs that It Is Demonism; Also, Who Are "the Spirits in Prison"? And Why Are They There?* Allegheny, Pa.: Watch Tower Bible and Tract Society, 1897.

Sabatier, A., Albert De Rochas, Arnaud De Gramont, J. Maxwell, Xavier Dariex, and C. De Watteville. "Expériences de l'Agnélas sur Eusapia Paladino." *Annales des Sciences Psychiques* 6 (1896): 1–55.

Salamanca, Lucy. *Fortress of Freedom: The Story of the Library of Congress.* Philadelphia: J. B. Lippincott, 1942.

Sargent, Epes. *Planchette; or, The Despair of Science.* Boston: Roberts Brothers, 1869.

———. *Proof Palpable of Immortality: Being an Account of the Materialization Phenomena of Modern Spiritualism.* Boston: Colby and Rich, 1881.

———. *The Scientific Basis of Spiritualism.* Boston: Colby and Rich, 1881.

Schaffer, Simon. "Babbage's Dancer and the Impresarios of Mechanism." In *Cultural Babbage: Technology, Time, and Invention,* edited by Francis Spufford and Jennifer S. Uglow, 54–80. London: Faber, 1996.

Schaper, Eva. "Fiction and the Suspension of Disbelief." *British Journal of Aesthetics* 18, no. 1 (1978): 31–44.

Schechner, Richard. *The Future of Ritual: Writings on Culture and Performance.* London: Routledge, 1993.

Schmidt, Leigh Eric. *Hearing Things: Religion, Illusion, and the American Enlightenment.* Cambridge: Harvard University Press, 2000.

Schoonover, Karl. "Ectoplasms, Evanescence, and Photography." *Art Journal* 62, no. 3 (2003): 31–43.

Schüttpelz, Erhard. "Mediumismus und moderne Medien. Die Prüfung des europäischen Medienbegriffs." *Deutsche Vierteljahrsschrift für Literaturwissenschaft und Geistesgeschichte* 86, no. 1 (2012): 121–44.

Schwartz, Vanessa R. *Spectacular Realities: Early Mass Culture in Fin-de-Siècle Paris.* Berkeley: University of California Press, 1998.

Sconce, Jeffrey. *Haunted Media: Electronic Presence from Telegraphy to Television.* Durham: Duke University Press, 2000.

Scott, Donald. "The Popular Lecture and the Creation of a Public in Mid-Nineteenth-Century America." *Journal of American History* 66, no. 4 (1980): 791–809.

Senex. "The Diffusion of Spiritualism: Mediumship in Literature." *Medium and Daybreak* 13, no. 633 (1882): 313–14.

Sexton, George. *Spirit Mediums and Conjurers: An Oration Delivered in the Cavendish Rooms, London, on Sunday Evening, June 15th, 1873.* London: J. Burns, 1873.

Seybert Commission for Investigating Modern Spiritualism. *Preliminary Report of the Commission Appointed by the University of Pennsylvania to Investigate Modern Spiritualism in Accordance with the Request of the Late Henry Seybert.* Philadelphia: J. B. Lippincott, 1887.

Sharp, Lynn L. "Fighting for the Afterlife: Spiritists, Catholics, and Popular Religion in Nineteenth-Century France." *Journal of Religious History* 23, no. 3 (1999): 282–95.

Shea, Daniel B. *The Patience of Pearl: Spiritualism and Authorship in the Writings of Pearl Curran.* Columbia: University of Missouri Press, 2012.

Shindler, Mary Dana. *A Southerner Among the Spirits: A Record of Investigations into the Spiritual Phenomena.* Memphis: Southern Baptist Publication Society, 1877.

Shorter, Thomas. "Emma Hardinge." *Spiritual Magazine* 6, no. 9 (1865): 385–402.

Sidgwick, Eleanor Mildred. "On Spirit Photographs: A Reply to Mr. A. R. Wallace." *Proceedings of the Society for Psychical Research* 7 (1891–92): 268–89.

Sidgwick, Henry. "Exit Eusapia." *British Medical Journal* 2, no. 1820 (1895): 1263–64.

Siegel, Steffen. "Daguerreotypie auf Papier: Ein Fotografisches Gedankenexperiment um 1840." *Fotogeschichte* 122 (2011): 5–12.

Simpson, J. Wharton. "Spiritual Photography." *Photographic News* 12, no. 562 (1869): 285.

Sketch of the Life, Personal Appearance, Character, and Manners of Charles S. Stratton. New York: Samuel Booth, 1871.

"Sleep." *Spiritual Magazine* 3, no. 1 (1862): 30–35.

Smajic, Srdjan. *Ghost-Seers, Detectives, and Spiritualists: Theories of Vision in Victorian Literature and Science.* Cambridge: Cambridge University Press, 2010.

Smith, Sidonie. "Performativity, Autobiographical Practice, Resistance." *Auto/Biography Studies* 10, no. 1 (1995): 17–33.

Snelson, Tim. "The Ghost in the Machine: World War II, Popular Occultism, and Hollywood's 'Serious' Ghost Films." *Media History* 17, no. 1 (2011): 17–32.

Snow, Herman. *Spirit-Intercourse: Containing Incidents of Personal Experience While Investigating the New Phenomena of Spirit Thought and Action.* Boston: Crosby, Nichols, 1853.

Solomon, Matthew. *Disappearing Tricks: Silent Film, Houdini, and the New Magic of the Twentieth Century.* Urbana: University of Illinois Press, 2010.

———. "Magic, Spiritualism, and Cinema, Circa 1895." *Cinema & Cie* 3 (2003): 39–45.

Solomons, Leon M., and Gertrude Stein. "Normal Motor Automatism." *Psychological Review* 3, no. 5 (1896): 492–512.

Sommer, Andreas. "Psychical Research and the Origins of American Psychology: Hugo Münsterberg, William James, and Eusapia Palladino." *History of the Human Sciences* 25, no. 2 (2012): 23–44.

Spencer, Wayne. "To Absent Friends: Classical Spiritualist Mediumship and New Age Channelling Compared and Contrasted." *Journal of Contemporary Religion* 16, no. 3 (2001): 343–60.

"Spirit Cartes de Visite." *Photographic News* 13, no. 572 (1869): 405.

"Spirit Photographs." *Chemical News* 4, no. 5 (1869): 269.

"Spirit Photographs." *Spiritual Magazine* 4, no. 1 (1863): 34–41.

"Spirit Photographs, and Modes of Producing Them." *Photographic News* 12, no. 561 (1869): 270.

"Spirits at Sea Conjured on Liner: Italian Medium Gives Seances on Way Here." *New York Tribune*, 11 November 1909, 4.

Spooner, Catherine. "'Spiritual Garments': Fashioning the Victorian Séance in Sarah Waters' *Affinity*." In *Styling Texts: Dress and Fashion in Literature*, edited by Cynthia G. Kuhn and Cindy L. Carlson, 351–68. Amherst: Cambria Press, 2007.

Sprenger, Florian. *Medien des Immediaten: Elektrizität, Telegraphie, Mcluhan.* Berlin: Kadmos, 2012.

Springhall, John. *The Genesis of Mass Culture: Show Business Live in America, 1840 to 1940.* New York: Palgrave Macmillan, 2008.

Stacey, Michelle. *The Fasting Girl: A True Victorian Medical Mystery.* New York: Jeremy P. Tarcher / Putnam, 2002.

Stainton Moses, William. "Researches in Spiritualism." *Human Nature* 8 (1874): 385–97, 425–30, 473–88, 514–27.

———. *Spirit-Identity.* London: W. H. Harrison, 1879.

Staiti, Paul. "Con Artists: Harnett, Haberle, and Their American Accomplices." In *Deceptions and Illusions: Five Centuries of Trompe l'Oeil Painting,* edited by Sybille Ebert-Schifferer, 90–103. Washington, D.C.: National Gallery of Art, 2002.

Stashower, Daniel. "The Medium and the Magician." *American History* 34, no. 3 (1999): 38–46.

Statham, F. F. "On Photographic Surprises." *British Journal of Photography* 17, no. 1032 (1880): 79.

Staubermann, Klaus B. "Tying the Knot: Skill, Judgement, and Authority in the 1870s Leipzig Spiritistic Experiments." *British Journal for the History of Science* 34, no. 1 (2001): 67–79.

Stein, Gertrude. "Cultivated Motor Automatism: A Study of Character in Its Relation to Attention." *Psychological Review* 5 (1898): 195.

Stewart, Victoria. "Spiritualism, Detective Fiction, and the Aftermath of War." *Clues* 27, no. 2 (2009): 75.

Stolow, Jeremy. *Orthodox by Design: Judaism, Print Politics, and the Artscroll Revolution.* Berkeley: University of California Press, 2010.

———. "Salvation by Electricity." In *Religion: Beyond a Concept.* Future of the Religious Past 1, edited by Hent De Vries, 668–86. New York: Fordham University Press, 2008.

Styers, Randall. *Making Magic: Religion, Magic, and Science in the Modern World.* New York: Oxford University Press, 2004.

"Subscription Price of the Medium for the Year 1884 in Britain." *Medium and Daybreak* 15, no. 723 (1884): 88.

Sussman, Mark. "Performing the Intelligent Machine: Deception and Enchantment in the Life of the Automaton Chess Player." *The Drama Review (TDR)* 43, no. 3 (1999): 81–96.

Sutherland, Meghan. "Populism and Spectacle." *Cultural Studies* 26, no. 2–3 (2012): 330–45.

Sword, Helen. *Ghostwriting Modernism.* Ithaca: Cornell University Press, 2002.

Taft, Robert. *Photography and the American Scene: A Social History, 1839–1889.* New York: Macmillan, 1938.

Taussig, Michael. *The Magic of the State.* London: Routledge, 1997.

———. "Viscerality, Faith, and Skepticism: Another Theory of Magic." In *In Near Ruins: Cultural Theory at the End of the Century,* edited by Nicholas B. Dirks, 221–56. Minneapolis: University of Minnesota Press, 1998.

Taylor, Kelly S. "Exploiting the Medium: Anna Cora Mowatt's Creation of Self Through Performance." *Text and Performance Quarterly* 16, no. 4 (1996): 321–35.

"Thackeray and Dickens on Spiritualism." *Spiritual Magazine* 1, no. 9 (1960): 385–93.

"Thirty-Fourth Anniversary of Modern Spiritualism." *Medium and Daybreak* 13, no. 630 (1882): 257–63.

Thornton, Brian. "The Moon Hoax: Debates About Ethics in 1835 New York Newspapers." *Journal of Mass Media Ethics* 15, no. 2 (2000): 89–100.

Thurschwell, Pamela. *Literature, Technology, and Magical Thinking, 1880–1920.* Cambridge: Cambridge University Press, 2001.

Toll, Robert C. *On with the Show! The First Century of Show Business in America.*

New York: Oxford University Press, 1976.

"Topics of the Times: Palladino Not yet Conquered." *New York Times*, 13 May 1910, 8.

Trachtenberg, Alan. "Mirror in the Marketplace: American Responses to the Daguerreotype, 1839–51." In *Lincoln's Smile and Other Enigmas*, 3–25. New York: Hill and Wang, 2007.

———. *Reading American Photographs: Images as History, Mathew Brady to Walker Evans*. New York, N.Y.: Hill and Wang, 1989.

Tresch, John. "The Potent Magic of Verisimilitude: Edgar Allan Poe Within the Mechanical Age." *British Journal for the History of Science* 30, no. 3 (1997): 275–90.

———. "The Prophet and the Pendulum: Sensational Science and Audiovisual Phantasmagoria Around 1848." *Grey Room* 43 (2011): 16–41.

———. *The Romantic Machine: Utopian Science and Technology After Napoleon*. Chicago: University of Chicago Press, 2012.

"Tributes to the Memory of Ercole Chiaia." *Annals of Psychical Science* 4 (1905): 261–63.

Triplett, Norman. "The Psychology of Conjuring Deceptions." *American Journal of Psychology* 11, no. 4 (1900): 439–510.

Tromp, Marlene. *Altered States: Sex, Nation, Drugs, and Self-Transformation in Victorian Spiritualism*. Albany: SUNY Press, 2006.

———. *Victorian Freaks: The Social Context of Freakery in Britain*. Columbus: Ohio State University Press, 2008.

Troyer, J. "Embalmed Vision." *Mortality* 12, no. 1 (2007): 22–47.

Tuchinsky, Adam-Max. *Horace Greeley's New-York Tribune: Civil War–Era Socialism and the Crisis of Free Labor*. Ithaca: Cornell University Press, 2009.

Tucker, Jennifer. *Nature Exposed: Photography as Eyewitness in Victorian Science*. Baltimore: Johns Hopkins University Press, 2005.

Turley, David. "A Usable Life: Representations of Abraham Lincoln." In *Imitating Art: Essays on Biography*, edited by David Ellis, 53–66. London: Pluto Press, 1993.

Turner, Graeme, Frances Bonner, and P. David Marshall. "Producing Celebrity." In *The Celebrity Culture Reader*, edited by P. David Marshall, 771–98. New York: Routledge, 2006.

Turner, Victor W. *The Anthropology of Performance*. New York: PAJ, 1986.

Turzio, Silvana, Villa Renzo, and Alessandra Violi. *Locus solus*. Vol. 2, *Lombroso e la fotografia*. Milan: Paravia Bruno Mondadori, 2005.

Tuttle, Hudson. *Arcana of Spiritualism: A Manual of Spiritual Science and Philosophy*. Boston: Adams, 1871.

Tymn, Michael E. "Etta Wriedt: The Best Medium Ever?" *Journal of Spirituality and Paranormal Studies* 34, no. 4 (2011): 229–39.

Underhill, Ann Leah. *The Missing Link in Modern Spiritualism*. New York: Thomas R. Knox, 1885.

Van de Port, Mattijs. "Priests and Stars: Candomble, Celebrity Discourses, and the Authentication of Religious Authority in Bahia's Public Sphere." *Postscripts: The Journal of Sacred Texts and Contemporary Worlds* 1, no. 2–3 (2005): 301–24.

Van Deusen, Glyndon G. *Horace Greeley, Nineteenth-Century Crusader*. Philadelphia: University of Pennsylvania Press, 1953.

Van Rensselaer, John King. *The Devil's Picture-Books: A History of Playing Cards*. New York: Dodd, Mead, 1890.

Vesme, Cesare. "Le misteriose fotografie di Pisa." *Rivista di Studi Psichici* 4, no. 9 (1898): 210–15.

Violi, Alessandra. "Shuffling the Times of Modernism: Primitive Magic and the Making of Modernity." *Textus* 26, no. 2 (2013): 31–46.

———. *Il teatro dei nervi: Fantasmi del moderno da Mesmer a Charcot*. Milan: Bruno Mondadori, 2004.

Vorderer, Peter, and Silvia Knobloch. "Conflict and Suspense in Drama." In *Media Entertainment: The Psychology of Its Appeal*, edited by Dolf Zillmann and Peter Vorderer, 56–68. Mahwah, N.J.: Lawrence Erlbaum Associates, 2000.

Voss, Ehler. "California Dreamin': Die Erfindung des Neoschamanismus als mediumistische Probe des 20. Jahrhunderts." *Historische Anthropologie* 21, no. 3 (2013): 367–86.

Walker, Barbara. *Out of the Ordinary: Folklore and the Supernatural*. Logan: Utah State University Press, 1995.

Walker, David. "The Humbug in American Religion: Ritual Theories of Nineteenth-Century Spiritualism." *Religion and American Culture: A Journal of Interpretation* 23, no.1 (2013): 30–74.

Walkowitz, Judith R. "Science and the Seance: Transgressions of Gender and Genre in Late Victorian London." *Representations* 22 (1988): 3–29.

Wallace, Alfred Russell. *A Defence of Modern Spiritualism*. Boston: Colby and Rich, 1874.

Wallis, E. W. "The Story of My Life; and Developments and Experiences as a Medium." *Medium and Daybreak* 16, no. 792 (1885): 353–59.

Walsh-Pasulka, Diana. "'Passion Tickets Bear Mark of Beast!' Otherworldly Realism, Religious Authority, and Popular Film." *Journal of Religion and Popular Culture* 11, no. 1 (2005): 44–53.

Ward, Pete. *Gods Behaving Badly: Media, Religion, and Celebrity Culture*. Waco: Baylor University Press, 2011.

Warner, Marina. *Phantasmagoria: Spirit Visions, Metaphors, and Media into the Twenty-First Century*. Oxford: Oxford University Press, 2006.

Waters, Sarah. "Ghosting the Interface: Cyberspace and Spiritualism." *Science as Culture* 6, no. 3 (1997): 414–43.

Watson, Samuel. *The Religion of Spiritualism: Its Phenomena and Philosophy*. Boston: Colby and Rich, 1880.

Weatherly, Lionel A. *The Supernatural?* Bristol: Arrowsmith, 1891.

"Weird Scenes on Ocean Liner." *Aberdeen Daily News*, 17 November 1909, 7.

Werrett, Simon. "The Arsenal as Spectacle." *Nineteenth Century Theatre and Film* 37, no. 1 (2010): 14–22.

West, Nancy Martha. "Fantasy, Photography, and the Marketplace: Oliver Wendell Holmes and the Stereoscope." *Nineteenth-Century Contexts* 19, no. 3 (1996): 231–58.

Wetherbee, John. *Shadows: Being a Familiar Presentation of Thoughts and Experiences in Spiritual Matters*. Boston: Colby and Rich, 1885.

Whalen, Terence. Introduction to *The Life of P. T. Barnum, Written by Himself*, by Phineas T. Barnum, vii–xxxvii. Urbana: University of Illinois Press, 2000.

"What the Phonograph Said About Vaccination." *Medium and Daybreak* 9, no. 426 (1878): 346.

White, Nathan Francis. *Voices from Spirit-Land*. New York: Partridge and Brittan, 1854.

"Who Are Spiritualists?" *Medium and Daybreak* 13, no. 629 (1882): 245–46.

Wicclair, Mark R. "Film Theory and Hugo Münsterberg's *The Film: A Psychological Study*." *Journal of Aesthetic Education* 12, no. 3 (1978): 33–50.

Williams, Robert Chadwell. *Horace Greeley: Champion of American Freedom*. New York: New York University Press, 2006.

Willis, Martin. *Mesmerists, Monsters, and Machines: Science Fiction and the Cultures of Science in the Nineteenth Century*. Kent: Kent State University Press, 2006.

———. "On Wonder: Situating the Spectacle in Spiritualism and Performance Magic." In *Popular Exhibitions, Science, and Showmanship, 1840–1910*, edited by Joe Kember, John Plunkett, and Jill A. Sullivan, 167–82. London: Pickering and Chatto, 2012.

Willis, Martin, and Catherine Wynne, eds. *Victorian Literary Mesmerism*. Amsterdam: Rodopi, 2006.

Willmann, Carl. *Moderne Wunder: Natürliche Erklärung der älteren wie neueren Geheimnisse der Spiritisten und Antispiritisten, Geisterritierer, Hellseher, Gedankenleser, Heilmedien, Mnemotechniker und Rechenkünstler*. Leipzig: Otto Spamer, 1886.

Winslow, L. S. Forbes. *Spiritualistic Madness*. London: Baillières, Tindall, and Cox, 1877.

Winter, Alison. *Mesmerized: Powers of Mind in Victorian Britain*. Chicago: University of Chicago Press, 1998.

Wiseman, Richard, Emma Greening, and Matthew Smith. "Belief in the Paranormal and Suggestion in the Seance Room." *British Journal of Psychology* 94, no. 3 (2003): 285–97.

Witness, Eve. "A Private Sitting with Mrs. Mellon." *Medium and Daybreak* 16, no. 825 (1885): 705–6.

Wolf-Braun, Barbara. "Parapsychologische und psychiatrische Konstruktionen des Mediumismus um 1900." In *Trancemedien und neue Medien um 1900: Ein anderer Blick auf die Moderne*, edited by Marcus Hahn and Erhard Schüttpelz, 145–71. Bielefeld: Transcript, 2009.

Wolfe, Napoleon Bonaparte. *Startling Facts in Modern Spiritualism*. Chicago: Religio-Philosophical, 1875.

Wolfreys, Julian. *Victorian Hauntings: Spectrality, Gothic, the Uncanny, and Literature*. Houndmills, Basingstoke: Palgrave, 2002.

"Woman's World: Eusapia Palladino." *Evening News*, 5 January 1910, 2.

Wood, R. W. "Report of an Investigation of the Phenomena Connected with Eusapia Palladino." *Science* 31, no. 803 (1910): 776–80.

Wright, Sarah. "Dropping the Mask: Theatricality and Absorption in Sáenz de Heredia's *Don Juan*." *Screen* 46, no. 4 (2005): 415–33.

Zabriskie, Francis Nicoll. *Horace Greeley, the Editor*. New York: Funk & Wagnalls, 1890.

Zielinski, Siegfried. *Deep Time of the Media: Toward an Archaeology of Hearing and Seeing by Technical Means*. Cambridge: MIT Press, 2006.

Zimmerman, D. A. "Frank Norris, Market Panic, and the Mesmeric Sublime." *American Literature* 75, no. 1 (2003): 61–90.

Zon, Bennett, ed. *Music and Performance Culture in Nineteenth-Century Britain: Essays in Honour of Nicholas Temperley*. Farnham: Ashgate, 2012.

INDEX

absorption, 40
Adorno, Theodor W., 13
alcoholism, 89–91
Anderson, John Henry, 76
advertising, 67, 73–74, 114, 147
amateur magicians, 56
American Society for Psychical Research, 98
anecdotes, 120
angels, 124–25
animal magnetism. *See* mesmerism
Armitage, Joseph, 119
artistic creation, 39
astrology, 13
audience, 7. *See also* paying public
authenticity, 10, 30, 66, 93, 121, 171
authorship, 126–27
automata, 38
automatism, 36, 38–39, 124, 126–32

Bazin, André, 135, 165
belief, 15, 22, 78–80, 170
    and entertainment, 117
    and fiction, 194 n. 44
Barnum, P. T., 66–69, 86, 147
Barnum's Hotel (New York City), 24, 72
Berry, Catherine, 2, 24, 44, 55
Berry sisters, 21
Bielfield, Henry, 113
Bly, Martin Van Buren, 79
Borderland, 75
Bottazzi, Filippo, 92
Brady, William A., 99
Brewster, David, 59–60, 149–50
broadcasting, 109, 113. *See also* religious preaching
Buguet, Édouard, 138, 142, 144
Burns, James, 109–10, 112–14, 123, 133, 157–58
Byron, Lord George Gordon, 86

camp meetings, 26
Capron, Eliab Wilkinson, 65–66, 71–73
card games, 53
Carrington, Hereward, 94, 98–99, 102
Carter, Lizzie, 143
celebrity, 34, 82–105, 146
Chiaia, Ercole, 96–98
childhood, 37, 119
cinema. *See* film
clairvoyance, 158
Columbia University, 101–2
commodity, 14, 84–85, 89, 114, 132, 137
Conan Doyle, Arthur, 36, 123
conjuring. *See* stage magic
consumerism, 14, 61, 137, 137, 153
controversy, 65–81, 91, 141–42
conversation, 45–46
Cook, Florence, 87–88
copyright laws, 126
Corinthian Hall (Rochester), 1, 24, 71
Crookes, William, 47, 75, 87–88
cultural intermediaries, 91
Curie, Pierre and Marie, 97
curiosity, 4, 79–80, 171, 175 nn. 9, 11
Curtis Blair, Lucie Marie, 33

dance mediumship, 33, 55
Davenport brothers, 29–31, 76–77, 161
deception, 67–68, 77, 79–80. *See also* trickery
Dickens, Charles (spirit of), 121
Dickson, Antonia, and William Kennedy, 154
diva, 104. *See also* celebrity
domestic entertainment, 2, 13, 56, 61
Doyle, Arthur Conan, 71
dreaming, 39–40
Duguid, David, 123–25

Eglinton, William, 127

Egyptan Hall (London), 167–68
electricity, 58, 70, 128–29
electroscope, 102
Elliotson, John, 50
emotions, 45, 48, 55, 95–96, 117, 144
entertainment industry, 6–7, 66–67, 171–73
escapism, 29–30, 78, 161
evidence, 36, 48, 57–58, 128, 141
  experiment, 9, 49–50, 79, 97, 127
  human testimony, 143–45
exhibitionary complex, 4, 25, 116
exhibition pamphlets, 115

Fairland, Annie, 91
fame. *See* celebrity
Fanciullacci, Gino, 121
Faraday, Michael, 74
fear, 48–49. *See also* emotions
fiction, 48, 111–12, 136, 117. *See also* spiritualism and literature
  fictional representations of ghosts, 48, 116–17, 153–54, 166, 171–72, 181 n. 37
  gothic literature, 116, 153, 172
film
  early cinema, 13, 123, 157, 159, 165–68
  horror film, 172
  film theory, 101
  invention of, 6
  kinetoscope, 154
  pre-cinema, 10, 61, 135–69
  trick film, 165–68
Fox sisters (Kate and Margaret), 1, 24, 37, 42, 65–66, 71–73, 89–90
Fox, Leah, 42, 65, 72
Fowler, Edward P., 129
frame analysis, 22–23, 41, 169
Franklin, Benjamin (spirit of), 129, 188 n. 29
fraud, 32, 67, 75, 88, 102, 136
freak shows, 69

George, Grace, 99
ghosting, 86–88
gospels, apocryphal, 124
Greeley, Horace, 65

Guppy, Samuel, 147

Hafed Prince of Persia, 123–25
Hayden, Maria B., 5
Hardinge, Emma, 32, 113, 133
Hare, Robert, 57
Harry, Thomas Lake, 122
Hatman, Jay J., 143, 147
Hartman, Joseph, 37
Hayden, Maria, 74
healing, 114, 119
hearing, 54
Herr Dobler. *See* Smith-Buck, George
Heth, Joice, 68
Holmes, Oliver Wendell, 145, 149
Home, Daniel Dunglas, 34–36, 142
Houdini, Harry, 33, 77, 161, 168
Houghton, Georgiana, 54, 147, 150, 158
Hudson, Frederick A., 147–48, 150, 158

illusion, 76–77, 160. *See also* trickery
illustrations in spiritualist publications, 113, 124
international exchange, 96, 115. *See also* transatlantic exchange
invisibility, 135, 165
Italy, representations of, 99–100, 122–23

James, William, 127

Kardec, Allan, 131
Kellar, Harry, 29, 77
Kellogg, James L., 102
Kennard Novelty Company, 58
King, Katie (spirit of), 87–88, 113
King, John (spirit of), 87, 93
Kipling, Rudyard, 129
Koons, Jonathan, 25

The Lady's Oracle, 56
laughter, 11, 55
leisure, 13, 45–46, 53, 55
levitation, 35
Lincoln, Mary Todd, 147
Lombroso, Cesare, 97–98

magic lantern, 156–59
magnetism, 70

manifestation. *See* spirit phenomena
Maskelyne, John Nevil, 76–78, 161, 167–68
material culture, 12, 51–52, 132, 146, 148–49
McKinstry, Carla, 123
media archaeology, 8, 61
media culture, 2, 8
media history, 49, 128, 130, 170. *See also* media archaeology
media representation, 88
mediatisation, 85
Medium and Daybreak, 26, 112–14, 118, 122–23, 147–48, 157–58
mediumship
  aesthetic value of, 39
  afterlife of mediums, 87
  as acting, 38, 88, 93
  assistants and managers of mediums, 91–92, 96–97, 99
  biographies and autobiographies of mediums, 75, 89, 99, 117–21, 144
  education of mediums, 38, 95, 119, 122
  itinerant performers and mediums, 25, 31
  mediumistic powers in children, 37, 117
  physical, 94
  private life of mediums, 89–90
  as profession, 14–15, 22, 31–33, 90
  as skill, 32, 119
  social background of mediums, 37, 94–95
Méliès, Georges, 166–68
memory, 87
Mendeleev, Dmitrij I., 28
mesmerism, 31, 50
Miller, Dickinson S., 101–2
mirth. *See* laughter
money. *See* spiritualism and money
Morse, J. J., 25–26, 28, 31, 38
Morselli, Enrico, 94–95
Moses, William Stainton, 142
mourning, 73
multiple exposure, 136, 150, 161, 165–67. *See also* photography; superimposition

Mumler, William, 68, 137–40, 144, 146–47, 150, 158
Münsterberg, Hugo, 100–101
music, 25–26, 53–55, 157
  musical instruments, 30, 54–55
  piano, 54–55
  popular songs, 133
Muybridge, Eadweard, 151–53

narrative, 119–21
New Age, 171
Newcastle Spiritualist Society, 91
New York Tribune, 65, 72–73
newspaper. *See* popular press
noise, 53–54
nontheatrical attractions, 2, 38, 69

objectivity, 36, 132, 138, 142–43
O'Key sisters, 50
Orientalism, 124
Ouija board, 58–59, 114
Owen, Robert Dale, 55

Palladino, Eusapia, 15, 82, 92–102
Paracelsus (spirit of), 123
patents, 58
paying public, 28
Pepper, John Henry, 70
performance, 22, 29, 31–32, 40–41, 76, 131–32
phantasmagoria, 156
phenakistoscope, 59, 60
philosophical toys, 59–61, 145
photography, 85, 87–88, 89, 135. *See also* spirit photography
  cartes de visite, 89, 145–46
  combination printing, 153–54
  interior photography, 151–53
  photographic amusements, 159–60
  photographic retouching, 150
  photographic trick, 136, 138, 142, 149–54, 159–61, 168
  portrait photography, 138, 145–46
  postmortem photography, 147
  spirit photography, 14, 68, 114, 135–64, 169
Plaetz, Julius, 143
planchette, 126–27, 132–34

popular culture, 17, 110, 116–17, 121, 130, 175 n. 2
postal service, 114
prestidigitation, 56. *See also* stage magic
print media, 14, 85, 109–34
    book market, 110–11, 125, 130, 132–34
    journalism, 69–70, 72–73, 75
    press and periodicals, 2, 68, 71–75, 96, 115, 138
    press conference, 99
    printing, 110, 130
    spiritualist periodicals, 112–16
programs of spiritualist demonstrations, 28
Progressive Library and Spiritual Institution, 113
projection. *See* magic lantern
psychology, 101, 127
public events, 26
public speaking, 25
Pyne, Warner, 102

radioactivity, 98
rational amusements, 59, 61, 145
rationality and irrationality, 13, 60
realism, 10
Redman, George, 119–20
Rejlander, Oscar Gustave, 153
religion
    and celebrity, 82–83, 104
    material religion, 12
    and print media, 110–11
    and theatricality, 12
    religious preaching, 49, 109–10
    religious ritual, 80–81
renown, 84. *See also* celebrity
repetition, 60
Rice, Dan, 69
Richet, Charles, 32
Rinn, Joseph F., 102
Robertson, Étienne-Gaspard, 156
Robinson, Henry Peach, 153
Royal Polytechnic (London), 4, 60
Roubaud, Felix, 45

Sargent, Epes, 132–33, 142
Sargent, John W., 102

scientific and technological lectures, 4, 58, 70
scientists, 74–75, 98, 104–5
séances
    composition of, 45
    devices used in. *See* Ouija board; planchette; spiritoscope
    entertaining character of, 21–22, 53
    as media events, 98–99
    open nature of, 9–10, 30, 45, 80–81
    private, 40–50
    private *vs.* public, 16, 43, 44, 50
    public, 21–31, 99
    séance reports, 49, 115–16
    séance room, 44
    séance table, 2, 50–53
    setting of, 43, 45, 51
    sexual connotations of, 46–47, 88, 90–91
    as social events, 43–44
Sears Roebuck, 58
sensation, 69, 74–75, 182 n. 81
sex. *See* séances, sexual connotations of
Seybert, Henry, 146
show business, 7, 67, 85, 90–92, 98–99, 115–16
skepticism, 11, 32, 71, 75–81, 159–65, 171
    response to, 192 n. 118
Slade, Henry, 127
sleep, 39–40
sleights of hand, 56. *See also* stage magic
Smith, Albert A., 166–67
Smith, Hester Travers, 123
Smith-Buck, George, 29
sociality, 43, 52–53, 56, 96
Society for Psychical Research (Great Britain), 98, 127
Solomons, Leon M., 127
sound, 53–54
spectacle, 8–9
spectacularism, 15, 31, 33, 94
spectacular realities, 10
spectator, 9–11, 23, 36–40, 117, 171–73
spirit board. *See* Ouija board; planchette
spirit cabinet, 29, 76
spirit circle, 51
spirit control, 25, 87
spiritoscope, 57–58

spirit phenomena
    interpretations of, 11, 97, 171
    innovations in, 33–34
    rappings, 65–66, 72
    spirit concert, 25
    spirit drawing, 55, 124
    spirit pantomime, 42
    table tipping, 2, 50–51
    types of, 33, 35, 42, 55, 94
spirits
    identity of, 48, 143–44
    temperament of, 49
spirit table. *See* séance table
spiritualism
    diffusion of, 175 n. 4
    British vs American spiritualism, 5–6
    commercialization of, 14–15, 31
    debunking of. *See* spiritualist exposé
    demonstrations of. *See* séances, public
    faith in, 12, 80, 109
    and gender, 103–4
    institutionalization of, 115
    and literature, 111–12, 116–17, 121, 123
    and media, 5, 61, 128–30
    and money, 14, 32, 71, 72, 96, 146–49
    and science, 4, 97–98, 104–5, 141
    and social class, 6, 37, 94
    as spectacle, 8–12, 33, 36–41, 76
    vs. stage magic, 29, 78–79, 160–61
spiritualist exposé, 76–81, 101–2, 159–65, 167. *See also* skepticism
spirit world, 56
spirit writings, 121–32
    automatic writing, 126–32
    direct writing, 127–28
    slate writing, 127
stage magic, 10, 29, 76–79, 160–63
stardom. *See* celebrity
Stead, W. T., 75
Stein, Gertrude, 127
stereoscope, 59, 144–45
superimposition, 135–69. *See also* multiple exposure
suspense, 22, 28, 48
suspension of disbelief, 41, 117
sympathy, 48

table games, 53
technology, 5, 36, 128, 142
telegraph, 8, 58, 73, 128–30
telepathy, 75
theater, 24, 86–87, 103
    parlor or domestic, 43
    theatrical afterlife, 86
theatricality, 23–24, 40, 47. *See also* religion and theatricality
trance, 36–41, 50, 121, 126
    as reverie, 39
    trance lectures, 24–25, 33, 157
transatlantic exchange, 5, 69, 85–86, 98–99, 115
trickery, 93, 101–2, 147. *See also* photographic trick
telephone, 61
television, 172
toys, 56–57, 133, 183 n. 93
Tuttle, Hudson, 49
typewriter, 129
Two Worlds Publishing, 58, 133

unconscious, 39–40, 74, 127

Valentino, Rudolph (spirit of), 123
Varley, Cromwell Fleetwood, 58
visual media, 135–69. *See also* film; photography

Watson, Samuel, 130
Weatherly, Lionel A., 161
Wetherbee, John, 21, 29
Wilde, Oscar (spirit of), 123
Willman, Carl, 161
wireless telegraphy, 129
women, condition of, 25. *See also* spiritualism and gender
wonder, 4, 56, 171, 175 n. 9
Wood, Catherine, 91
Wren, Cristopher (spirit of), 122

www.ingramcontent.com/pod-product-compliance
Lightning Source LLC
Chambersburg PA
CBHW021942290426
44108CB00012B/933